"Our kids now have access to more information than ever before, including objections to Christianity and the existence of God. Young people encounter skepticism long before they enter universities and colleges. They encounter it online while they are still *living at home*. That's why we, as *parents*, are the most important apologists our kids will ever know. *Mama Bear Apologetics* will help you understand the challenges so you can navigate your kids' questions and prepare them to become committed Christ followers."

J. Warner Wallace
Dateline featured cold-case detective; Adjunct Professor of Apologetics at Biola University; author of *Cold-Case Christianity*, *God's Crime Scene*, and *Forensic Faith*; and creator of the *Case Makers Academy for Kids*

"*Mama Bear Apologetics* is an incisive and witty look at the false ideas kids are drowning in today, often under the watch of well-meaning but unaware Christian moms. I love that it cuts right to the heart of the problem in each chapter—just enough information to provide helpful context and key points of understanding, but not so much that it will leave you feeling overwhelmed. If every Christian mom would read and thoughtfully apply this book in her parenting, it would profoundly transform the next generation. *Please* read this, then share it with a friend."

Natasha Crain
National speaker, blogger, and author of *Keeping Your Kids on God's Side* and *Talking with Your Kids About God*

"It is such a thrill to see this book come to fruition. Recently there has been a significant movement of women in the church embracing the important role apologetics has in raising the next generation. *Mama Bear Apologetics* is the result of their collaboration, prayer, and experience. This offers both insight into our contemporary culture as well as practical ways to engage young people with biblical truth. I wish every Christian woman would read this book and pass it on to a friend."

Sean McDowell, PhD
Author, speaker, professor

"I'm thrilled to see a book of this caliber written for moms! *Mama Bear Apologetics* is engaging and accessible without minimizing the seriousness of the subject matter. I'm particularly pleased by the inclusion of chapters on so-called progressive Christianity and postmodernism. Readers will gain effective tools for dismantling some of the more dangerous ideologies that pervade contemporary culture—and be able to equip their children to follow suit."

Melissa Cain Travis, PhD
Author of *Science and the Mind of the Maker:*
What the Conversation Between Faith and Science Reveals About God

"Outstanding! *Mama Bear Apologetics* deftly describes cultural lies, how to recognize them, and how to defeat them logically and compassionately. Humor abounds, such as their chew-and-spit method of discerning where progressivism, feminism, socialism, and more agree with or go astray from biblical teaching. Chapters end with discussion questions perfect for small group settings."

Jean E. Jones
Coauthor of *Discovering Joy in Philippians*
and *Discovering Jesus in the Old Testament*

"This team of women thinkers, under the leadership of Hillary Morgan Ferrer, has put together one of the most engaging, accessible, clever, and relevant books on apologetics available today. They take on and answer the questions that intimidate Christian parents—and they do it with joy, humor, and rare skill. This is the kind of book that should be ordered by churches in case lots so that everyone can read it and discuss it. This book will surely be a confidence builder and a game changer for Christian families far and wide."

Craig J. Hazen, PhD
Biola University Apologetics,
author of *Fearless Prayer*

"Brilliant, humorous, conversational, must-read book about the importance of apologetics for anyone who gives a hoot about the current and next generations. This fresh perspective—by women—is exactly what apologetics needs. Everyone, not just parents, needs to learn the chew-and-spit method of discernment, how to ROAR like a mother, and grasp the consequences of linguistic theft. The Mama Bear clarion call is providential—'Mess with our kids, and we will demolish your arguments!'"

Laurie A. Stewart
President, Women in Apologetics

"*Mama Bear Apologetics* is a brilliant collaboration for every woman concerned about lies and ideologies that have crept into both society and the church—and have come against the knowledge of God. It's for those mothers who want to protect the minds and souls of their children. *Mama Bear* will equip you with the answers to the tough questions, engage you and your children's critical thinking, and encourage you—through prayer and discussion—on your faith journey. This book will inspire and strengthen your family and I highly recommend it for every home, in small groups, and in your church."

Rodney Lake
National Director, Thinking Matters New Zealand Foundation

"The *Mama Bear* book bounds onto the apologetics scene coming to the aid of Christian moms navigating the swift-moving—and often dangerous—ideological waters of postmodern Western culture. These authors understand that while moms have difficulty finding time to learn apologetics, they are still concerned about what their kids are ingesting from cultural influencers. So the Mama Bears have provided answers at an accessible level using stories and humor for an experience that is as informative as it is enjoyable, all the while maintaining a loving and compassionate approach to tough issues. This book will have Christian moms ready to 'ROAR like a mother'!"

Mary Jo Sharp
Assistant Professor of Apologetics, Houston Baptist University;
director of Confident Christianity Apologetics Ministry

MAMA BEAR

BEAR

Apologetics®

HILLARY MORGAN FERRER
GENERAL EDITOR

HARVEST HOUSE PUBLISHERS
EUGENE, OREGON

Cover by Faceout Studio

Cover photo © CSA-Archive / Getty Images

MAMA BEAR APOLOGETICS is a trademark of Hillary Morgan Ferrer. Harvest House Publishers, Inc., is the exclusive licensee of the trademark MAMA BEAR APOLOGETICS.

Mama Bear Apologetics®
Copyright © 2019 Hillary Morgan Ferrer
Published by Harvest House Publishers
Eugene, Oregon 97408
www.harvesthousepublishers.com

ISBN 978-0-7369-7615-2 (pbk.)
ISBN 978-0-7369-7616-9 (eBook)

Library of Congress Cataloging-in-Publication Data

Names: Ferrer, Hillary Morgan, editor.
Title: Mama Bear apologetics / Hillary Morgan Ferrer, general editor.
Description: Eugene, Oregon : Harvest House Publishers, [2019] | Includes
    bibliographical references.
Identifiers: LCCN 2018046459 (print) | LCCN 2019006939 (ebook) | ISBN
    9780736976169 (ebook) | ISBN 9780736976152 (trade)
Subjects: LCSH: Mothers--Religious life. | Apologetics. | Christian education
    of children.
Classification: LCC BV4529.18 (ebook) | LCC BV4529.18 .M355 2019 (print) |
    DDC 248.8/431--dc23
LC record available at https://lccn.loc.gov/2018046459

Printed in the United States of America
21 22 23 24 25 26 / VP-GL / 15 14 13

For Leslie, Ann, and Jan—Mama Bears who were taken before their time

Dedicated to all our little bears. May you learn to "chew and spit,"
but not at the dinner table.

Luke and Joe

Elijah and Jonah

Hannah and Rachel

Will and Dalton

Dyllan and Ayden

Carli, Ben, and Sam

Connor and Luke

Kai, Levi, and Toby

Morgan and Carter

Darby, Avery, Riley, and Bret

Acknowledgments

To start out with, we all want to thank our amazing husbands—John, Todd, Howard, Bill, Lee, Kyle, and Mike—for the way they supported us during this project. You put up with our late-night skype calls, our endless text chains, and the hours of writing and rewriting. We are honored to be called your beloveds. (Each individually. Not collectively. This isn't a cult.)

I would like to thank the Mama Bears who worked so tirelessly to make this group project a success. I am so proud of the work we have accomplished, and even though we have our names on our chapters, each chapter has a little bit of all of us. A special thank you to Hillary Short for being the citation ninja and fixing the hot mess that was the chapter 1 endnotes. There are special rewards for you in heaven, my friend. Also thanks to the friends and scholars who reviewed the chapters and provided feedback—Chris and Alice Morgan and their small group, Beth Barber, Amanda Burke, Jody Vise, Leslie Horton, Lindsey Medenwaldt, Blake Reas, Justin Bass, Katie Peterson, Elena Doepel, Gordon Sterling, Marcia Montenegro, Diane Woerner, Ryan Huxley, and Steve Cable for their tireless work on the youth exodus.

And thank you for the many who lent their emotional support during our first project—Natasha Crain, for always lending an ear to bounce ideas off of. For Sean McDowell, for helping me navigate my first compilation book. Nancy Pearcey, for believing in the mission of Mama Bear Apologetics. For Craig Hazen, who is never too busy to talk when I need guidance. For Terry and Steve, amazing editors. And finally, for our Lord Jesus, without whom we would have nothing of substance to say.

Contents

Foreword

Nancy Pearcey

I abandoned my Christian upbringing midway through high school—
and that's why I strongly support the mission of Mama Bear Apologetics.

God has given parents the primary responsibility for the spiritual education of their children. In a previous era, it was not unusual for parents
to slide that responsibility off to their church, youth group, or Christian
school. But that is no longer possible. In an increasingly secular age, it's
more obvious than ever that parents are on the front lines in preparing
their children to face a society that responds to Christianity with puzzle-
ment or outright hostility.

Already decades ago, when I was a teenager, the pressures of living in
a secular culture were severe enough to cause me to question the Christianity my parents taught me. (And not just me: Out of my five siblings,
only two remained Christian into adulthood.) At the public high school
I attended, the teachers were secular, the textbooks were secular, and my
friends were mostly secular or Jewish. I did know a few Christians, but
they were theologically liberal. When I visited their church, they stood in
a circle, held hands, and sang the civil rights anthem "We Shall Overcome."
I was not impressed. They seemed to be merely putting a Christian veneer
on secular progressivism.

It was obvious that in my school and social circles, theologically conservative Christians were a tiny minority. I could not help wondering:
Why do they think they alone are right and everyone else is wrong?

So I started asking, "How do we know Christianity is true?"

Just that. Nothing about the problem of evil and suffering; nothing about how a good God could send people to hell; none of the typical questions young people ask. Only the most fundamental question of all: How do we know it is true?

No one could give me an answer.

My parents are ethnically Scandinavian. On my father's side, my grandparents crossed the ocean from Sweden, and on my mother's side, my great-grandparents were from Norway. In these countries, the state church for centuries has been Lutheran. As a result, my parents were baffled by my questions. Their mindset seemed to be, "But, but…we're Scandinavian! What else could you be, if not Lutheran?"

My pastor had not studied apologetics, so he had no answers to offer. An uncle was the dean of students at a Lutheran seminary, so I hoped he would have more substantial answers. But all he said was, "Don't worry, we all have doubts sometimes."

Where is a parent to get guidance on how to address their children's questions about God?

Mama Bear Apologetics is stepping into the breach. With real-life, down-to-earth examples from their own families and lives, they are making apologetics clear and accessible to ordinary parents. This book will equip you to get started with a basic awareness of the questions young people are raising today—questions your own children are also likely to ask.

Until recently, fewer women than men have been interested in apologetics. But that is changing rapidly—especially among women who have children. In 1991, I was the founding editor of "BreakPoint," a national daily radio program featuring Chuck Colson. Though the program was only five minutes long, my goal as the editor was to ensure that every "BreakPoint" program gave listeners a kernel of Christian worldview and apologetics teaching. Both in the radio commentaries I wrote myself and in those I edited written by staff and freelance writers, I made sure that the program used current events as a springboard to educate listeners on the underlying secular worldviews at the root of social trends. The goal was to educate listeners on how to think critically about secular worldviews and to offer a Christian response.

In short, "BreakPoint" aimed at teaching apologetics in a very accessible format. And here is what we discovered: When we covered topics of concern to parents, *that* is when we sparked by far the largest response.

The way we gauged responses was by call-ins. When listeners liked a program, they were encouraged to call in and request a transcript. (This lasted the first few years, until demand grew so high that we had to outsource the service.) It was blindingly obvious which topics attracted the highest number of call-ins: anything that helped parents to equip their children. The numbers always spiked when we talked about issues related to topics like education (what is being taught in the public schools), entertainment (children's movies and video games), literature (books for children or young adults), and evolution (giving parents tools to help their children answer questions raised by science).

What we learned was that many people may not be terribly interested in apologetics for their own sake. After all, by the time they are adults, many of them have settled whatever questions they had. But they are intensely interested in helping their kids stay Christian. And they are aware that their children are facing much tougher questions than any previous generation.

That's why the time is ripe for Mama Bear Apologetics. With each new generation, worldviews shift—which means the questions you and I had may not be the same questions our children have. We cannot simply rely on what we already know to pass on to our children. The best motivator for apologetics is love: We need to love our children enough to listen to them and do the hard work of finding answers to their questions.

In my view, mothers are especially well equipped for this task. Why? Because effective apologetics requires empathy. You have to be willing to listen to the other side intently enough to understand where the questions are coming from. What ideas are my children picking up? What cultural messages are they tuning in to? What are the unspoken assumptions behind those views? The sheer experience of daily interaction with young children gives moms the opportunity to develop skills in empathy and communication.

It's never too early to get started. A friend's eight-year-old son asked his parents, "People with other religions believe they're right about their gods, and we believe we're right about our God. How do we know who's *really* right?" Your child could be wondering the same thing. Do you know how to answer?

And there's a bonus: As you address your children's questions, at the same time, God is training you to help friends, family, church members, and neighbors—because the same skills are needed to communicate God's truth to *anyone*. My first professional writing job was a weekly science reader for first- through third-graders. A little later, I moved up in the organization and started writing for fourth- through sixth-graders. Later still, I wrote for junior high students, then high school students. Looking back, I can see that the job provided outstanding training in how to break concepts down and explain them simply and clearly for any audience. (I encourage my students who aspire to be writers to start by writing for children.) In the same way, as you accept the calling to educate your own children, God is preparing you for a broader ministry that will open up as your children mature and leave home.

Let me step aside now and introduce you to Mama Bear Apologetics. On the following pages, you will gain wisdom to help you listen well to your children—to discern their thoughts and questions, and then guide them in thinking critically and biblically about the postmodern culture they face. What an honor for each of us to be called by God to stand alongside young people, shaping their mind and understanding. Mama Bear Apologetics is an excellent support and guide along the way.

Nancy Pearcey
Author of *Total Truth* and *Finding Truth*

Protecting Your Kids
the Mama Bear Way

Several years ago, my husband and I were asked to be helpers at an apologetics class at my parents' church. It was here that we met a woman named Jody. One day, Jody stood up to give her story. She had raised two sons in the church. They attended Awana, youth group, and church every week. One of them even asked to be rebaptized after his first year in college. *That'll clinch it!* she thought. After her son got his first job post-college, her world was turned upside down. On a weekend visit, he declared that he no longer believed in God. He was following in the footsteps of his atheist boss, who had convinced him that "Jesus was just like Santa Claus and the tooth fairy." *What more could I have possibly done?* she wondered.

Jody then told the class how she handled the situation. On the inside she was freaking out. (Who wouldn't be?) On the outside, however, she listened to her son, asked him questions, and tried to see what had caused such a seismic shift in his life. She asked him to tell her his main objections and questions. When he left to return home, Jody—a fitness instructor—dove into the unfamiliar world of academia and Christian scholarship, frantically searching for evidences that would refute her son's objections. She didn't ask for this task. She didn't want it. But her baby's eternal destiny was in the balance! What else could a Mama Bear do? She saw the philosophical bulldozer crushing her son, and she jumped in with both hands—as all Mama Bears do—wanting to lift it off of him, even though it meant studying *apologetics* of all things.

Shocked that the church had not prepared her (or her son) for culture's antagonism toward Christianity, Jody spent the next several years attempting to help answer her son's questions and walking with other parents who had experienced the same thing with their children.

After hearing her story, a tiny seed was planted in my mind which, after several years, blossomed into both the ministry Mama Bear Apologetics and the book you're reading right now.

I would like to say that Jody's story is unique, but it is not. Kids are being introduced to challenges to Christianity at younger and younger ages (see chapter 1). In response, we can either focus on the questions themselves, *or* we can take a closer look at the worldly philosophies *behind* the questions. I compare the "just answer the questions" method to a game of whack-a-mole. Do you remember that game at the fair? Little stuffed moles would pop up unexpectedly from different holes while the player tried to bop them on the head for points. While answering the tough questions of the faith is important, doing so is a lot like playing whack-a-mole. As soon as you deal with one, another pops up.

What if we could prime our children to think biblically *before* they are presented with the questions that challenge the faith? Thinking biblically isn't merely about knowing Bible verses (though that's a great place to start!). No, thinking biblically is about taking what we know from the Bible and understanding how the principles presented in it apply to everyday situations. That's the kind of biblical thinkers we want our kids to become!

Think of ideas as being like seeds. Whether or not a seed grows is determined by the kind of soil it is placed in (and whether or not we water it). We want to nurture our children's intellectual soil so that *when* (not if!) bad ideas are planted there, *they won't grow.* We don't want our children to feel like they have to choose between God and science because we have already made an effort to till their intellectual soil so they know that science and faith are not at odds, and never were (chapter 6). We don't want our kids to look to the government as their savior because they know that the battle has already been won by *Christ*, and He alone is their Savior (chapter 13). We want them to know what constitutes trustworthy evidence so that they can never claim that "there is no evidence for God" (chapter 7). We want them to understand that truth is exclusive—it excludes falsehood (chapter 11).

These principles are foundational to everything Scripture teaches. Allow the foundation to erode, and we leave our kids prey to doubt and worldly thinking. After all, how can our little bears accept the *truth* of Christ unless they already know that *truth itself* exists and is not up for interpretation (chapter 8)? Or how will they know to reach out to Jesus for help if they are taught that all they need to do is look inside—that everything they need resides within (chapter 5)?

Culture's lies are like weeds that want to take over the garden of our children's minds. The lies need to be stopped, and they stop with you, Mama Bear! Afraid that apologetics isn't your cup of tea? That's totally fine. Don't read this book for yourself. Read it if for no other reason than *you need to know what the world is telling your kids the eight-plus hours a day that they are away from you.* Read it so that you can recognize the lies and help your little bears to recognize them too.

We have structured this book to be informative, not condemning. We are not out to point fingers at every belief we dislike. Rather, our goal is to raise up an army of *discerning* Mama Bears who can take an idea, identify the good aspects, distinguish them from the bad aspects, and accept the good while rejecting the bad (chapter 3). Our job as Mama Bears is to protect our children no matter where the threats may come from. Protection may mean sheltering our kids for a time, but that's a short-term solution. We need to prepare our children so they aren't left unprotected for the future. *The greatest protection we can give our kids is to equip them to face the cultural lies head-on while remaining gracious, loving, and winsome.* It is not enough to simply tell them *which* ideas are raised against the knowledge of God (2 Corinthians 10:5). We must train them to understand *why* those ideas are flawed. We want to train them to use their critical thinking skills during every lecture, every movie, every song, and—yes—even every sermon!

We don't want our children to see everything around them as black and white, because, frankly, we don't live in a comic-book world. We want them to realize that biblical truths and cultural lies can appear anywhere at any time. We don't want our children to live in fear, but with discernment. We want our kids to be able to see Christ in art, movies, science, history, music—in all things because He is Lord over all. Yet we don't want them to assume that everything they encounter in art, movies, science, history, or music is speaking His truth.

With enough practice, our children won't even have to think about the way they receive or reject the various ideas or views espoused in our world. It's like breathing. We don't inhale 100% oxygen. We inhale a combination of oxygen, carbon dioxide, nitrogen, and atmosphere. Our bodies were designed to take in the oxygen and exhale everything else. If we as Mama Bears do our jobs well, and we hope this book will help you on that journey, then our little bears will be able to interact with this culture with grace, love, and critical thinking—inhaling the spiritual oxygen and exhaling everything else—in a way that is as natural as breathing. This skill doesn't come overnight, and we need it to teach ourselves first.

So get ready, Mama Bears! It's time to learn about culture's lies and #RoarLikeAMother.

Part 1:

Rise Up, Mama Bears

Chapter 1

Calling All Mama Bears

My kid has a cheerio shoved up his nose.
Why am I reading this book?

HILLARY MORGAN FERRER AND JULIE LOOS

I rather enjoy the phone conversations I have with my mom friends—especially those who are moms of young children. Where else can I hear someone yell nonsensical statements like "Don't put the chicken on the trampoline!"?

I did a survey asking our Mama Bears for the weirdest statements they'd ever had to utter as a mom. There were quite a few responses regarding things that should *not* be licked (for example, eyeballs, cars, an elephant's butt...). My favorite response was "We do *not* put wise men in the toilet!" As a mom, I'm sure there are plenty of phrases you never thought would leave your mouth. Let's be honest: Who has to clarify that "poop is not paint"? Moms, that's who.

Mom life is a special calling and *not* for the faint of heart. Most moms will tell you that it is the hardest *and* the best job in the world. On one hand, there is no alone time for about the first eight years, and you don't get to call in sick. On the other hand, what other job allows you to snuggle with your clients while they show you how big of a spit bubble they can make?

Moms are like managers, except they don't just *manage* people; they *create* them. As a mother, you have the honor of training, molding, and educating your offspring from birth until (hopefully) they become functioning members of society. William Ross Wallace rightly described motherhood in his nineteenth-century poem titled "The Hand That Rocks the Cradle Rules the World." In other words, if children are our future, it is moms (and dads) who are in a position to help determine what kind of future that will be.

As parents—as well as aunts, uncles, grandparents, and guardians—one of our most important jobs is preparing kids for the real world. Our children are growing up in a society that is vastly different than the one in which we grew up. I loved memorizing Bible verses as a child, but I didn't have to deal with the culture telling me that the Bible was full of contradictions or that it was just a book of fairy tales. The trustworthiness of Scripture was *presumed*. That is not the case anymore. We can no longer rely on Western culture to reinforce our Christian beliefs, and we cannot ignore the fact that youth are leaving the church in droves. What many parents don't know is that some of the reasons for their departure are totally preventable.

Why Do We Care About Apologetics?

Julie and I (Hillary) have had very different experiences when it comes to apologetics. Julie discovered the importance of apologetics after having children, whereas I discovered its importance as a child. I like to share my story because I think it is important for parents to have a long-term vision of what apologetics training can do for their kids. Many apologists' stories are filled with regret that they didn't get their training sooner. I am among those whose hindsight is not filled with regret, but rather full of appreciation for the training I received as a youngster.

I was a churchgoing kid who loved Jesus and wanted to be a missionary. I remember wanting to become a nun and being bummed when my mom informed me that only Catholics could do that. During my growing-up years, if Mom and Dad said it, I believed it. They said Christianity was true, so I didn't question it.

Had the Internet been around when I was a kid, my story might have ended *very* differently. I was a question-asker. Even my kindergarten "report card" has a handwritten note from my teacher that says, "Asks a lot of questions." Fast-forward to when my parents met one of my favorite grad school professors. The *first* thing he said to them? "She asks a lot of really good questions!" So I come by this trait honestly. It's been there since I could talk.

Growing up, the only people to whom I could direct my spiritual questions were Mom, Dad, Pastor Tim, and a handful of Sunday school teachers. Given access to the Internet, I might have looked up "God" on Google and been introduced to not only the Judeo-Christian God, but also the god(s) of Islam, Baha'i, and Zoroastrianism. If your kids are anything like me, they might have then searched "Which God is the real God?" Last I checked, at the top of the list was the Wikipedia entry for God. Entry number two was "Is God Real?" on Mormon.org. If your kids go a little further down the screen, they will be told by a HuffPost article that "Approaching God, or rejecting the very idea (atheism), ought to be a *personal matter,* something like happiness as defined in the Declaration of Independence: *a pursuit by each in their own way*"[1] (emphasis mine). Postmodernism agrees. Naturalism agrees, and so do emotionalism and moral relativism. A lot of the popular worldviews in this book agree with that statement.

So if our kids have mom, dad, and Pastor Whoever saying one thing, and Wikipedia, HuffPost, and their school friends and teachers saying another, which worldview do you think will ultimately win out? You could cross your fingers and hope that your kids stick with what you've taught them and don't succumb to other ways of thinking, but I don't recommend that approach.

What Apologetics Did for My Faith

As mentioned earlier, I was among the few who experienced apologetics at a young age—and I hope your children have that privilege as well. I was introduced to apologetics by my pastor when I was 12. He was a former atheist who came to Christ the same way as Lee Strobel, the author of *The Case for Christ*: by trying to disprove Christianity, and then discovering that he couldn't because it was actually true. As a responsible pastor, he taught a few series on defending the Christian faith. The first was on the "liar, lunatic, Lord" trilemma, in which he showed that Jesus being Lord was the most reasonable conclusion out of the three. The next was on the historical evidences for New Testament reliability. Finally, he examined the biblical and historical accounts of the resurrection by refuting every alternate theory ever proposed by a skeptic, showing how the resurrection, as reported in the Gospels, was the most plausible explanation.

Those three series still serve as the foundation for my Christian faith. I've had plenty of opportunities to be angry at God (my mom's cancer, my cancer, my sister's terminal cancer and recent death, my depression, childlessness, you name it). Many who have gone through similar hardships have simply concluded that God must not exist. However, rejecting Christianity as untrue has never been an option for me. To reject the existence of God would be the most irrational conclusion I could come to, and I refuse to be irrational!

Sure, there are days when I don't *feel* God's presence or *feel* peaceful. But no matter what I *feel*, I can't *un*know what I know. My faith is not based on feelings. It is based on the immovable, absolute truth of Christ's life, death, and resurrection. The evidences for Christianity and God's unmistakable thumbprint upon creation are my beacons of sanity amidst the tumultuous sea of uncertain emotions. Sometimes my emotions agree with truth and I feel loved, peaceful, and close to God. Sometimes my emotions disagree with truth and I don't feel those things. Either way, I am thankful that my faith does not rely on the shifting sands of my emotions because on some days, my emotions are all over the place.

Peaceful emotions, closeness, and mountaintop experiences are important to our relationship with God, but they are more like the decor inside a house. Decor helps make a house a home, and we *should* enjoy our home in Christ! But it's the foundation that enables a home to stand firm. Yet how often do you hear of someone who takes great pleasure in a foundation? That's not the purpose of a foundation—its job is to create the *stability* by which we can enjoy all the other things that come with having a home. The only time people notice foundations is when there's something wrong with them. In our culture, we have massive foundational issues, and the ideological cracks can be seen everywhere.

We know that we are to build on the foundational rock of Christ (Matthew 7), but I have noticed a growing trend of people confusing their feelings *about* Jesus for Jesus Himself. There is a fundamental difference between teaching our kids to base their spiritual foundation on the *experience* of Jesus and basing it *on* Jesus. They need something that doesn't change, which is the immovable, absolute truth of Christ's life, death, and resurrection. Experiences and emotion? Those change over time and in unpredictable ways.

How to Get People Excited About Apologetics

Most people do not gravitate toward the topic of apologetics. Interest is usually preceded by an "Aha!" moment when they realize *why* they need to have reasons for their faith. I'm hoping this book will be your "Aha!" moment.

These lightbulb moments can occur when a person either experiences or witnesses a crisis of faith that leaves them asking "Why *am* I a Christian?" Sometimes it is when they are challenged by a person of another religion. One of the more mobilizing experiences is when a person witnesses firsthand the spiritual slaughter that is taking place on college and university campuses.

My husband and I once attended a church led by a pastor who didn't understand why apologetics was necessary. To him, it was a cool hobby that John and I had, not something to which all Christians are called. In his sermons he would say that "love is all we need" to preach the gospel, and he encouraged the congregation to "stop all that theologizing and just love Jesus."

John decided to invite our pastor to his debate at the local university. By the end of the night, our pastor was on "Team Apologetics"! What caused him to change his mind in a single evening? While there, he saw a standing-room-only crowd full of Christians, atheists, skeptics, and seekers. These people weren't just outliers; they were the kind of individuals we see all around us every day. As John answered audience questions, our pastor came to realize how many Christian students were being spiritually rerouted in college. He saw the stronghold of secular thought and how youth who had grown up in church were being seduced away—until they encountered John's rebuttals, possibly the first intellectual rebuttals they had ever heard from a Christian.

Apologetics may not seem important until you witness firsthand the consequences of bad ideas.

You could almost see the lightbulb going on in our pastor's mind. Seeing this reminded me of that scene from *Gone with the Wind* where the camera pans out over the endless field of wounded soldiers and the audience is confronted with the magnitude of Civil War casualties. From that night on, our pastor was our biggest cheerleader. Conclusion: It is easy to miss the importance of apologetics if you haven't witnessed the sheer number of victims being held captive to bad philosophy (see Colossians 2:8). Apologetics may not seem important until you witness firsthand the consequences of bad ideas.

As you look at your children trying to remove the Cheerio, or Lego, or whatever they have shoved up their nose, you may be asking, "Why am I reading this book?" The answer is simple: *because you are a Mama Bear.* When you saw the words *Mama Bear* on the cover, something inside you said, "That's me." Nobody had to explain to you what a Mama Bear was. The moment you first held your child, you knew that if anyone or anything ever threatened him or her, you would do whatever it took to deal with that threat. That's what Mama Bears do. We will talk more in the next chapter about what it means to be a Mama Bear, but first, like that scene in *Gone with the Wind*, we want to give you a snapshot of *why* we are writing this book, and it all begins with what research calls "the youth exodus." It may not be pretty, but if we do our jobs well, you will come away from this chapter ready to become a Mama Bear Apologist who says, "Mess with my kids, and I will demolish your arguments!"

So What Is the Youth Exodus?

Julie here! You know those never-ending piles of laundry? Yes, the one waiting to be separated and the other one waiting to be folded? They are about as immense as the amount of research done on the issue commonly referred to in apologetics circles as "the youth exodus." It's probably the largest exodus since Moses, but this one has no assurances that the wanderers will return to the "promised land."

The youth exodus refers to the percentage of Christian youth who stop attending church. This includes those who go on to declare themselves atheists, agnostics, or more recently, "none" (that is, of no religious affiliation). This exodus has been widely researched, documented, and discussed, but in many Christian circles it's also widely *ignored*. And while there are some varying opinions (and what can look like contradictory statistics), the bottom line is it's real, it's bad, and it's now becoming more rampant among young people prior to entering college, which used to be the exit ramp.

The reasons for this exodus are varied, nuanced, and somewhat complicated. Unfortunately, there's no one "tumor" we can treat and thereby cure the disease. Instead, there are tentacles of cancer growing all throughout our youth's spiritual experiences. Apologetics is not the only solution, but it is a large part of the solution, and one that is ignored far too often.

Come On—How Big Is the Problem Really?

Most studies indicate between 45%-48% of youth leave church after their freshman year in college and never return.[2] The percentages vary based on denomination, but the problem is the same. David Kinnaman found that after age 15, almost 60% of young Christians had disconnected from their church.[3] More than half (54%) of high school students attend church. But once they hit college, the problem gets worse. *Frequent* attendance drops from 44% in high school to 25% in college; *nonattendance* goes up from 20% in high school to 38% in college.[4] In a 2006 Barna study, 61% of twenty-somethings who had attended church as teens were no longer spiritually engaged.[5] One study showed that 70% of teens who attended youth group stopped attending church within two years of their high school graduation![6]

For many years, most people assumed that the problem originated in college (probably because that's when we see the church attendance numbers take their most drastic drop). However, we must take into account that college is when kids no longer have good ol' mom and dad waking them up and driving them to Sunday school. *So while college is and remains a contributing factor, these numbers are an external manifestation of an internal disconnection that started years earlier.* The ticket was already purchased. College was just their first opportunity to use it.

What Exactly Have They Left?

That's a good question with sort of a complicated answer. Leaving the faith and leaving the church are not necessarily the same thing. Whether they are saying goodbye to church attendance, separating from orthodox doctrine, or saying hello to atheism, they are still leaving, and no form of leaving is good. From Millennials to Gen Z, while some leave with their feet (due to life events and changes), many leave with their hearts and minds due to emotional, behavioral, or intellectual reasons. When youth describe their religion, you'll hear statements like "I'm spiritual, but not religious," or "I am no longer affiliated with any certain religion or denomination." (Pew Research Center calls these "the nones.") And then of course there are those who either renounce all belief in God (atheist) or are no longer sure that they *can* know whether He exists (agnostic).

Some are leaving organized religion. Others are leaving biblical authority. They want to create a religious buffet to suit their own tastes.[7] Many have left the biblical definition of who God is. They have redefined Him to be somewhat like a big genie in the sky who wants them to be nice to others, will help them when they are in trouble, and wants them to be happy. This is called Therapeutic Moralistic Deism.[8] Those who have left the more orthodox views of theology have adopted beliefs that are closer to historical heresies. They may call themselves Christian, but their views don't support that label.[9]

For example, in three independent surveys conducted by Josh McDowell, the Barna Group, and researcher Mike Nappa, it was discovered that among self-proclaimed "Christian" teens,

- 41% were uncertain whether Jesus was physically resurrected.[10]
- 63% didn't believe Jesus to be the son of the one true God.[11]
- 44% believed the Bible to be just one of many authoritative voices about Jesus.[12]
- 33% believed that Jesus is not the only way to heaven.[13]
- only 5% studied the Bible daily (down from 8% in 1991).[14]
- a growing majority believe the Holy Spirit is only a symbol of God's presence or power rather than a person of the Trinity.[15]
- 60% are uncertain, unsettled, or confused about whether the Bible can be trusted.[16]
- 70% express persistent, measurable doubts that what the Bible says about Jesus is true.[17]

An Increasingly Hostile World

In the 12 years since I (Julie) began studying apologetics, my eldest son has gone from prepubescent middle-schooler to college graduate. During that time, the cultural hostility exhibited toward Christianity has increased as exponentially as his shoe size. Because this accelerated trend has been going on for some time now, the first generations of the youth exodus (Gen X and Millennials) are now the ones hiring, teaching, and influencing the younger generation (currently that's Gen Z). We are also now seeing—gulp—the first generation of these "religious exiles" parenting their own brood. This has huge implications for society because we are now post-truth, post-Christian, void of gospel influence, and waiting to see which way the "spiritual but not religious" will finally fall.

Myths About the Youth Exodus

You know how you have to fight to get that precious alone time in the bathroom (I see that chocolate bar tucked away in your book—high five!) but your children just—will—not—leave—you—alone!? In a similar way, Satan will work through peer pressure and cultural chaos to pursue your kids, and won't leave them alone. Our proverbial locks on the doors no longer work as well as they used to. The enemy is constantly picking at them. We can't lighten your laundry load (so sorry!), but we can help address some of the myths surrounding the youth exodus. The truth is, when it comes to this trend, there is some stinkin' thinkin' going on. Ain't no place for that in your mind!

Myth #1: They All Walk Away but Then Come Back

For years, the common reasoning in Christian circles has been "All kids rebel. It's part of growing up. Let them sow their wild oats." And then the ace of spades gets thrown down: "You know what the Bible says: 'Train a child in the way he should go, and when he is old he will not turn from it'" (Proverbs 22:6). In other words, *we've depended on our Christian kids to be boomerangs.*

What's wrong with this thinking?

1. *We shouldn't "expect" that our kids might walk away just because others say it is "inevitable."* God has entrusted the stewardship of our children's faith to us, and we are to do all within our power to train them. Yes, what our children decide to do (especially as they get older) is ultimately their choice. But we need to strive for a clear conscience in our spiritual guidance of them, knowing that we did all we could to clearly communicate the truthfulness and validity of the Christian faith.

2. *Not all kids rebel.* I didn't walk away. My kids haven't. Hillary didn't.

I know many others who haven't. When it comes to parenting, don't roll over and play dead just because someone says a certain outcome is inevitable.

3. *The statistics regarding the youth exodus change over time.* Research has shown a general trend of young adults returning to church after they get married and have kids of their own. That trend drastically slowed starting with Gen Xers, who are now raising kids in a less religious world than that of their childhood.[18] A Lifeway study found that out of the 70% of teens who left church during their college years, only about half of them eventually returned.[19] For those of you (like me) who are a bit slow at math, this means that with each successive generation, we are essentially losing about 35% of our church population. As Steve Cable noted in his book *Cultural Captives*, "If America continues on its current trend, the number of 18-29-year-old Americans who state, 'My religious preference is none or a non-Christian religion' will grow to over 50% of the population by the year 2030."[20]

Christianity has gradually become less socially accepted, which means that not only are we losing the nonboomerang youth exodus adults, but also the nonbelieving adults who never had faith yet, in the past, would explore it for the sake of their kids. Bottom line, you can no longer count on the boomerang effect. It's more like the sail-away effect.

So if Gen X is not returning to church like the generations before, and if the older Millennials are even less religious than Gen X, then what will happen to Gen Z (the largest current generation)?[21] It is the first truly post-Christian generation, with less than half attending church.[22]

Myth #2: Because My Kids Go to Awana/Youth Group/ Christian School/Homeschool, They'll Be Okay

Then there's the myth of the Christian "insurance plan." "My child has been in church since he was in my belly." "I piped in the Word of God via books on tape, so she could hear it in utero." "They've been to Awana, youth group, church camp, Christian school, and homeschool."

Check. Check. Double check. Good for you. Good for them. Seriously. And don't stop what you're doing (okay, maybe except for the books on tape). These things are great, but they are not guarantees. Desiring to probe the reasons for youth exodus, Ken Ham commissioned America's Research Group to do a study. In a stunning finding, the research revealed that Sunday school was actually *detrimental* to spiritual health! Kids who grew up in a Sunday school environment were *more* likely to have a secular worldview than those who didn't.[23] Wait…what?! I mean…HOW?!

Surprisingly enough, coloring pictures of animals in a boat and acting out "stories" on a felt board doesn't actually teach kids that what you are saying is *true*. It turns out they believe exactly what we tell them: that these are Bible *stories*.

For the most part, we are not teaching doctrine or skills that can help our children think critically from a biblical perspective about what they are learning in school. And as they get older, most church youth groups focus on entertaining kids (to retain attendance), not training them to become disciples. Apologist Frank Turek has astutely noted that "what we win them *with* we win them *to*."[24] Ed Stetzer has remarked that "too many youth groups are holding tanks with pizza."[25] The sad truth is that in many cases, we've won our kids to fun, friends, and pizza, but not necessarily to *Christ*.

Myth #3: They Won't Need Apologetics Training Until College

Steve Cable points out in *Cultural Captives* that "the culture itself has become just as corrosive as the college."[26] It used to be that a quick course in apologetics during their senior year of high school would give our kids the necessary spiritual booster shot before college. No longer. The infestation of anti-Christian teaching is trending younger and younger. Moms, truly: Elementary age is not too young to begin. In fact, some research indicates that up to 46% of youth have spiritually "checked out" by the end of middle school. They may attend church just to please their parents, but their Christian faith is in name only.[27] The American Research Group study noted,

We've always been trying to prepare our kids for college (and I still think that's a critical thing to do, of course), but it turns out that only 11 percent of those who have left the Church did so during the college years. Almost 90 percent of them were lost in middle school and high school. By the time they got to college they were already gone! About 40 percent are leaving the Church during elementary and middle school years![28]

Let those numbers sink in for a moment. *Forty %* are mentally leaving the church in *elementary and middle school.* Let's consider how early formative experiences typically occur: Morals are set by age 9; most salvation experiences happen by age 13; most worldviews are established by age 13.[29,30] If the way our kids choose their favorite sports team is any indication, they have "chosen sides" by third grade—that's typically eight years old. This means that from mid-elementary age onward, we need to be on our toes.

Okay, Okay, I Get It! But What Can I Do?

We must start our worldview training at a young age, teaching theology and apologetics. Because we aren't the only ones who are training children. Atheists now have their own alternative summer camp options—like "Camp Quest." The LGBT+ advocates are introducing propaganda in public schools as early as kindergarten. Maybe starting in utero is not such a bad idea after all!

The good news is that concerned Christians are answering the call for developing resources and curriculum designed to help teach children as early as the preschool years. For example, Melissa Cain Travis has her Young Defenders picture book series. Elizabeth Urbanowicz has just released her Foundations curriculum for third- through fifth-grade children. Deep Roots Bible curriculum is currently available for first through fourth grades (with more scheduled to be published). Tom Griffin has materials for those in fifth through eighth grades. (See our complete resource list at www.mamabearapologetics.com/resources.)

The parents and pastors who are introducing theology, apologetics, and worldview training to younger children are often amazed by the questions they ask and their ability to think through various issues. In fact, Kevin Duffy of Ratio Christi College Prep (RCCP) has found that churches that use the RCCP training materials have reported attrition levels falling from 75% to as low as 13%, helping to reverse the youth exodus in at least a few churches. We can all be encouraged by this kind of news! Our children are sponges. The question is, what are they going to soak up?

The youth exodus is real. Now that you are aware, alert, and no longer susceptible to the common myths about it, you are ready to discover what it means to be a Mama Bear and learn how to start counteracting the popular cultural lies that are coming for your cubs. By the time you're done with this book, we pray that you are hungry for apologetics and equipped to teach your cubs how to swallow the sweet honey of God's truth.

Discussion Questions

1. **Icebreaker:** What have you said to your kids that you never thought you would have to say? (Any elephant-booty licker parents in the room?)

2. **Main theme:** *Youth Exodus*—Do you know another parent who has experienced their child walking away from the faith? Which statistic shocked you the most?

3. **Self-evaluation:** Have you ever found yourself saying or thinking any of the myths about the youth exodus? How has your perspective changed? Did any of the myths hit close to home?

4. **Brainstorm:** What are some tough questions you've heard your child ask about the faith that you could start researching?

5. **Release the bear:** Check out the resources on the Mama Bear Apologetics website. What is *one* resource that you can start implementing into your weekly routine? (After reading *Mama Bear Apologetics: Empowering Your Kids to Challenge Cultural Lies,* of course!)

Chapter 2

How to Be a Mama Bear

Is this code for being the weirdest
mom on the playground?

Hillary Short

S everal years ago my husband and I went rafting in Washington state. The water, which came from melted glacier ice, was emerald green and sparkled brightly. Pine trees hugged the shorelines on both sides, and the scene proved absolutely breathtaking. In the raft were myself and my husband, his mom and dad, and his sister and her husband. We six Texans were ready for a grand adventure on a gorgeous river! I even wore my new wool socks bought specifically for this trip because I read they keep you warm when wet. What else could I do to prepare for this excursion? In my mind, the right outfit meant the right level of preparedness.

Yet I hadn't anticipated such strong rapids. The calm, glistening river on which our journey began soon transformed into rushing white waters shaped and jarred by boulders below. What happened to our scenic tour? Nobody told us we were going to have to work.

Suddenly, the river's force tipped our raft sideways and knocked my sister in-law and me overboard. She managed to hold onto a rope on the side of the raft and was working her way back in when my 60-year-old mother-in-law leapt with the force of a thousand stunt doubles, grabbed her full-grown daughter by the waist, and hoisted her back into the raft. It was an amazing sight to behold—one of those moments of motherly adrenaline you typically only hear about. It was even more amazing to witness such prowess from my vantage point in the river, sloshing amongst the rushing rapids, trying not to let them fully sweep me under the boat (after all, my mama wasn't there).

My mother in-law's impromptu heroism perfectly depicts a Mama Bear—she is instinctual, prepared, and strong. She doesn't need time to make a decision in a moment of crisis; the decision to ferociously protect her young was made the first time she held her child. She will do anything to save her cub.

Not all mothering is glamourous feats of prowess to protect our young. I love the way Melanie Shankle describes motherhood in her book *Sparkly Green Earrings*:

> There is really no better indicator you're a mother than acquiring the ability to catch throw-up in a plastic bag, disinfect your hands, and immediately ask your friend to pass the beef jerky as you put on another Taylor Swift song and act as if nothing happened. It's a unique skill set.[1]

Moms do whatever it takes, no matter how hard, and no matter how gross. While this kind of dedication is important for our children's physical development, it is especially imperative when it comes to our children's *spiritual development*. We may not *want* to jump into the deep end of theology and apologetics, but we *will*, lest we see our kids dragged down by the rushing rapids of bad ideas. We're Mama Bears. That's what we do! A Mama Bear does whatever it takes, even if that means studying apologetics.

Every generation faces its own kind of spiritual rapids. For our kids, the battle is especially fierce around ideas and morality. Christianity is no longer the accepted norm, and the number of openly atheistic families is growing.[2] Evangelistic atheistic organizations and even children's camps are popping up all over the country with the express purpose of training young people to argue *against* Christianity. In her book *Talking with Your*

Kids About God, Natasha Crain highlights two such organizations: Kids Without God (an initiative of the American Humanist Association) and a nationwide kids' program called Camp Quest. Crain gives an example of what goes on at these camps:

> One of the popular freethought activities is the Invisible Unicorn Challenge. Campers are told there are two invisible unicorns that live at Camp Quest but cannot be seen, heard, tasted, smelled, or touched. An ancient book handed down over countless generations contains the only proof of their existence. The challenge? Try to disprove their existence. (Campers learn they can't.)[3]

The campers then make the connection that only things measurable by the scientific method can be evaluated and therefore taken seriously. This belief is known as scientism and it is a flavor of naturalism, which we will discuss in chapter 6. I ask you, dear reader: Is that very belief able to be seen, heard, tasted, smelled, or touched?

Apolo...What? What Are We Apologizing For?

We need to teach our children critical thinking skills and prepare them to defend their faith—if not to others, at least to themselves. This isn't just a "good idea." Scripture commands us to do so. Peter said, "Always [be] prepared to make a defense to anyone who asks you for a reason for the hope that is in you; yet do it with gentleness and respect" (1 Peter 3:15). The word translated "defense," in the original Greek text, is *apologia.* In ancient Greece, *apologia* referred to a lawyer arguing for a case in court. This is not arguing or being defensive in the negative sense. Instead, it refers to giving reasons to support a conclusion, and doing so in a way that, ideally, is persuasive in nature. This is where our word *apologetics* comes from. No, we are not apologizing for our faith, nor are we being defensive about it. Rather, we are giving *reasons* and *evidence* for what we believe, preferably with the kind of skill and tact that is necessary for persuading others to accept the truth of Christ. A Christian apologist is a person who presents a case for the Christian faith.

We are apologists for many things in our lives. We give *reasons* for why such and such is the best cake recipe, or why our favorite TV show should have won the Emmy. We use *evidence* for why we trust one babysitter the most, and we would never appeal to blind faith when choosing an accountant. Why should we think the truth on whom our eternal salvation is placed should be supported by anything less?

Some people think studying apologetics means that you go looking for a fight. In our culture, we "look" for ways to defend our beliefs as much as I went "looking" for rapids. You don't have to search for opportunities; they find you, and they find your children. The command from 1 Peter 3:15 is for us to be *prepared* for when these occasions present themselves. Mama Bear Apologetics is about preparing our children so that when they encounter submerged boulders of bad ideas, the rapids don't capsize their faith.

A Call for Moms

In 2014, Hillary Morgan Ferrer recognized that out of all the demographics currently involved in apologetics, moms seemed to make up the fewest participants. She also realized that out of all the demographics that *need* apologetics, moms are among the *most* important! It's not necessarily that moms are uninterested—there is huge interest. Rather, the materials currently on the market don't cater to the practical needs of moms who want to figure out how to best explain biblical truths and concepts to their kids. In response to this growing desire and need among parents to become better equipped in obeying 1 Peter 3:15, Ferrer began Mama Bear Apologetics.

The website MamaBearApologetics.com hosts an array of articles, blogs, and podcasts. Each resource is geared toward teaching parents to answer their kids' questions in age-appropriate ways. Ferrer recognized that moms often don't have much time to sit down and read, so she made sure that audio resources were a prominent part of the ministry. The Mama Bear Apologetics Podcast is a conversational-style podcast where she and a partner discuss various apologetics topics. I don't know about you, but I can't follow a university lecture while I'm driving or packing lunches. But I (like most women) possess the ability to follow a conversation no matter what else I'm doing.

One of our other Mama Bears, Robin Lopez, also provides weekly blogcasts through the Audio Apologetics Blog. Robin finds helpful apologetics articles and simply reads them to her listeners. That way, while we Mama Bears scramble around all day, we can still feel "well read," even if we don't have the spare time to actually sit down to do it.

What a Mama Bear Is (and Isn't)

While Papa Bears undoubtedly play an integral role in their children's faith, more often than not it's Mom who spends the majority of the time with the kids. When spiritual questions are asked, they are likely being fielded by mom. For that reason alone moms will end up doing apologetics the most! You are your family's front-line defense, Mama Bear! Moms can have a profound influence on their children's spiritual development. Learning and teaching apologetics is one of the best things we can do in that role. Before we dive into exactly what a Mama Bear Apologist is, let's make sure we know what she's not.

A Mama Bear is not necessarily a mom—I know this to be true because the founder of Mama Bear Apologetics doesn't have kids herself! A Mama Bear is any woman who recognizes that the children in the body of Christ need guidance, role models, and solid answers to the tough questions about the faith. She is a Mama Bear to the church's kids (and let's be honest—don't you love it when someone *else* helps reinforce the truths that you want your children to hear?).

A Mama Bear isn't necessarily formally educated in apologetics— We don't need a formal degree in apologetics to read and listen to great apologetics materials. While higher-ed apologetic programs are wonderful, equipping yourself can be as simple as listening to a podcast while you unload the dishwasher or participating in an online reading discussion group.

A Mama Bear is not abrasive or argumentative—She models the last part of 1 Peter 3:15—"with gentleness and respect" just as much as the first part of the verse, which tells us to be prepared with a defense. Often the defense part of the verse gets all the attention, but that's not the full command. *Clearly, we are to defend in a very specific way.* Thus, the Mama Bear Apologist responds not only to the question or critique, but also to the person. A Mama Bear apologist answers the *person* as much as she does the question.

A Mama Bear isn't one stereotype—Mama Bears can be sorority sisters, volleyball coaches, soccer moms, engineers, homeschoolers, CEOs, scientists, teachers, bakers, runners, and software programmers. Mama Bears live all over the world; the common denominators are a passion for Christ, the pursuit of truth and, well, probably the fact that we're all really tired. Mama Bears are women who have realized that the Kingdom needs them right where they are!

Theodore Roosevelt said, "Do what you can, with what you have, where you are."[4] If every Christian woman took advantage of her conversations with nonbelievers at the playground bench, or the soccer field sidelines, or in the stands at her daughter's dance competition, the kingdom would have so many foot soldiers on the ground that it would grow exponentially! You are needed to do apologetics right where you are, even if that means teaching the words *true* or *evidence* to your toddler while you cut a grilled cheese sandwich into what should be appeasing shapes.

Four Key Traits of Mama Bears

As you begin this journey, pay attention to the four *H*'s of Mama Bears—honesty, humility, humor, and heroism:

1. *Honesty*—As Mama Bear apologists, we must be intellectually honest. If someone showed you Christ's body and could somehow

prove without a shadow of a doubt that it was His and He had never risen from the dead, would you still be a Christian? This scenario is difficult to imagine in reality, but the point is that we are to be careful followers of truth—scientific, historical, and metaphysical. We are not blind believers who practice Christianity because it's our culture or tradition. We hold up the claims of Christianity as the best and most reasonable explanation for who we are, where we came from, and why we're here. The Mama Bear Apologist is convinced that seeking the truth will land her at the foot of the cross and at the empty tomb that followed.

2. *Humility*—The Mama Bear realizes her life on Earth is finite, and she wants to make it purposeful. She knows her legacy is not wrapped up in the jewelry and china she passes down, but in the pearls of wisdom and character she gifts her children. She admits when she lacks the answer, yet is willing to search for it. She corrects course and mends fences when she has erred in fact, tone, or deed. Above all, she recognizes the dignity in the questioner behind the question because she loves others as God's creatures and as fellow passengers on this ball we call home that hurtles through space at 67,000 miles per hour.

3. *Humor*—Perhaps no skill is more needed in today's world than humor. It is the universal tension cutter and can even promote peace when used strategically. It is truly a skill—one that can be learned, developed, and honed. Why do you think four-year old boys deliver what they find to be a well-timed potty joke? It's a survival skill they've developed to change the serious tone of the conversation that you're *trying* to have with them about picking up their fruit pouches off the living room floor. (Totally hypothetical, of course…MY child would *never* do such a thing.) Humor is not much different in a conversation about apologetics. Often the topics have very personal implications and it's all too easy for either party to become emotionally heated. Enter humor—the

great tone-reset. Did you know humor can physiologically take people out of fight-or-flight mode?[5] It's an incredible salve, one you should practice using, albeit preferably above the level of a four-year-old.

4. *Heroism*—Even though a Mama Bear loves her cave of comfort and familiarity, she is willing to leave it to prepare her children for the real world. What worked for our generation growing up (attending church, Awana, and reading the Bible) is no longer sufficient. Are we saying that Scripture is insufficient? Absolutely not. However, we must realize that our kids are facing attacks on their faith that we never had to, and that means it's time to play catch-up. Yet it's tempting to take the easy way out and decide that we're exhausted from endless debates and therefore we would much rather just avoid talking about anything of substance. (Facepalm.)

I understand. The last few years haven't been a pretty scene for productive dialogue. No matter how much our culture wants the pendulum to swing toward fluffy, feel-good conversations, we cannot follow suit by ignoring opportunities to share the truth of Christ. That would be a grave mistake. His truth is not about political affiliations, it's about how we view the world. And that is exactly how Mama Bears can serve on the front lines—by bringing well-developed thoughts back into society. We must brave the world and leave our caves of comfort.

I'm New to Apologetics. Where Do I Even Start?

Now that we've established some of what a Mama Bear is and is not, let's look at what it means to be a Mama Bear apologist to the people around us.

1. *Know Your Bible*—We minister to our families first, and in order to do that well, we have to practice what we preach. We need to remain in God's Word and in regular prayer to Him. After all, we can't defend Scripture if we don't know it.

2. *Gather Resources*—Often, women are intimidated by the idea of getting into apologetics because they think it requires that they know all the answers right away. This is not the case. We need to model a thirst for learning if we want our kids to do the same, but we don't need to know everything at once. Great apologetics materials abound both in print and online. Not a reader? Listen to a podcast. Need to see and hear what's going on? Check out YouTube apologetics resources. Want community? There are some great Facebook groups whose sole purpose is discussing apologetics questions. The main thing is to get started.

3. *Carve Out Regular Family Time to Study*—After you have gathered resources, create time and space with your family for regular discussion. Intentionally ask your children difficult questions about Christianity. We aren't merely teaching them to know the answers; we are also teaching them how to *find* answers. We can look to the example of other faith systems that have successfully established certain routines within their families. Islam, Mormonism, and Orthodox Judaism prescribe specific times each day during which they stop to pray, study their religious texts, or disciple their kids. We may not be able to handle doing multiple daily lessons, but we can start out with once-a-week family studies and intentional conversations during the day. Let's commit to being the generation of mothers who restores Christianity to a state of thoughtfulness, academia, and real-life practice by making a regular and purposeful focus on Christ and His truths part of our family's daily routine.

4. *Find Like-Minded Mamas*—Next, we need to take this foundation of thoughtful focus and learning from our homes to our fellow brothers and sisters in Christ. As Mama Bears, we can share our excitement and confidence in defending the truths of Christianity by starting apologetics book clubs in our churches, incorporating more apologetics into Sunday school classes for all ages, and

participating in online discussion groups. As a piece of coal cannot stay hot on its own, so enthusiasm will dissipate if we keep it to ourselves. Discussing apologetics ideas with others is how we will experience iron sharpening iron (Proverbs 27:17).

5. *Practice, Practice, Practice*—Finally, take what you are learning and practice having conversations, even if it is with strangers. I know this sounds scary, but this is where we Mama Bears must exercise courage. I would never ask you to do something that I don't practice myself. On the Mama Bear Apologetics website, I write a blog series called Playground Apologetics, in which I discuss exactly what this step looks like. I share my real-life experiences (like an apologetics field reporter, if you will) of conversations I have started when I take my son to the playground. In the Playground Apologetics series, I discuss the nuanced skills you need, like how to recognize an opportunity in a conversation. I've found that a key element for success is to be asking people questions about *their* beliefs and reasons. Another key is lots of practice.

   Some people mistakenly assume that defending the faith means you do all the talking, but usually it's best to do as little talking as possible. Let the other person share her ideas and the reasons for why she believes what she does. It's a great way not only to learn about the other person's view (and so avoid misconceptions of it), but also to gently and respectfully help the other person discover areas where her reasoning might fall short. All it takes is asking the right questions. For more practical guidance on how to carry out an apologetics conversation, read Greg Koukl's book *Tactics in Defending the Faith*. It's an essential apologetics resource, one that I reference often in my blog series.

Mama Bears, we are so excited for you to embark on this great adventure, and we are honored to be a part of it. I know that you will find enlightenment in the pages to come and fulfillment in your role as a mama and a daughter of the King as you venture into the important work of apologetics. We need you! As we say at Mama Bear, "Apologetics might not affect *your* faith, but it might affect your children's."

Discussion Questions

1. **Icebreaker:** What have you witnessed (either in yourself or in someone else) that demonstrates the strength and ferocity of a Mama Bear protecting her kids?

2. **Main theme:** *You can do this!* What are some misconceptions you have had about apologetics in the past? Did this chapter help clarify how you, as a mom, can be a Christian apologist? What stood out to you?

3. **Self-evaluation:** Review the four "h" attributes on pages 40-42. Which characteristic comes most easily to you? Which is the hardest, and why? From the "Where Do I Even Start?" section, which suggestion would be the easiest for you to implement, and which is most outside your comfort zone? Why?

4. **Brainstorm:** What are some ways you and other moms can encourage and reinforce learning apologetics for each other and in your church community?

5. **Release the bear:** Would you be willing to talk to your pastor or other church leaders about their thoughts on apologetics and the importance of worldview training aimed at helping youth? You could share with your pastor or leaders some of the statistics you read on page 29. What are some ways we could help the church to reverse this trend of young people leaving?

Chapter 3

The Discerning Mama Bear

The refined art of "chew and spit"

Hillary Morgan Ferrer

Say the word *discernment*, and everybody thinks of something different. My friend's church class instructor had an interesting take on it. Apparently when it came to discernment among believers, he claimed that the Spirit would never reveal anything "negative" about another believer. If you "discerned" something negative, then it wasn't from the Holy Spirit. Ummm…excuse me? The Lord is never going to let me discern something negative about another believer? Where is *that* verse in the Bible? (I bet Nathan the prophet would beg to differ.)[1]

I've also known respected Christian leaders who implicity define discernment in the exact opposite way. Instead of *never* identifying negative things they see going on around them, they *only* point out the bad stuff. They may not come right out and say, "Discernment means pointing out everything you disagree with." However, when they claim to be exercising biblical discernment, it's often one big finger-pointing rant from beginning to end. They might as well title it "Everything That's Wrong with _____." Take your pick—a movie, a book, another Christian's theology.

Still others equate discernment with a feeling, like intuition. This is what the Bible refers to as "discerning of spirits" (see 1 Corinthians 12:10;

47

1 John 4:1). While that is part of discernment, it is not the whole part, or even a major part of what we are talking about here. We are talking about using discernment when it comes to ideas and worldviews, the discerning of truth from nontruth. This requires a commitment to understanding the Bible's teachings, and not just single verses.

The Party Nobody Wants to Attend

A friend of mine's young son said to her, "You always tell me no! You are the party of no! Nobody wants to go to *that* party, Mom." I suspect it was one of those moments where my friend felt torn between disciplining him for disrespect or laughing because what he said was funny. As a former teacher, I've felt this same conflict. But disrespectful or not, her son had a point. If we Christians are constantly focusing on our areas of disagreement, then we've basically become the food critics of Christianity. We sit back, create nothing, but tear down anyone else brave enough to try. What a cushy job! Who wouldn't want that gig?

We never want Christianity to be known as "the party of no." Rather, we should be known for our love, wisdom, and devotion to Christ and each other. True, part of keeping ourselves unpolluted by the world means rejecting certain parts of culture, but that should never be our main message to the people around us.[2]

So How *Are* We Defining Discernment?

Biblical discernment means identifying *both* the good and the bad. I compare biblical discernment to having a food allergy. For example, I can't eat peas. (Or rather, I *can*, but it is an unpleasant experience for everyone afterward.) If someone were to serve me a delicious plate of fried rice with vegetables, the first thing I would do is pick out the peas. I don't accept all the food, and I don't reject all of it. You could call this "culinary discernment." As Mama Bears, our job is to help separate the good from the bad, accept the good, and reject the bad.

Kids are natural culinary discerners. Raise your hand if you have a picky eater. (I'm assuming most of you are raising your hands.) Kids instinctively pick through their food as soon as you hand them their meal. Very rarely will they chow down without a thorough inspection. They want to make absolutely sure that you aren't pulling one of your mom-sneaking-an-unfamiliar-vegetable-into-the-meal tricks. If there are elements they don't like, they will immediately pick them out. (This is usually accompanied by grunts of frustration and loud sighing to dissuade you from including these ingredients in future meals.)

As Mama Bears, our job is to help separate the good from the bad, accept the good, and reject the bad.

Needless to say, we don't need to train our children to be picky when it comes to what they feed their bodies—they do this on their own. But we *do* have to train them to be discerning about what they feed their minds. I am reminded of the old Sunday school song that says, "Oh be careful, little eyes, what you see…" Everything our children watch and hear is either nourishing or harming their spiritual body.

Most parents will probably say, "I'm *very* careful what my children watch or listen to." That is good! Children progress through both physical *and* moral developmental stages. New parents baby-proof their homes because they know that a child beneath a certain age has no concept of right and wrong. Similarly, parents often childproof the media their kids are allowed to watch. If that's true in your case, I applaud you for this! However, we must realize that this is essentially like cutting up our kids' food for them. While parental supervision is appropriate for young children, at some point your kids will need to learn the skills to make wise decisions on their own, without you hovering over them. *We want to keep our kids safe, but part of keeping them safe is teaching them to discern for themselves.* When it comes to media, we cannot do this by simply labeling things as "safe/dangerous" or "Christian/non-Christian."

I have seen this safe/dangerous tactic used by many parents. The problem with so many aspects of culture is that they cannot be picked apart like food. For example, while listening to a song, we cannot pick which parts we want to hear and which parts we don't. We live in a world where the good is mixed in with the bad. There is very little that is all safe or all dangerous. Most everything requires discernment.

The Chew-and-Spit Method of Discernment

I have a shocking little statement for you: There are no Christians so theologically sound that they're never wrong, and there are no atheists so bad that they're never right. It doesn't happen. There is only one perfect man—Jesus, and one perfect book—the Bible. Most everything else will be a mixture of truth and error.[3]

The danger of dividing up the world into simplistic "safe" and "dangerous" or even "Christian" and "non-Christian" categories is that our kids will eventually (and perhaps accidentally) swallow a lie from something they thought was safe or Christian, or reject a truth from something they thought was dangerous or non-Christian. It is here that the picky-eater method for discernment is no longer viable. We need a new model. And as gross as it sounds, it's called the chew-and-spit method.

I am a proud Texan, and beef is a part of our cultural heritage. I *love* a good steak! Most steak eaters know that there are some pieces that make you keep chewing…and chewing…These are known as *gristle*. From a young age, we were trained to discreetly spit the gristle into a napkin without drawing attention to ourselves, then continue on with our meal. Chew and spit. We have to do it with certain types of food, and we have to do it with culture.

I'll use rated R movies as an example. The R-rated movies of the 1980s and 1990s are today's PG-13. Nowadays it is very difficult for me to sit through a movie with an R rating because of the amount of swearing and sexual content. That's why I generally avoid them, but I don't make it a hard rule to do so.[4]

I do not dismiss all rated R movies because there are some that have content that Christians can find to be of value. They may not outline the steps of salvation or show an atheist accepting Christ, but they do depict a kind of raw reality that is valuable to acknowledge and which can't be accurately depicted without disturbing content. For example, there was one movie produced in the late 1990s that portrayed the journey of a guy and a girl descending into the world of drugs. The movie showed the various physical and psychological stages that accompany addiction, and the (cough) lengths people will go to get their next fix. It was a brilliant movie, spectacularly produced, and images from it *still* haunt me to this day. What did I do after I finished watching it? I got on my knees and praised God for what He had protected me from. The movie reminded me how, with a few wrong decisions, I could have easily been one of those teenagers who got caught up with the wrong crowd and descended into drug culture.

The movie was brilliant in the way it showed the slow decay that occurs as a normal teenager becomes a junkie. And in *no way* did the film glorify the process. I can wager that not a single viewer left that movie thinking, *Oooh, that looks like fun! I want to try drugs!* The next time any of them went to a party where drugs were offered, I bet they thought twice. The movie had graphically exposed the deception of drugs, and in that sense, I think it was God-honoring. Did every part honor God? No. But the film was definitely worth a chew-and-spit experience.

My point is that *a mature, informed, discerning worldview does not need to fear the false messages that this world churns out if it has already been trained to identify which aspects to reject.* I'm not saying that every R-rated movie is as redeeming as this one (and especially not the ones being produced nowadays). But on the occasion such a movie comes along that appears to have redeeming value, I am well practiced in chewing and spitting—mentally swallowing what is spiritually useful, and spitting out the rest.

Not only do I use this method when I am interacting with culture, but also when I am listening to a sermon. There are many excellent theologians out there, but no one is 100% biblical and balanced all the time. We cannot listen to pastors without the occasional chew and spit. Not even Paul was immune from scrutiny. When he showed up to teach the Bereans, they were all, "Who is this fool? Fact check everything he says!" And they were *praised* for doing so! (Acts 17:11...with creative liberties taken.)

The Consequences of Not Teaching Our Kids to Chew and Spit

As I mentioned above, dividing the world into safe/good/Christian or dangerous/bad/non-Christian is like cutting your kids' food for them. This TV show is good. That one is bad. You can listen to this musician, but not that one. While this method is appropriate for children still in the black-and-white stage of thinking, it becomes counterproductive as they mature. Why? Because it gives them the mistaken impression that as long as they *categorize* something correctly, they can turn their brains off and operate on autopilot. However, there is no such thing as autopilot in the Christian life. I've heard F-bombs from a pastor during a sermon, and I was surprised at some of the excellent points Karl Marx made in *The Communist Manifesto*. Most everything is a mix of good and bad. (Or as Rebekah [one of the contributors to this book] always says, we're all a mixture of marble and mud.)

As tiring as it is to do so, we must exercise discernment in response to *everything* we hear and see, and we are to train our kids to do the same. Otherwise, what happens when your freshman goes off to college and assumes that professors, pastors, or Christians are safe when they're not? I have seen strong Christians go down weird and dangerous theological trails all because they thought a pastor or Christian leader's doctrine was trustworthy. Most anyone can spot a wolf among sheep. It's much harder to spot the wolf in sheep's clothing, and yet *that* is our command (Matthew 7:15).

Second, what happens when your children are under the impression that certain artists, speakers, or books are dangerous when they aren't? I can almost guarantee that at some point, they will find something redeemable, good, or true within what they were told was in the bad category. As your children get older and explore the world for themselves, they will discover that some of the "forbidden fruit" you've urged them to avoid are not dens of iniquity full of sex and Satan worship. At this point, they feel lied to. And lied to by whom? By you, of course! Or their pastor, or church, maybe by Christianity in general. And once they feel lied to about one thing, they will start wondering about what else has been a lie. At that point, you will have lost all credibility and for what? For children who were "safer" for a few more years, only to make a beeline for all the things you denied them in their youth? Except now, when it comes time for them to interact more with the world, it'll be like they are walking into a junkyard with virtually no immune system.

The most potent lies are wrapped in partial truths.

We need to train kids the refined art of chew and spit. We must build up their spiritual immune systems. We must teach them how to interact with contemporary culture, swallow what is good, and spit out what is bad. But we cannot teach them how to do this if we do not know how to ourselves! So what can we do?

ROAR Like a Mother!

Discernment is a process, and it doesn't stop at *identifying* the good and bad elements within culture. We must know *why* certain things are considered good or bad. That's why we here at Mama Bear Apologetics have created this handy-dandy guide for you! We won't guarantee that by utilizing these steps your children will develop perfect discernment and never go wrong. However, by regularly practicing these steps, they will learn the necessary tools to protect their own minds and hearts from popular lies wrapped in partial truths. Because that's the most effective kind of lie, is it not?

Truth is powerful, and the most potent lies are wrapped in partial truths. If a spoonful of sugar helps the medicine go down, then partial truths help the lies go down. The all safe/dangerous method teaches kids that lies are easy to spot. The chew-and-spit method teaches them that most lies are wrapped in attractive packages.

Being a Mama Bear isn't limited to protecting your kids from the dangers in this world, although that is part of it. The best Mama Bears *teach their kids how to spot danger on their own* and avoid it! We here at Mama Bear Apologetics use the ROAR method. ROAR is an acronym for:

Recognize the message

Offer discernment (affirm the good and reject the bad)

Argue for a healthier approach

Reinforce through discussion, discipleship, and prayer

Each chapter in this book will take you through these four steps. We are in a culture war, and unfortunately, a lot of people are talking past each other. Why? Because neither side will recognize the good that their opponent is offering! The ROAR method is intended to identify a message and analyze its ideas with grace and truth. Doing this requires identifying the good intentions, separating them from the bad ideas, synthesizing a healthier approach, and strategically praying through the battle of ideas.

Step 1: Recognize the Message

All media—movies, books, music, and art—have a message. The question is this: Can we identify the message? Going back to our chew-and-spit analogy, the only way for me to know whether I should spit something out is by correctly identifying the food to begin with. Is it squishy when it's supposed to be firm? Is it crunchy when it's supposed to be smooth? If I bit into a piece of broccoli and it had the texture of pudding, I would spit that nastiness out immediately! I know what broccoli is supposed to feel like in my mouth, and it ain't like pudding.

When it comes to media, here are some habits you will find helpful:

1. Identify the messages that are being presented. They all have one or more. (Except maybe that song about there being millions of peaches...I think those dudes were just high.)
2. Along with your kids, identify which values the creators are elevating. (Freedom? Autonomy? Sex? Drugs? Pride?) Which values

are they demeaning? (Humility? Responsibility? Traditional gender roles?)

3. Try to piece together the worldview behind the message. What do you think the artist's definition of good and bad is? What about moral and immoral? What is the good life—the life that reflects success (according to their art or writing)? Is it money? Lots of romantic relationships? Freedom from rules?

4. If you are watching a movie, identify which characters and qualities are presented in an attractive way. Pay attention to the traits that are exhibited by the villains. The protagonist and antagonist are often archetypes, or representations of ideas.

Accurately identifying the message is the first step toward exercising discernment. There are many ways you can cultivate this skill with your kids. When you go see a film, choose movie theaters that are further away than you would normally go. On the long drive home, discuss the movie. Ask your children to identify the overall message. Can they do it? Can you?

What about the music your kids listen to? What are their favorite songs? Print out the lyrics, get together for family night, go through the songs line by line. Identify the message underlying each one. What is being communicated as truth? What is being glorified? What is being shamed?

Part of the biblical process of sanctification—or spiritual growth—is *training* our appetites to crave what is good and be repulsed by what is not. What is the song, movie, art piece, or story prompting the consumer to crave? Identify it. Discuss it together. Is it something the Bible wants us to crave? I am sure that you will get your share of eye rolls, but that's part of being a parent, right? (I personally believe eye rolls are a God-given sign that you're doing something right.)

Step 2: Offer Discernment

There is a big difference between *offering* discernment and being a finger pointer. Nobody wants to have a conversation with someone lecturing from their soapbox, so keep this step conversational. Young kids tend to be black-and-white thinkers, so it is important for us to model discernment in a way that doesn't encourage them to be "terrifying truth tellers." Do not be mistaken: A person can be absolutely in the right yet be totally obnoxious about it. Our goal is for God's truth to be the aroma of Christ, not the stench of self-righteousness.

There are three skills necessary for practicing discernment: (1) seeing things accurately, (2) correctly identifying the good, and (3) correctly identifying the bad. If we don't see things accurately, we may end up condemning a strawman version (or a false representation) of an idea. A strawman argument is a type of logical fallacy—it happens when a person presents an oversimplified and distorted version of an idea and then offers a rebuttal to it. It got its name because doing this is like getting into a fight with a lifeless scarecrow. You may "win the fight," but only because you set the situation up in such a way that it was hardly a fair match.

Here are two examples of strawman statements: (1) "Evolutionists think that our great-great-grandfather was a monkey," and (2) "Pro-life advocates think women should go back to being barefoot and pregnant in the kitchen." An evolutionist would never agree with the first statement, and a pro-lifer would never agree with the second. In both cases, a strawman version of a specific viewpoint has been set up. We must avoid doing this if we want to earn the right to speak into culture. Our goal in discernment is to offer up an accurate representation of what our opponents believe—to the point they would agree with what we say about them. Think of it as the golden rule of apologetics: Treat other people's ideas the way you would like yours to be treated.

The second necessity in discernment is to accurately identify the good. This could be in the form of good ideas, good values, or good motives. There are a lot of bad things people do with good motives. Having correct motives doesn't make their actions right, nor does it make their statements true. Pointing out that someone's cherished beliefs are incorrect is akin to doing worldview surgery. How does a surgeon approach a patient?

He doesn't run quickly into the operating room from out of nowhere, waving a scalpel and slicing away. No. The doctor builds a relationship with the person. Together they talk about the procedure to be performed and why it will be helpful. Over time, trust is established.

Similarly, we establish trust with people by acknowledging their good intentions. Few people think that they are on the wrong side of history. Everyone sees themselves as crusading for the greater good. We must try to see their idea from *their* perspective. What are they valuing? What are they trying to accomplish? What is their ultimate goal? A person who believes in communism is often motivated by the corruption she or he sees in large corporations. He or she may know people who work three jobs yet can't seem to pay the bills. This person may ache for the plight of the poor and genuinely want to lift them up to a higher station in life. All of these motivations are things that we can affirm! We *should* stand against corruption. We *should* want to help the poor.

It should go without saying that there are *massive* issues with communism that we should stand against. However, before we point all of them out, let's stand on the same side as our misguided comrade and affirm all the good that we can. It is easier to fight with people when you are standing opposite of them. It is much harder to take a swing when you are standing on the same side. When we affirm the good intentions of the other person, we build bridges of trust. These bridges tell the person, "I see you. I hear you. I understand you." That trust *must* be built before we can attempt to start "remodeling" unhealthy beliefs.

That is why the step of affirming the good must come first. People may think that their belief is their identity, but it is not. Scripture tells us in Colossians 2:8, "See to it that no one takes you *captive* through hollow and deceptive philosophy." *We are not dealing with enemies. We are dealing with captives.* Think of it like a hostage situation. All good cops know that if a kidnapper is holding a hostage, you do not take a shot unless you can separate the hostage enough to ensure that your bullet hits the abductor and not the abductee. In the battle of ideas, we cannot drop a truth bomb and let the chips fall where they may. We must maintain love for the person while we demolish the idea.

The final requirement for discernment is to identify the bad. People often fall into one of two categories—they either dread this step (or avoid it all together), or this is their favorite step and they rush through all the other steps so they can start pointing out everything that's wrong in the world. There is a time and a place to speak up against lies that are being smuggled in through virtuous motives. When people don't speak up, lies snowball. A friend of mine used to tell his kids, "What you tolerate today, you accept tomorrow. What you accept today, you embrace tomorrow." I would add a third statement to that: "What you embrace today, you promote tomorrow." We have seen this progression within the realm of sexual ethics, have we not?

Step 3: Argue for a Healthier Approach

I can already hear the moms' nostrils flaring with this one. "What? No way am I teaching my kid to argue. I'm always trying to get them to *stop* arguing!" Before we can appreciate this step, we need to first rid ourselves of the colloquial definition of *argue*. The Oxford English Dictionary defines *argue* as to "give reasons or cite evidence in support of an idea, action, or theory, typically with the aim of persuading others to share one's view." That is what we at Mama Bear Apologetics mean by an argument.

When we argue for a healthier worldview, we are providing *reasons* for why we affirm that which we say is good and reject that which we say is evil. We need reasons for calling one idea *truth* and another idea a *lie*. We cannot tear someone's worldview apart and just leave it there. We need to propose an alternative worldview, one that retains all the good elements that we've affirmed while replacing the lies with biblical wisdom.

Biblical wisdom is not ignorant of the world. It doesn't think that this life is always full of rainbows and puppies. Rather, it takes human nature into account. It anticipates evil, selfishness, and suffering. It isn't under the impression that we will ever achieve utopia here in this world. A biblical worldview sees the world for the broken mess that it is, but at the same time understands the hope that Christ provides.

Having a biblical worldview doesn't mean that we just attach Bible verses to a statement and call it a day. We should realize by now that anyone can take a verse out of context to justify their own agenda. Not only must we know Scripture, but we need to *know God, and know the heart of God.* The heart of God will never conflict with the Word of God, but the words of God can be twisted, as happened in the garden of Eden.

Furthermore, while we as Christians believe that a healthy worldview *is* a biblical worldview, we don't have to limit ourselves to verses when it comes to supporting our stance. Scripture is a great starting point when talking with other Christians, but most non-Christians don't care what the Bible says. We need to find common ground that gives them a reason to want to talk with us.

It's amazing how many truths in Scripture were ignored until modern science finally showed them to be true. A biblical worldview helps us flourish with insights into human nature, principles of discernment, guidelines for society, and truths about ultimately reality. It allows us to see things as they really are. Common sense and fair-minded science reinforce a good biblical worldview. For this reason, we will not only share verses that reflect the truth and lies that we discuss in this book, but we will also seek to give practical, real-world, common-sense evidence that supports what the Word of God teaches. Your children need to know that God's wisdom isn't just valid in church. It can be taken into the arenas of science, sociology, and psychology and shown to be true there as well.

Step 4: Reinforce Through Discussion, Discipleship, and Prayer

It is not enough to discern between good and evil, or even to provide the reasons for the conclusions we've reached as a result of our discernment. If we stop there, it's like we have trained for a test and then slept in on exam day. The way we live our lives is evidence that a biblical worldview is coherent, reasonable, rational, and good. It isn't enough for our kids to hear us *talk* about the truth; they must understand how we are to *live* the truth.

At the end of each chapter, we will provide some helpful conversation starters for you and your kids. We will also recommend some activities that will help reinforce the truths that we are upholding and the lies that we are rejecting. And finally, we cannot be ignorant of the fact that our war is not a battle between people. It's not even a battle between ideas! Our war is predominantly a *spiritual* battle, and we need to prepare ourselves accordingly. Thus, in Part 2 of this book, we have also included a PAWS for Prayer section at the end of each chapter, written by Julie Loos, with prayers specifically tailored to address each of the lies we discuss. We can talk all day long, but the real battle takes place on our knees. May we never forget that!

Discussion Questions

1. **Icebreaker:** What is the grossest thing you've ever accidentally eaten?

2. **Main theme:** *Discernment means both affirming the good and rejecting the bad.* What are some examples of things in pop culture that polarize people? Have you ever completely disagreed with someone about something you thought was "bad"? Pick something to discuss (such as a TV show, a movie, a book, political view, or a way of thinking), and talk about the good and the bad. What good can be swallowed? What needs to be spit out?

3. **Self-evaluation:** Do you have a tendency to label things as either safe or dangerous for your children? For what ages and personality types do you think this method is appropriate? For what ages or personality types might this method be inappropriate? Why?

4. **Brainstorm:** What are some ways that you can take your children's media or interests and teach them to chew and spit?

5. **Release the bear:** Pick one song or movie that your child likes and listen to or watch it together. Identify the good aspects that align with God's truth. Identify the aspects that don't. Remind your children how important it is that they practice this kind of discernment with all books, movies, music, and ideas.

Chapter 4

Linguistic Theft

Redefining words to get your way and avoid reality

I was in fifth grade when I first encountered the concept of linguistic theft. I had just transferred from my private Christian school the year before to a rural public school. As I walked through the hall one day, I had an incredible feeling of peace and joy, so I decided to express myself by letting out a contented sigh and proclaiming, "I feel so gay!" I knew instantly, from the looks on the other students' faces, that I had said something wrong.

My mom used to sing the "Kookaburra" song to me as a kid. Apparently living a gay life is okay for birds sitting in gum trees (or the Flinstones), but not for a fifth grader walking through school halls in the late 1980s. Needless to say, I learned *a lot* that first year in public school. What a sheltered little creature I had been before!

Linguistic theft is much more sinister than just the evolution of language. *Linguistic theft refers to purposefully hijacking words, changing their definitions, and then using those same words as tools of propaganda.* This is not a new technique (it's an especially virulent form of the equivocation fallacy), but it is extremely prevalent right now. Not only are words in general being commandeered to promote the lies we discuss in this book, but *Christian* words, virtues, and concepts are being kidnapped as well. And the ransom—acquiescence to the new definition—is too high a price to pay.

63

Far too often I see Christians succumb to these dangerous demands. We've lost the word *gay*. But that's okay because we have other words for happy. There are other words we are currently losing that are far more precious, such as *marriage, love, hate, equality, justice, male, female, tolerance, bigotry, oppression, war*, and *crisis*. These words and more are all under siege, and if we want our children to properly understand Scripture, we cannot afford to let them go without a fight.

Who Cares About Words? Words Are Just a Social Construct, Right?

Wrong. Words are important. As apologist Holly Ordway says, "Once language becomes routinely distorted, it becomes increasingly easy to justify and promote evil—while at the same time hiding behind positive words."[1] In fact, words are *so* important that John 1 uses the Greek term *logos* to describe Jesus Himself: "In the beginning was the *Word*, and the *Word* was with God, and the *Word* was God...The *Word* became flesh and made his dwelling among us" (verses 1, 14). In fact, now that I think about it, the war on words is essentially the same as the war on God. Postmodern culture is trying to mold God's created reality into a reality that they approve of, one that fits *their* definitions of love, tolerance, etc. It's a repackaged form of idolatry. No one is bowing down to an idol in their closet, but we have plenty of people bowing to a Jesus of their own design.

We as parents, guardians, and caregivers need to be especially aware of how words are being used. We can teach our children to love God, love their neighbor, and love their enemy. But what do we do when the concept of love is replaced by the shallow concept of comfort? For us to say or do anything that makes someone uncomfortable or offended is now considered unloving, and thus we are labeled as haters. Psalm 10:18 extols God as a defender of the oppressed, so what will our kids do when taking a stand against sin is interpreted as oppressive? According to the new definition, to "defend the oppressed" now requires affirming sin! We are seeing an unraveling of the basic moral fabric of society *as we speak*, and it is all being done through creatively redefining words affirmed in Scripture.

How Linguistic Theft Works

In this chapter we'll look at some of the most common words being hijacked, and how they are being used to advocate decidedly unbiblical agendas. Then in the following chapters, we will help identify the abducted vocabulary for which to be on the lookout. They are often smooth-sounding ideas wrapped in secular principles and smuggled in through Christian-sounding virtues. Before we move on, though, let's first understand the reasons for this tug-of-war over words, and how these new definitions are being used as a means for certain people to get what they want and avoid reality. Linguistic theft is effective in the following ways:

1. Stops a Discussion in Its Tracks

Certain word choices are strategically used to stop conversation by appealing to people's innate sense of right and wrong. Abuse is wrong. Love is right. Hate is wrong. Truth is how you define it. Tolerance is right. Intolerance is wrong. If a person changes the definitions or connotations of these words, they effectively control the conversation. Our job as Mama Bears can be as simple as asking, "What do you mean by that?" (I am reminded of that scene from *The Princess Bride* in which the Spaniard says, "You keep using that word. I do not think it means what you think it means.")

As Mama Bears, not only do we advocate for open communication, but communication based on truth. If someone is using a bogus definition for a word, we need to call it out (in love, grace, and kindness of course...but call it out nonetheless). That's because fake definitions obscure the issues, and it doesn't make sense to attempt to carry on a discussion when we're working with two different meanings for the same word.

2. Compels People to Act Without Thinking Through the Issues

Emotions are great responders, but horrible leaders. Unfortunately, when a person has an emotional reaction to a statement, it becomes difficult to think about it rationally. This is actually the brain's physiological response to emotion. Turning on the amygdala (the site of emotional processing) turns *off* the prefrontal cortex (the site of rational thought). A person doesn't *choose* for this to happen, it just happens. Research has shown that when the amygdala and prefrontal cortex compete, initially the amygdala (emotional center) wins.[2] People can be talked down from this state, but they must first realize that the switch from rational to emotional thinking occurred in the first place! (Most people don't even realize it.) You can see why propaganda writers phrase their "arguments" with inflammatory language intended to trigger the emotions. It's much more efficient than presenting *actual* information.

Those who hijack words figure that most people aren't going to take the time to respond thoughtfully to a crisis. That's good news for them! If they want to promote an agenda without getting much pushback, they will keep presenting a situation as a crisis. "Desperate times call for desperate measures!" they say. *Crisis* isn't the only word they'll use—they also use the terms *abuse* or *war*. "Stop analyzing! We're at war here! No time for thinking!"

When people use emotionally charged words in an attempt to persuade others, they are *trying* to elicit an emotional reaction. They know that an emotional respondent will tend to act without thinking, which is perfect for the manipulator! As Hitler supposedly said, "How fortunate for leaders that men do not think."

Picture that scene in Star Wars episode IV when Obi-Wan Kenobi used the Force to get out of a sticky situation. He could have said, "Are you profiling? I am so offended! Do you know how racist you sound right now? How would you feel if it was your droid being stopped at every turn? Stop oppressing these droids. They are not the droids you're looking for, you intolerant bigot!" That's probably how the script would read nowadays. Mix in some guilt, fear, anger, pity, and compassion, and you've got the recipe for pushing an agenda! And the perfect cover for it all is linguistic thievery.

3. Blurs the Details

Not sure what everyone is so upset about? You've probably seen linguistic theft in action. What exactly constitutes a crisis? Or a war? Or bigotry? Or intolerance? Or violence? If you hear a buzzword and you are left thinking, "Okay, so what *actually* happened…?" you are probably dealing with propaganda, not actual information. The buzzwords give the illusion of offering information, but the real purpose for using such words is it allows people to use their imaginations and fill in the details with what *they* think the word means. We saw this happen during the March for Women in 2017. I can't count the number of ladies who posted on Facebook with comments like, "I don't understand what this march is about. Can someone explain?"

That's why I posted a blog article titled "So You Marched for Women This Weekend? 8 Things You Probably Didn't Know You Were Marching For." It caused a bit of a ruckus, but all I did was peel back the curtain and expose the real agenda for the march, which was stated on the organizer's own website. (I learned that word thieves don't like it when you fill in the missing details with actual information.)

4. Vilifies the Opposing Viewpoint

Unfortunately, people on all sides of an argument do this. Everyone wants to look like the good guys, but some people won't be forthright about what they really want to say. For example, not many people will stand on a street corner with a sign that says, "Everyone should be able to have sex with whomever they want, no matter the gender, age, relation, or number of participants." However, you *will* see signs that say, "Love is love." Or how about anti-free speech rallies that equate free speech with fascism? You may think I'm kidding, but on many college campuses, advocating for free speech will get you branded a fascist.[3]

And don't forget Hitler. Ohhhh, Hitler. He's the kid nobody wants on their kickball team. The Christians claim he was an atheist, the atheists claim he was a Christian, the right says he was left, the left says he was right. If your camp can make the opposing camp share *anything* in common with Hitler, then you have won, hands down. (Apparently, "Hitler was bad" is the only thing we can *all* agree on.)

There's a big difference between being heard and being understood and persuasive.

But in all seriousness, pay attention to this in the way you treat opposing ideas. As we hope to show in this book, most people swallow the whoppers discussed in the upcoming chapters thinking that they are serving the greater good. The road to hell may be paved with good intentions, but before you loudly point out that others are marching off to hell, please at least acknowledge their good intentions first. You may be right, and they may be the devil incarnate…but then again, maybe they aren't. Maybe they are just captives to bad ideas. When you try to warn people by adopting an alarmist tone, you will be heard, but you won't necessarily be understood and persuasive. There's a big difference between being heard and being understood and persuasive.

5. Turns a Negative into a Positive (or Vice Versa)

You'll see this happen especially during pro-life/pro-choice debates. What exactly do those who are pro-choice mean by *choice*? If we want to get technical, they are referring to the *choice* for a woman to scald, dismember, or suction out her in-utero, fetal human—if she no longer wants it to grow in her body. You'll likely never see a protester holding *that* sign though. *Choice* or *reproductive justice* sounds much more positive!

A few years ago, there was a brouhaha over a popular ministry whose new CEO began taking this well-known organization in a different direction. The concept of sin was oddly missing from their explanation of "the gospel." Worried leaders in all states began petitioning the board of directors to clarify this new position. When their concerns went unheeded, many stepped down. In response to this mass exodus of state leaders, the national leadership sent out a memo condemning those who did not like this new direction. In it they emphasized how they would not back down and would continue to shout love and hope even louder to anyone willing to listen. Notice the change? A refusal to acknowledge sin is redefined as shouting *love* and *hope.*

Words That Are Being Stolen

Now that we've discussed how to identify when someone is engaging in linguistic theft, let's talk about some of the most commonly commandeered words.

Love

This one little word is an all-around favorite. Everyone loves *love*, provided they get to define it. I think part of the battle was lost when our English language started utilizing one word for a concept that can have many meanings. In ancient Greek, there are four different kinds of love: *phileo* (brotherly love), *eros* (sexual love), *agape* (unconditional love) and *storge* (natural, instinctual affection, like parent to child love).

Love used to be defined as "to will the good of another." (Of course, this is also problematic when our world can't agree on the definition of *good* anymore, or that good even exists apart from our own opinions!) Anything that makes someone uncomfortable is now deemed unloving. Today, to love someone means to blindly accept whatever that person believes, even if his or her belief contradicts reality.

Because God *is* love, I vote that He gets to define it. One of the most overlooked points in 1 Corinthians 13—also known as the love chapter— is that love "does not rejoice in unrighteousness, *but rejoices with the truth*" (verse 6 NASB). When our kids are confused about where their loyalties should lie regarding love, we should point them to the side of truth.

Granted, that means they need to know what truth is...

Truth

Have you noticed this season's hot new phrase? It puts a possessive pronoun in front of truth. (Remember your seventh-grade grammar rules?) We are no longer dealing with *the* truth. Nope. That's way too narrow. Our kids are now encouraged to "live *their* truth." This is *my* truth. He's being authentic to *his* truth.

I can't even begin to tell you how dangerous this one lie is. When our society messes with the definition of truth, it is messing with our kids' very foundation of reality. If our children no longer feel comfortable using *reality* as their arbiter of truth, they will be insecure and timid about having any convictions whatsoever.

Truth has become whatever an individual's buffet-style worldview happens to be, and none of us can say anything against it. After all, that would be unloving, bigoted, and intolerant. Even science is ignored if it contradicts the paradigm of tolerance.

> **When our society messes with the definition of truth, it is messing with our kids' very foundation of reality.**

Tolerance

This one is *huge* right now. When I say huge, I mean that students at the University of Wisconsin-Madison would rather agree that a medium-height white male interviewer was actually a 6'4" Chinese woman than be accused of being intolerant.[4] I'm not kidding. There is a video that documents this. The word *tolerance* no longer means to live peaceably with people of different beliefs. It now means that all beliefs, no matter how bogus, must be treated as equally legitimate.

Tolerance (like political correctness) started out as a good idea that responded to a valid critique of culture—then the term got hijacked and it went off the rails. The concept of tolerance is very biblical. Romans 14 is devoted to tolerance within the Christian community regarding convictions about eating meat that had been sacrificed to idols and other disputable matters. Tolerance is implied in the many verses that encourage church unity.[5]

Thankfully, the Oxford Dictionary has not been rewritten yet, and tolerance is still defined there as "the ability or willingness to tolerate the existence of opinions or behavior that one dislikes or disagrees with."

According to the *actual* definition, for tolerance to exist, there must be (1) dislike or (2) disagreement. I cannot stress to you enough the importance of repeating this to your children on a regular basis. Whenever you hear someone talking about intolerance, ask your kids, "Are they asking for people to accept their belief as equally true, or to live with them in peace despite disagreement?"

Tolerance has essentially been relegated to a place of neutrality, where a person is prohibited from having strong convictions about anything. The only strong conviction a person is permitted to have is to say that everyone is equally right. Deny anyone's right to be right, and you are intolerant.

Do not let your kids be bullied into silence by adopting this bogus definition of tolerance. Teach them how to graciously define the word and how to respectfully coexist with people of differing beliefs without having to change their own. Modeling this begins in the home. There are usually plenty of opportunities, especially if siblings are involved. Just think about how many times your kids disagree on something. Be purposeful about reminding them the definition of *tolerate*, and then have them practice their new skills on their brother or sister.

Justice and Equality

Unless you're a Luddite living off the grid, you've probably heard a lot about justice and equality in the media. At every turn, there is some group demanding justice because situations are said to be unequal.

Every social problem is now being defined in terms of justice and equality. Want to redefine marriage? Fight for marriage equality! Want to organize a women's march? Fight for gender justice! Do people make different wages? Economic injustice! If you say anything against any of these movements, it *must* be because you are content with injustice and inequality. In fact, using these two little words actually utilizes *all five* of the tactics described earlier in the chapter!

The side that controls the words *love, truth, tolerance, justice,* and *equality* is the side that can shut the conversation down, compel people to act without thinking, blur the issues, vilify the opponent, and basically win the argument on emotions alone. Why? *Because everyone already believes in love, tolerance, justice, and equality!*

Justice is a frequent theme in both the Old and New Testaments and is even an attribute of God.[6] However, the way it is currently being used is a far cry from how it is defined in Scripture. In today's culture, justice no longer means "what is merited." When someone talks about equality, they are no longer referring to equality of access or worth. They mean equality of *outcome.* For example, Harvard decided that there were too many Asians being admitted to the school, and that this was *unjust* to other races. Their solution? Change the criteria for admittance based on race. This practice has landed them in a legal battle. To be considered for admittance, Asian students must have SAT scores that, on average, are 140 points higher than their white classmates, 270 points higher than Hispanics, and 450 points higher than African Americans![7,8] How's that for justice and equality?

Bigot

These days, anyone who makes what is perceived to be an exclusive statement is automatically labeled a bigot. Do you believe Jesus is the only way? Well that's a bigoted claim. Do you believe in the biblical definition of marriage—that is, one man and one woman for life? Bigot. Do you deny that all paths lead to the same God? Again, bigot.

The irony is that people who use the term *bigot* in this manner are actually living out the very definition of the word. According to the Merriam-Webster's dictionary, a bigot is "a person who is obstinately or intolerantly devoted to his or her own opinions and prejudices." Popular opinion right now is that all ideas are equally legitimate, and anyone who does not agree is a bigot.

Authentic

This is another buzzword, one that has even worked its way into most Western churches. In times gone by, many Christians tried their best to appear perfect. After all, they reasoned, how could people believe that Christianity was true unless all churchgoers' lives appeared perfectly ordered? I am thankful to not be burdened with having to pretend my life is perfect. I'm not very good at hiding my thoughts. My family will readily attest that if my mouth doesn't say it, my face will. Luckily for me, my inability to maintain my "Christian game face" works to my advantage because perfection is no longer considered to be the primary evidence of a growing faith. Nope. Openly admitting to *imperfections* is all the rage now. Woo-hoo!

One of the "delightful" skills we possess as humans is the ability to make an idol out of anything. Currently, one of the more popular idols is this abstract (and often bogus) concept of authenticity. Authenticity is said to be the highest goal one can aspire to, and openly claiming to "have it all together" will draw concerned whispers from friends who wonder if they should plot an intervention for you.

So what am I saying? Is authenticity bad? Should we go back to the days of glossing over our imperfections and longing for the winter of our discontent, during which we could be honest to *no one* about our current struggles? By no means! However, we must also look at how the word *authentic* has been hijacked.

In a Christian context, encouraging people toward authenticity was originally intended to help them to admit their sinfulness, experience conviction (as opposed to shame and condemnation), and love one another despite their struggles. All of us should work toward sanctification and holiness while maintaining the humility that comes from understanding how far we are from Christ's perfection. That's the biblical take.

Enter today's authenticity, which is actually a Trojan horse for rebellion. This new and more popular definition says, "You are perfect just the way you are" or, "We are all messy. Learn to love your beautiful, messy life!" These are code for "God would rather you be 'real' than striving for holiness." This kind of authenticity says that if something doesn't come naturally, or doesn't feel natural, then it is inauthentic and therefore fake. Newsflash: Much of the Christian life is uncomfortable. What if Jesus had said, "You know, I really don't *feel* like being crucified today. It doesn't feel like the right time. I just need to be *authentic* with you all, and I don't want to try to be someone I'm *not* right now, like a Savior. Thanks for understanding." Thank God Jesus did not do that!

If a person is using the word *authentic* to describe a person who doesn't hide their struggles, that is healthy. But if the word is used to describe someone's apathy about struggling over sin, or a blatant acceptance of sin, then that is *not* healthy. That's just flat-out rebellion cloaked in Christian lingo. Paul warned against this in 1 Corinthians 5, where an entire community was so "proud" of God's grace that they exulted in their sin.

Healthy authenticity stops where *unhealthy* tolerance of sin begins. If you're not perfect, don't pretend to be. If you are imperfect, don't revel in it. The purpose of authenticity is to loosen the chains of silence so that people can pursue freedom from the sin that binds them, not so they can live comfortably with their chains without feeling judged by anyone. Big difference. Like, REALLY big difference.

> **True authenticity loosens chains so that people can pursue freedom.**

How to Fight Back Without Being a Jerk

All in all, what can we do about this mass theft taking place under our noses? How do we teach our kids to see through these verbal hijackings?

1. ***Know the biblical definitions of these words***—What does God say about love? What does He say about truth? You might want to find a dictionary from before 1950 and look at some of the definitions before agendas started creeping in. If the word isn't in the Bible (like *bigot*), then study how that word is defined, and talk about examples of actual bigotry. (Ahem…1960s desegregation much?)

2. ***Teach your kids to identify buzzwords***—To do that, however, we need to recognize them ourselves. (In the following chapters, we have made an effort to highlight the buzzwords that accompany the "ism" lies.)

Take the word *deserve*. Who knows how many advertisements that little word appears in? (No wonder we live in such an entitled society.) When you are shopping with your kids and you see a sign that says someone "deserves" something (a new bathroom, a better set of golf clubs, etc.), ask your children, "What if a person gives wedgies to handicapped kids? Do you think he or she deserves a new XYZ? What does the Bible say about what we deserve?" (Hint: Romans 6:23.)

3. ***Identify when you are embarrassed to state your position***—Let me be clear: An intellectual position on any given issue should not be embarrassing to admit unless your position has been culturally stigmatized. With words like *love / hate, tolerant / intolerant, bigot / inclusive*, we are being told that our biblical principles land us in very unattractive territory. Do not allow this to happen. When one faction claims association with a positive word, the opposite faction is by default associated with the negative counterpart of that positive word. Why do we sit back and allow ourselves to be the punching bags? Stop it.

   We are called to be loving, but in love we should recognize and point out false definitions. Disagreement does not equal hate. Disparities are not always due to injustice. Exclusive beliefs do not equal intolerance. If that were the case, then everyone would qualify as intolerant. Even the person telling everyone else that we should be more tolerant is being intolerant of the people he claims are intolerant. It's a self-refuting statement.

4. ***Decide to be salt and light***—Salt and light have two properties: one is to prevent decay, and the other is to act as an irritant. Light in the midst of darkness is very useful, but it can also be very irritating. Salt is used to prevent decay, but it is also painful if you accidentally get it in an open wound or in your eyes. Being salt and light is a mixed bag. Not everyone will welcome your being "the salt of the earth…[and] the light of the world" (Matthew 5:13-14).

But that doesn't excuse us from fulfilling the role God has called us to.

Bad ideas start with bad logic, and it is no beatific virtue to agree with bad logic. Matthew 5:9 says "blessed are the peacemakers," not "blessed are the peacekeepers." A peace*keeper* will not rock the boat, and the peace is a shallow one based on silence in the face of destructive evil. A peace*maker* is someone who *creates* peace by getting everyone on the same page. We cannot do this without making a few waves, or without countering bad logic with good. We don't have to be jerks about it, but it is wise to address these issues as they come up rather than shirk and hide.

Whooooooo Let the Bears Out?

Now that you understand *why* we are writing this book, *how* to be a Mama Bear, *what* it means to be a discerning Mama Bear, and *where* the battle is taking place (i.e., words), it's time to turn you loose! In the upcoming chapters, we will discuss the most popular lies of contemporary society, where they came from, and how we Mama Bears can ROAR against them. Time to get your game face on—and roar like a mother!

Discussion Questions

1. **Icebreaker:** Give an example of a word that people use incorrectly. What bothers you about this usage, and how can you communicate the right meaning of the word?

2. **Main theme:** *People change word definitions to make their agenda sound more appealing or to hide their true motives.* How have you seen this strategy at work in our culture and affecting it?

3. **Self-evaluation:** Have you caught yourself inadvertently adopting culture's new definitions? If so, which ones? What made it hard to discern the agenda behind the way those words were being used?

4. **Brainstorm:** What are some ways that you can start teaching your kids about the real (and biblical) definitions of *love*, *truth*, *tolerance*,

justice, equality, bigotry, and *authenticity?* If you are in a group, have everyone pick a word and study it this week. Come back next week and share what the Bible says about that word or concept, and how it differs from what culture says.

5. **Release the bear:** Listen closely to your kids' conversations this week. What words have they absorbed from the culture that need to be corrected? If you hear them use a linguistically hijacked word, set aside time to talk about it. Ask, "What do you think that word means?" Make sure your children know the *real* definition. You would be amazed at how adopting a correct definition changes someone's perspective.

Part 2

Lies You've Probably Heard but Didn't Know What They Were Called

Chapter 5

God Helps Those Who Help Themselves

Self-Helpism

Teasi Cannon

When I was in high school, my family had a very large console television. That thing weighed about a ton and stuck nearly three feet out from the wall due to the huge cathode-ray tube mechanism in the back (definitely *not* a flat screen), but the picture was large and in color, and we loved it—until the sound went out.

We didn't lose the sound all at once. At first the glitches were minor, and all it took was a solid WHACK to the top and voila!—the volume worked again. But at some point our television had enough of being slapped around and decided to go silent for good. We were left watching our family favorites without hearing any of what was going on. Something was wrong, and it needed to be fixed.

And "fixed" it was. But not the way you're probably thinking.

Most people would have called a professional repair person to come take a look and change out a few broken parts (per the manufacturer's recommendation). *My* parents, however, decided to fix the problem themselves—the cost-free way. Their solution? Get a second television that had sound but no picture and place it on *top* of the first console. Technically, when both televisions were on at the same time, the problem was "solved." We had picture and sound. Did it work? Yes. Was it cheap and easy? Yes. Was it the best? No. And as a teenager who was desperately trying to be cool, it was a total embarrassment anytime friends came over.

Thinking about our silly tower of television sets reminds me of the human plight. We are all broken. Due to sin, not much works according to the factory presets. And as moms, we don't usually need any help admitting that. In fact, we could likely recite all our faults and failures in a moment's notice—which isn't a totally bad thing. Self-awareness is healthy and being willing to admit we aren't perfect is one of the best things we can do for our children. It's what we do with our brokenness, however, that we must be mindful of. Someday our little babies will become aware of their own brokenness, and we will want them to know how to diagnose it correctly, what to seek as a remedy, and who to turn to for help. We want them to turn to their "manufacturer" rather than relying on themselves—the latter is what the masterfully influential self-help industry would much prefer.

What Exactly Is "Self-Helpism"?

Self-helpism starts with a good idea—that we should do what we can, within our power, to work for a better life for ourselves and others. We can become better educated, set worthy goals and strive for them, discipline ourselves for positive ends, and encourage others to do the same. However, in the final analysis, we can't fix what is *fundamentally broken* within ourselves. Only God can do that. As the term *self-helpism* suggests, self-help is a completely unbiblical take on human brokenness. Its message (boiled way, way down) is that we need search no further than within ourselves to find both the cause and remedies for our brokenness.

That is a dangerous lie, one that people inside and outside the church are buying like crazy. The self-improvement market, which was worth $9.9 billion in 2016 in America alone, is predicted to have average yearly gains of about 5.6%. That means in 2022, it will be worth something like $13.2 billion![1]

To be fair, self-help isn't all bad. It's not like Scripture tells us to sit back and just pray about all our bad habits and watch them magically disappear. Rather, the message we would like to emphasize is that self-helpism has limits. There is a line between being good stewards of our bodies, emotions, and behaviors versus trying to change our own hearts or sin nature apart from the Holy Spirit's sanctifying work. The message within self-helpism (and within every "ism" mentioned in this book) is idolatry: Humanity takes something good and even powerful, and then mistakes it for God—giving it powers that are God's alone.

A Brief History of Self-Helpism

Statistics give us a glimpse of what the future could hold for self-helpism (especially in terms of dollar signs). But what about its history? When did society first become obsessed with navel-gazing? From what we see in Genesis, the seeds of self-helpism were planted by the very first humans way back in the Garden of Eden.

When Eve decided to take things into her own hands (and bring Adam along with her), our ancestors helped themselves…albeit to a heaping portion of death.

A deeper dive into the history of self-helpism takes us into the teachings of Socrates, the philosophy of the Stoics, Greco-Roman and Renaissance literature, and proverbs from antiquity around the world.[2] But for our purposes here, let's start a little closer to home with more recent contributions. Consider the oft-touted maxim "God helps those who help themselves."

Contrary to what some might believe, you won't find that promise anywhere in the Bible. That statement was popularized by the 1773 edition of *Poor Richard's Almanac*, written by Benjamin Franklin, who likely got the idea from Aesop's fable "Hercules and the Wagoner." Written for the masses rather than the elite, Franklin's almanacs made it into the hands of thousands of colonists and eventually into Europe, and they provided the perfect vehicle for spreading his deistic worldview.

Though deism broadly acknowledges the existence of God, it characterizes him as detached and uninvolved with creation. Franklin's god was not the God of the Judeo-Christian worldview, but rather like a divine watchmaker who wound up the world and then sat back to watch it tick. With a god like that, it's easy to see why people would embrace self-helpism! Nobody's coming to help you, honey. All you got is you.

In 1859, the proverb was adapted by Scottish writer and social reformer Samuel Smiles in his book titled *Self-Help,* said to be the first book of this genre. In the very first paragraph of chapter 1, Smiles summarized his worldview. He wrote:

> "HEAVEN helps those who help themselves" is a well-tried maxim, embodying in a small compass the results of vast human experience. The spirit of self-help is the root of all genuine growth in the individual; and, exhibited in the lives of many, it constitutes the true source of national vigor and strength. Help from without is often enfeebling in its effects, but help from within invariably invigorates.[3]

More than a quarter million copies of this book were sold by the time of Smile's death in 1904. Like Darwin's *Origin of Species* (also published in 1859), which championed a survival-of-the-fittest perspective, *Self-Help* played a major role in stressing the importance of individual hard work, character, independence, and perseverance for social reform and survival (not necessarily bad in themselves).

Book sales continued to play a huge role in the spread of self-helpism over the years. In 1902, James Allen, a poet and pioneer in the self-help movement, wrote *As a Man Thinketh,* in which he states,

> The aphorism, "As a man thinketh in his heart, so is he," not only embraces the whole of man's being, but is so

comprehensive as to reach out to every condition and circumstance of his life. A man is literally what he thinks, his
character being the complete sum of his thoughts.[4]

And before you accuse us Mama Bears of being Negative Nellies, we
readily admit there is some truth to this statement. We *are* called, in Scripture, to bring every thought captive.[5] However, our ability to do so does
not determine our entire destiny, nor is it a comprehensive balm to "every
condition and circumstance" in our lives.

Not long after Allen's contribution came the ever-popular book *How
to Win Friends and Influence People* by Dale Carnegie, published in 1936.
(Flashback: I can totally remember my parents assigning that book to
me as summer reading when I was in fifth or sixth grade. They hoped
Carnegie's message of success through self-confidence would cure my
bad attitudes and limited social connectiveness. Yeah…it didn't.) In 1937,
Napoleon Hill's *Think and Grow Rich* delivered more of the same: a focus
on the power and prosperity of positive thinking.

The late twentieth century ushered in a virtual battalion of gurus, each
hocking their own personal flavor of self-helpism: Tony Robbins, Deepak
Chopra, Eckhart Tolle, and of course, Oprah Winfrey. But I'd like to take
a moment here to highlight a man who was very influential for bringing
self-helpism into the church: Norman Vincent Peale.

Peale was born in 1898 and raised in a Christian home. His father
was a Methodist minister, and Peale followed in his footsteps, eventually
becoming one of Christianity's best-known preachers. He earned a bach-
elor's degree in sacred theology and a master's in social ethics before going
on to pastor several churches, author multiple books, host his own radio
and television shows, and start the popular magazine *Guideposts*. Somewhere along the way, Peale was asked by his parishioners to preach more
topically on issues related to life's problems. So he turned from his theological roots and began exploring psychology and eventually embraced the
principles of Christian Science and other mystical inspirations.[6]

The first paragraph in chapter 1 of Peale's best-selling *The Power of Positive Thinking* (published in 1952) reveals the type of "doctrine" he was delivering to his parishioners and his millions of readers:

> BELIEVE IN YOURSELF! Have faith in your abilities! Without a humble but reasonable confidence in your own powers you cannot be successful or happy. But with sound self-confidence you can succeed. A sense of inferiority and inadequacy interferes with the attainments of your hopes, but self-confidence leads to self-realization and successful achievement. Because of the importance of this mental attitude, this book will help you believe in yourself and release your inner powers.[7]

Did you catch that? *Faith* and *belief* lead to success, happiness, and power. Unfortunately, Peale was not talking about faith and belief *in God*. Rather, he was basically presenting Humanism 101.[8] Peale, of course, baptized his humanistic teachings with Scripture, reassuring audiences that "God" (aka their divine genie) was always eager and ready to help them in their journey toward achieving inner peace and releasing their inner power. His use of Bible verses, unfortunately, made his teachings *sound* safe to the average layperson. Many Christian leaders were no wiser and embraced his platform with open ears and arms.

One such leader was the highly influential Reverend Robert Schuller, pastor of one of the nation's first megachurches (The Crystal Cathedral) and host of the globally popular Sunday morning program *Hour of Power*. Schuller took Peale's message of positive thinking and tweaked it a little by using the term *possibility thinking*, a self-improvement philosophy he first explained in his 1967 book *Move Ahead with Possibility Thinking*.

Robert Schuller was only one of the major influencers who adopted and advanced Peale's ever-appealing message of self-empowerment and the good life. As we'll see later in the chapter, the echoes of this philosophy can still be heard today not only in the secular world, but also within the church.

ROAR Like a Mother!

RECOGNIZE the Message

That gives you some idea of how self-helpism got its start and what makes it problematic. Now let's take time to focus on some of the specific ideas coming from the self-empowerment camp and where we will likely find them.

> ## Ultimately, self-helpism points people toward self-reliance rather than God-reliance.

One thing self-helpism presupposes—and I think most people would agree with—is that we are in need of help. Things aren't the way they should be, or at least they're not as good as they could be. True enough. But we need to go beyond self-helpism's definition of the problem, what it recommends as a remedy, and who it recommends people turn to as a source of help. That's because ultimately, self-helpism points people toward self-reliance rather than God-reliance.

The Diagnosis

The problem, according to self-helpism, is that we are experiencing far less than what we think we have a right to experience. We aren't happy enough, and we *deserve* to be. We aren't achieving financial prosperity, and every one of us should be enjoying the finer things in life. We feel empty when we should feel content. We are enslaved to Oreos, but we should be enjoying perfect satisfaction with both food and our bodies. Bottom line, we are lacking (which brings angst), and we deserve to be flourishing in comfort. Anything short of that is wrong. What do people mean when they say, "I deserve..."? Sounds like some linguistic theft!

In self-helpism, the most reliable way to test how bad our problems are is to focus on how we *feel*. We should pay attention to how situations and other people affect our emotions and sense of self-worth and security. The better we are at identifying our triggers, motivators, core talents, personality strengths, dreams, and attractions, the better we will be at determining what's getting in the way of our journey toward living our best life now. And we should expect this to look different for everyone, because everyone's needs are different.

What we will discover, however, is that when we scatter a few seeds of self-helpism, along with a few seeds of moral relativism, we won't get happiness. Instead, we will end up with a lush growth of self-centeredness blooming in our hearts.

The Remedy

Simply stated, the remedy for our problems, according to self-helpism, is *self-discovery*. Whatever has been stolen, broken, or remained underdeveloped is within us, waiting to be found. And once we finally tap into it (by following simple steps to guaranteed results, of course), the life we were meant to live will be within our reach!

For some, what's needed is more self-love. (Repeat after me: You are good enough, you are smart enough, and gosh darnit, people like you!) Other solutions are materialistic (stuff brings pleasure, and pleasure—not the Hokey Pokey—is what it's all about). Some solutions are pantheistic (you are a unique piece of God, what's not to love?). And still others center on our thought lives: Think it, and you will be it, have it, and do it. Whatever the reason, and whatever the tactic, it's *all* inside you, grasshopper.

The Source

In the self-help world, *I* am the source in my life and *you* are the source in your life. We are all our own source of strength. We are the power source to solve the problems we think we have. Closely related to the remedy (me digging deeply into me), the ultimate desire and power to dig comes *from* me. I am both source and solution. It's a closed system.

The overall effect of this diagnosis, remedy, and source is that we elevate the power of self-reliance past the point of healthy self-care and well into the realm of self-worship. I don't think it's hard to see the attraction of self-helpism. It creates a beautiful throne for each and every one of us to sit on, making us our own ruler. Any song, podcast, TED talk, animated series, sermon series, or Christian book (and there are many) that elevates you, your feelings, or even your calling—making you the hero in the story—is an agent of self-helpism.

OFFER Discernment

Anyone who says they don't desire happiness, prosperity, or firmer abs is probably lying (or inanimate). I asked Siri. She didn't seem to care. Desiring these things doesn't make someone a selfish pig—it makes them human. Our earliest ancestors, Adam and Eve, had everything they could ever want or need. They lived in paradise, which is what we are made for. With paradise lost, the human heart experienced brokenness and separation from the source of all emotional, physical, and spiritual freedom. Since then, we've been trying to remedy the problem and recreate our own paradise. History repeats itself again and again as we bypass the wisdom of our maker and grasp for happiness on our own terms.

> Be aware when you hear people touting rights.
> Often, what they call a right is really a gift to
> which they feel entitled.

With that in mind, let's take a quick look at what is appealing and even right within self-helpism and compare it to what the Bible says about our three issues: diagnosis, remedy, and source.

The Diagnosis

As mentioned above, our problem, according to self-helpism, is that we are not living the life we could be living—that we are missing out on what God originally intended. However, we have mistaken God's gifts for "rights," or what we feel *entitled* to. But we must remember, Mama Bears, that the only reason we have anything good coming our way is because *God* is good, not because we are. Be aware when you hear people touting rights. Often, what they call a right is really a gift to which they feel entitled.

Self-helpism has a very low view of just how big of a problem sin is. It diminishes (if not eliminates) the power and consequence of sin, waving sin away as mere bad habits or character defects rather than the soul-wounding, spiritual (and sometimes physical) scar-creating force that sin is.[9] As Jonathan Edwards said in his fire-and-brimstone message "Sinners in the Hands of an Angry God,"

> Sin is the ruin and misery of the soul; it is destructive in its nature; and if God should leave it without restraint, there would need nothing else to make the soul perfectly miserable...[It is] boundless in its fury...it is like fire pent up...if it were let loose it would set on fire the course of nature.[10]

Edwards understood the real impact of our sin nature. Apart from salvation by grace through faith in Jesus, we remain alienated from the One who knows us best, loves us most, and who offers us the only real path toward redemption and healing.

For those of us who have been reconciled to God, our measuring rod for truth or success is not our feelings (which we will talk more about in the chapter on Emotionalism). Our goal is not merely to feel good or to have the most comfort or to live on Easy Street. Our goal is to be conformed to the image of Christ in word and deed, no matter the cost. While we may make strides toward that goal, we understand (contrary to what self-helpism promises) that we won't have it all this side of heaven. Sometimes temptations, struggles, and the lasting effects of our sinful choices follow us our entire earthly lives.

The Remedy

In self-helpism, the remedy for our brokenness is self-discovery because whatever we're looking for is supposedly already within. While there is a place for getting to know how God uniquely made us, being honest about past wounds, or reminding ourselves of former aspirations, the problem is that these efforts alone are not going to heal us.

Jesus, we are told in Scripture, is the One who heals. He is the One who understands every wound, every betrayal, and every temptation we've ever faced or will ever face *because He faced them too*. By His death, resurrection, and ascension, we have been set free from the ultimate penalty of sin (our real problem) and our enslavement to its power. We've been given the ultimate helper, the Holy Spirit, who guides us in all truth.

When we make Jesus the Lord of our lives and follow His earthly example of humility and obedience to the Father, we are changed day by day into His image. The more we choose God's truth and God's way, the easier it becomes to resist the lies of the enemy and turn away from the temptations of our flesh.

The hard part about this correct remedy is that it is costly—*much* costlier than a weekend seminar or a lifelong subscription to *O, The Oprah Magazine*. Self-discovery, however hard it may sound, is truly the easy way out. According to self-helpism, I don't have to deny myself or repent of anything. I only have to *find* myself. For Christ followers, it's the opposite.[11] We don't truly live until we die—die to selfish desires that exalt us against the wisdom, love, guidance, and righteousness of our maker. We are called to surrender all.

The Source

I'm pretty sure you see where I'm going with this. In self-helpism, we are the source—the solution to all our problems. Our own latent powers can supposedly save us. But according to Christianity, God is our source, and *He alone* has the solutions. That, however, doesn't mean we have no part to play. We have each been given free will, so each day we have the personal power to choose whom we will serve: self or God.

God doesn't help those who help themselves; He helps those who are helpless and know it.

Now, choosing God doesn't mean we just sit back and wait for Him to magically change us, expecting nothing of ourselves. Choosing God includes being willing to regularly practice spiritual disciplines such as prayer, studying the Bible, and living a lifestyle of repentance and forgiveness—things that keep us plugged into God's power and provision for our lives. And God has given us professionals (counselors and pastors) who can see blind spots that we can't. Science has done wonderful work in showing what happens to humans when something goes wrong in our minds, and providing tips for how to reverse the damage. These alone, however, do not heal us. They are the mechanism by which God has chosen to work in us and in our hearts. Being good stewards of the life God has given us means taking care of our bodies, working toward being godly parents and spouses, and participating in community. We need other believers spurring us toward holiness, reminding us that our help comes from the Lord, our power comes from His spirit, and that apart from Him, we can do nothing.[12]

God doesn't help those who help themselves; He helps those who are helpless and know it. Any philosophy that elevates man over God is humanism. Humanism claims that the problem is superficial and that we are both the source of and remedy to the brokenness. Using Christian terminology to promote self-reliant solutions only creates a funky form of religious humanism—a worldly ideological cupcake with a thin glaze of Christian icing.

ARGUE for a Healthier Approach

I remember becoming very aware of my own feelings of emptiness and despair sometime around seventh grade. Wearing garage-sale couture and having a mom who didn't believe in letting me shave my legs or wear makeup until age 13 didn't help (just call me Sasquatch). I suspect surviving those hellacious years is what imbued me with the unique superpower needed to teach middle-school students: lots of patience mixed with knowing we're all broken.

So, what's the best approach to our problem? It's as simple as fixing anything that's broken: duct tape and a paper clip.

Okay...not really.

What we need is our manufacturer. He knows exactly what our hearts need, and trying to fix ourselves is as futile as expecting a broken vacuum to fix itself. It won't happen. Not even if we gather the family around to shout, "You're an amazing vacuum! You can do it!"

No broken thing can fix itself, and that includes our hearts. Even though some self-help teachings may offer beneficial insights, they never go the distance to lasting growth—which keeps people coming back for another book, seminar, or guru. The number of self-help books on a gal's shelf is evidence enough that self-helpism fails. If it truly worked, you'd only see one.

There will be times we listen to podcasts or read books that offer useful insights covering topics that range from emotional health to organizational tips, and that's okay. The Bible is not exhaustive. It doesn't cover every single issue we'll face in life. No amount of in-depth Bible study will help you determine how many hours you should spend on Facebook, how to set healthy boundaries for your teens, or how to recognize when you're being manipulated by a narcissist. I am personally grateful to all the books that have helped me navigate those things and more.

Psychology must always bend the knee to theology.

But the Bible is *sufficient*, meaning that it tells us all we need to know about who God is, who we are, and what we need for the abundant life (as defined by God). Just remember—no matter what you're reading or listening to—psychology must always bend the knee to theology. Does the teaching you're listening to line up with who God says He is in the Bible? Or does it belittle Him by taking away from His character or ways?

Does the teaching line up with who the Bible says *we* are? Or does it elevate our callings or gifts higher than the Bible does? Does the teaching call out sin for what it is and include the absolute necessity of repentance? Or does it soften the definition of sin ("mistakes, messiness") and minimize its effects?

The bottom line for us as believers is this: We know enough about ourselves to know that we do not have what it takes to fix ourselves completely. In fact, when we rely only on our own strength or internal powers, we are sure to fail. And that's by design. While we should continue to do our part toward spiritual growth, we find joy in knowing our dependency upon God isn't weakness, it's true strength.

We can take encouragement in what God said to Paul, and Paul's response: "'My grace is sufficient for you, for My power is made perfect in weakness.' Therefore I will boast all the more gladly about my weaknesses, so that Christ's power may rest on me" (2 Corinthians 12:9).

REINFORCE Through Discussion, Discipleship, and Prayer

So, what can you do as a Mama Bear to help your children recognize the flaws of self-helpism and turn to the right source for answers?

1. When it comes to the issues we deal with on a daily basis, discuss with your children what is within *our* power to fix, and what is within *God's* power. Doing the dishes? Being kind to the unpopular kid at school? What about kindness and helpfulness coming naturally? We can control *what we do*, but it is God who creates the growth to change *who we are*.

2. When your children come to you with a problem, begin by telling them, "Let's see what the Bible says about it." Once you have identified the biblical principle that your children are to strive for, then you can equip them to find other helps that enable them to apply what they've learned. That's the most biblical form of self-help—turning first to the Bible, then searching for guidelines that help put God's Word into action.

PAWS for Prayer

Praise

Lord God, You and You alone are my helper. You are a good God who desires my good even if it comes through hardship and struggle. I praise You that Your strength is what helps me in my weaknesses. You reveal where I need help. Where does my help come from? It comes from You (Psalm 121:2).

Admit

Lord, I confess that I am broken. Forgive me for not always admitting that I need help and for believing the lie that I can fix myself. I am sorry for buying into popular teachings such as the power of positive thinking and humanism, which elevate our power and diminish Yours. I admit I am often guilty of a sense of entitlement that leads to self-centeredness, self-discovery, self-worship. Forgive me for not looking to You for my help.

Worship with Thanksgiving

Lord, thank You for the power and availability of the Holy Spirit to help me. I am thankful for Your Word's instruction to help me overcome sin. You are not a detached God who leaves me to figure out things on my own. Your strength is most effective in my weakness, and I am self-sufficient in your sufficiency (2 Corinthians 12:9; Philippians 4:13 AMP).

Supplication

Lord, as I move from the lie of self-helpism to God-helpism, I ask that You help me bring every thought captive to You. Empower me to discern Your gifts from the rights I demand. Help me to teach my children the balance between independent thinking and dependence on You. May I foster in them the desire to seek Your Holy Spirit as their ultimate helper. Expose, and help me to recognize, the wolves in sheep's clothing—to recognize psychology disguised as theology so I can protect my children. May

I teach my children to make the Bible their first self-help source. Help me to be a good steward of my mind and gifts, and to point others to You as the source for their help.

In the name of Jesus, my Helper, amen.

Discussion Questions

1. **Icebreaker:** If you feel comfortable sharing about this, what is one area of your life over which you feel completely powerless?

2. **Main theme:** *You are a steward, not your own savior.* One fruit of the Spirit is self-control. Yet the Lord also warns us against "striving" (Psalm 46:10 NASB). What do you think is the difference between taking responsibility for ourselves in a healthy way, and striving in an unhealthy way?

3. **Self-evaluation:** Most people are on a spectrum. Draw a line on a piece of paper and label one end "Passive Patty" and the other end "Striving Suzie." *Passive Patties* spiritualize their laziness, not recognizing that obedience is a necessary part of sanctification (or spiritual growth). *Striving Suzies* think that *everything* is their responsibility and forget that God sometimes works in us at a different speed than we would like. Where do you think you fall on the spectrum, and why? What can the Patties and Suzies learn from each other?

4. **Brainstorm:** Draw a vertical line down the center of a piece of paper and label one side "Me" and the other side "God." On one side, identify the things in life that are our own responsibility as stewards of God's gifts. On the other side, identify those areas of life in which God is the one responsible for making things happen. Are there any items on the "God" side of the paper for which you have been taking responsibility? Identify them. Talk with the group to get additional feedback on your assessment. (Remember, the answers aren't always "within"!)

5. **Release the bear:** Pick one responsibility in the "Me" list that you need to be a better steward over. What steps can you take to make that happen? Then pick one or two things you've taken control of that you need to offer up to God. Pray for the strength to be diligent in areas where diligence is needed and to release control in areas where only God should be holding the reins.

Chapter 6

My Brain Is Trustworthy...According to My Brain

Naturalism

Hillary Morgan Ferrer

Communication is impossible and words are useless. God is unknowable. All statements about God are meaningless. In fact, all truth is unknowable because all knowledge is mere opinion. We can't *really* know anything. You should doubt everything. Science is the only means to knowledge, the only path to truth, the only way to understand reality.

I hope you're thinking, *That doesn't sound very Christian*. If so, you're right because it's not! That entire paragraph is what logicians call "self-refuting statements," and you should start familiarizing yourself with them. In fact, make it a game with your kids to create your own! It is actually kind of fun to do this.

A self-refuting statement is a statement that, if true, contradicts itself. Let's look at each of the above statements again. I stated that communication is impossible, then used words that expressed the uselessness of words. If all truth is unknowable, then how can anyone *know* that to be true? What about the command to doubt everything—is that statement itself immune from scrutiny? And what about science being the only way to gain knowledge? Please tell me from which test tube you got that little nugget so I can empirically verify and reproduce it.

Naturalism is the belief that natural causes are sufficient to explain everything in our world, and *materialism* is the belief that nature (that is, material stuff) is all that exists. Material things can be studied with the five senses.[1] Immaterial things (morals, the human soul, angels, demons, and God) cannot.[2] The kind of naturalism that I'm talking about in this chapter is technically materialistic naturalism, but that's a mouthful, so we'll categorize it under the term *naturalism.*[3]

Naturalists, believing in only material stuff, often downplay philosophy and theology. However, the irony of claiming "The material world is all there is" is that this is a metaphysical—outside of the physical realm—or philosophical statement. The meaning of those words is not material. Not only is it immaterial and philosophical, but it is an *untestable assumption,* an allegation that is often brought against Christians.

Faith is a much-misunderstood word, and we need to make sure our kids know what faith is and what it isn't.

There is no lab in the world that can prove or disprove the existence of immaterial things because immaterial things, by nature, cannot be studied using material methods. We'll never be able to measure our souls in a beaker and we'll never be able to put God under a microscope. Naturalism is an untestable hypothesis that can be granted only on faith. Naturalists don't like to use the "f word" (faith). In their eyes, they alone hold the keys to reason and logic. To them, religion is silly, unprovable superstition. Science is all about evidence; religion is all about faith.

Faith is a much-misunderstood word, and we need to make sure our kids know what faith is and what it isn't.

When naturalists use the word *faith,* they are not talking about what is traditionally understood as faith. *We put faith in people and things that we have experienced to be trustworthy.* Nobody would proudly proclaim their "faith" in a babysitter they had never used or an accountant whom they had never worked with. However, when used in reference to religion, the word *faith* is frequently twisted beyond recognition. As evolutionary biologist Richard Dawkins stated, "Faith is the great cop-out, the great excuse to evade the need to think and evaluate evidence. Faith is belief in spite of, even perhaps because of, the lack of evidence."[4] Or, if you prefer the words of Mark Twain, "Faith is believing what you know ain't so."

The word *supernatural* has negative connotations within the scientific community. When people hear that word, their minds immediately conjure up images of psychics, aliens, or magic. However, the word *supernatural* simply means "outside of nature"—nothing more, nothing less. God is supernatural to the universe in the same way that I am superbook to this book. I am *outside* of my book. I can write myself into this book. (There once was a girl named Hillary, who loved Mamas, and Bears, and Apologetics…) Nothing inside this book created that sentence. A mind (and specifically *my* mind) *outside* this book created it.

We as Christians are supernaturalists because we *don't* believe that nature is all there is. We believe that real things exist outside of nature.[5] We believe that, like this book, nothing in creation could create our universe. Something outside of the universe is required, and particularly a *mind*.

As Christians, we acknowledge the existence of human souls and supernatural beings like angels and demons (but not ghosts!). I am more than my body. There is something about me that is not reducible to chemicals or moving electrical charges. Conversely, we don't (or shouldn't) discredit the material world. We are called to be good stewards (or caretakers) of the earth, our bodies, our families, and our communities. That was God's first commandment to Adam in Genesis. However, when it comes to knowledge and truth, we have more tools in our toolbox than just natural causes alone. To be a die-hard naturalist is to limit oneself to material tools only. I prefer the bigger toolbox.

A Brief History of Naturalism

We have a lot to cover in this chapter, so like the wedding ceremony in *Spaceballs*, I'm going to give you the short, short version. (But I will also provide extensive endnotes that will give additional insights rather than merely cite sources.)

The history of philosophy can be divided into three main periods: premodern, modern, and postmodern. I believe we are technically living in post-postmodern times, but it's not clear what we're supposed to call it. We are partial to the phrase *post truth* as that appears in many sources.

	Sources of Knowledge	**Ultimate Truth**
Premodern	God or gods Observation Common sense Authority	God or gods
Modern	Observation Experimentation	Man's collective reasoning ability
Postmodern	Observation Experimentation	Trick question, silly! There's no way to know for sure.
Now?	Observation Experimentation Experience Blend of all three periods	Strength of emotion Personal conviction

Premodernism spans from the beginning of man until the mid-seventeenth century. Premodernists were known for relying on authority and revelation as the main sources of truth. Religious leaders were seen as the preeminent authorities, and revelation was assumed to have come from God or the gods. When I speak of religious authorities, I am not talking only about Judeo-Christian priests and rabbis. The Greek, Mesopotamian, South American, African, and Asian religions all had spiritual figureheads as well. The supernatural realm was assumed to exist, and it didn't occur to most people to question it. In general, a denial of God was something that one had to be "educated" into.

The *modernists* moved beyond what they saw as superstitious nonsense. And to be fair, there *was* a lot of nonsense. For example, according to Greek mythology, the growing and winter seasons were attributed to the six pomegranate seeds Persephone ate while a prisoner of Pluto. And thunder was a sign the gods were fighting.

The modern period technically started about a hundred years after the Scientific Revolution (AD 1543).[6] Before this time, people believed that life's ultimate questions could only be answered by God or the gods. The modernist period marked the switch to the belief that people could answer these questions for themselves—using reason, observation, and experimentation.

Not all of the Scientific Revolution was motivated by a desire to dethrone God. In fact, the Judeo-Christian worldview played a significant role in science, though your kids won't learn about *that* in public school.[7] The gods of other cultures were hardly more than projections of extra-powerful humans (almost like superheroes). And like humans, the gods were fickle and temperamental. Thus, people assumed that nature (the material world) was no more reliable or predictable than the emotions of any volatile personality.

However, scientists who held to a Judeo-Christian worldview *expected* the world to reflect the characteristics of the unchanging God of Scripture. They expected the world to be rational, orderly, and law-like because God was rational and He "changed not."[8] This conviction allowed modern science to flourish, whereas paganism had stymied it.

But we humans are idol-creating machines. Science was a gift, and instead of using science (like Johann Kepler did) to "think God's thoughts after him," people started using science as a means of *replacing* God. We no longer had to worry about the battle between or within religions. Science could "prove" truth on neutral ground.

However, when man replaces God's authority with another authority (in this case, scientific authority), he tends to transfer the *attributes* of God onto the new crown-bearer. In fact, when reading *Origin of Species,* I was struck by a passage in which Darwin shifted from tedious observations about the number of hairs between pigeons' toes to a worshipful person-ification of natural selection.

> Can we wonder, then, that *nature's productions should be far 'truer' in character than man's productions*; that *they should be infinitely better adapted*...and should plainly bear the stamp of a *far higher workmanship*? [N]atural selection is daily and hourly *scrutinizing*, throughout the world...*rejecting* that which is bad, *preserving* and *adding up all that is good*...*[N]atu-ral selection can act only through and for the good of each being.*[9]

Is it just me, or does it sound like he's talking about God here? To Dar-win, natural selection, not God, was the source of moral character, sover-eignty, foreknowledge, humble servanthood, and unconditional goodness to all beings. Darwin 8:28 of course tells us that ~~Jesus~~ natural selection works all things for good according to its purposes. Evolution became the new religion, with Darwin as its Pope and scientists as the priests.

The history of science is like the history of all failed relationships, pro-gressing through three phases: infatuation, disillusionment, and rejection. In any new relationship, idealism runs high. The beloved can do no wrong. During the modern period, the scientific method—not Jesus—became the savior of mankind. Finally—we don't have to deal with that faith rub-bish! We can know things with *absolute certainty.*[10]

And as every young lover knows, there comes a day when infatua-tion wanes and you start seeing reality, complete with flaws and foibles. The grand hope of achieving absolute certainty failed miserably.[11] Theo-ries were changing, factions were forming, people were fighting. Science became just as dogmatic and divisive as religion (and still is) and Dar-winism morphed into social Darwinism—a deeply dehumanizing belief which taught that different races of people are at various stages of evolu-tion. This horrific philosophy paved the way for a supposedly "scientific" rationale for racism and justified new and creative evils like eugenics and the sickening experiments done on Jews during the Holocaust.[12]

Most relationships crumble under the weight of impossible expectations, resulting in broken trust and broken hearts. The poor young lover swears off love, convinced that true love is a fantasy. That's basically what happened here with truth. With the dream of achieving absolute certainty demolished, humanity entered the rejection phase of the relationship. Instead of concluding that *reasonable* certainty was close enough, an entire school of thought emerged that taught its followers to *trust nothing*. They swore off truth. It doesn't exist. It's just an illusion. Or if it does exist, we can never find it. Enter postmodernism, which teaches that there is no such thing as absolute truth, and nothing can be known. (Do you recognize two self-defeating statements here?)

Practical Implications of Naturalism

Naturalism isn't new—it dates as far back as 500 BC with the Greek atomists. The universal problem with denying the existence of God is the difficulty of explaining creation apart from a creator. Romans 1:20 says that God has made Himself plain to us through what has been made. Creation screams, "Creator!" To silence the voice of nature, man must construct ever more clever ways of shouting louder.

So, in our study of naturalism, we must wade through and evaluate the alternate theories postulated as a replacement for God. Your children *will* encounter these theories, and it is important for us Mama Bears to be able to *reason* through the plot holes.

If God didn't create the universe, who or what did?

There have been a whole schmear of hypotheses offered throughout history to explain away the existence a God who is uncreated, self-existent, and powerful enough to create the universe. The solution? Hypothesize something *else* that is uncreated, self-existent, and capable of creating. Mama Bears, listen closely when I say this: every hypothesis about origins is eventually reduced to something that (1) has always existed—is eternal, (2) needs no creator—is self-existent, and (3) is sufficiently powerful to create. Aristotle called this the "first cause." Do not let anyone tell you that their first cause is "more scientific" than yours. None of us can recreate the beginning of the universe, so all of us must take our respective "first causes" on faith. Here are a few that your kids might ask you about:

1. *The material world has always existed*—Carl Sagan's TV show *Cosmos* began with the infamous "The cosmos is all there is, was, and ever will be." Does that sound a lot like Hebrews 13:8, which says, "Jesus is the same yesterday, today, and forever"?[13] It should. Sagan basically scratched out "Jesus" and replaced it with "the cosmos." Until Edwin Hubble, belief in an eternal universe bypassed the perceived problem of God.[14] If the universe was never created, then there's no need for a creator. Genius! However…you are still left with an unprovable assumption based on faith. That's hardly a step forward, scientifically speaking.

2. *There are an infinite number of universes* according to multiverse theory. Why would someone postulate something so bizarre? Because within the last century, scientists have discovered how incredibly fine-tuned our world is for life. The charge ratio of protons to electrons, the gravitational constant, the temperature at which water boils, and about 140 other scientific constants must all simultaneously exist for life to be possible.[15] To claim all of these constants happened by mere chance is to essentially claim that earth won the cosmic lottery on the first try. The cosmic lottery is, however, much easier to win if you buy an infinite number of lottery tickets. That is the idea behind multiverse. It takes the "odds" of fine-tuning for life and says, "Since there are infinite universes, we just happen to be in the lucky one that has all the right constants. Hurray!" It pains me that the multiverse hypothesis is so prevalent and that we actually have to defend against it. What's more, my

sister called me a few years ago because my eight-year old nephew was asking her about this, so don't think you will have to wait until your kids are in college to deal with this.

Multiverse theory remains highly conjectural, bordering on theology rather than hard science. And even if the multiverse hypothesis were true, it doesn't solve the issue. It just moves the problem back a step and multiplies it. If there are infinite universes, then where did they all come from? I kid you not, the answer is that there is a "multiverse generator." And guess what properties it has? It is eternal, uncreated, and apparently capable of creating repeatedly. *Please* someone explain to me how this is a simpler and less faith-requiring hypothesis than belief in God?

3. *Natural laws are capable of creating*—Rebekah Valerius and I did an entire podcast on this titled "How Educated Do You Have to Be to Identify Nonsense?" It was based on an interaction between the late Stephen Hawking (a brilliant but atheist physicist) and John Lennox, an equally brilliant (and Christian) Oxford mathematician. Hawking claimed that "because the law of gravity exists, the universe can and will create itself from nothing." This led Lennox to respond that "nonsense is still nonsense, even when [spoken] by world-famous scientists."[16]

Here's the problem: Natural laws *describe* things. They don't *generate* things. Two plus two never put four dollars in anyone's pocket. Natural laws only act upon already-existing material. In fact, the definition of gravity is that it is the force pulling two objects together, and it depends on the mass and diameter of the objects. The diameter of nothing is nothing. There is no gravity without preexisting material.

4. *A smattering of theories for the origin of the universe*—Light, quantum particles, quantum vacuums, and probably a whole lot of other things with the word *quantum* in it because it sounds smart

and mysterious. But do not be fooled—every single hypothesis says the same thing: _____ is eternal, self-existent, and capable of creating. The most logical thing to place in that blank is not a *what*, but a *who*. Minds create. We'll discuss this more in the ROAR section.

Okay, fine. We'll skip the universe. Where did life come from?

When I taught the high school biology unit on cells, I would get the same question every year. According to cell theory, all cells come from pre-existing cells. Your kids will learn this from kindergarten on up. The question I got year after year was, "Where did the first cell come from?" An excellent question!

For centuries, the belief in *spontaneous generation* (that is, life coming from nonlife) was considered "scientific consensus." (And, as we know, scientific consensuses are supposedly *never* wrong—looking at you, geocentric model!) For example, it was widely observed that maggots showed up on rotting meat. So people concluded that rotting meat (nonliving material) could create life (maggots)! It is quite embarrassing how long and how ardently this belief was defended. In the mid-1800s, French scientist Louis Pasteur conducted experiments that once and for all slew the behemoth of spontaneous generation. (Thank you, Louis Pasteur, for putting that one to rest, due to your faith in God informing your science!)

However, like any good heresy, the ideas behind spontaneous generation keep coming back. They just get repackaged into things like "RNA world." Unfortunately, we do not have the space in this book to go through all the alternate theories that have arisen. Suffice it to say that with each small discovery of nucleotides forming spontaneously (nucleotides are the biological basis for life), none of these theories have gained real traction. We have applauded ourselves as we moved forward mere inches when the gap between life and nonlife is the size of the Grand Canyon.[17] There is a limit to what natural processes can do. Naturalists declare their unyielding assurance that one day we'll discover a natural cause for the beginning of life, but this hope is based on faith, not on observation.

ROAR Like a Mother!

RECOGNIZE the Message

The lie of naturalism is not confined to the classroom; it has been making its way into our churches as well. Here are the two most common (and most important) ways you will see naturalism packaged. Very rarely will it be stated in these terms, but look deeper. You'll see these kernels *everywhere*.

1. *The supernatural will eventually be explained away by science*—This theme is one we'll hear constantly in everything from science shows (like *Cosmos*) to kids' programming. If you watched Scooby-Doo when you were a kid, you'll remember that in almost every episode, the gang was investigating some sort of paranormal event. But as all Scooby-Doo fans know, the mystery was always solved by exposing some farmer Bob character in a mask. Similarly, a common tactic in the atheist community is to ask, "Can you tell me one thing that we originally thought was natural that turned out to be supernatural?" There is no way for Christians to rebut this because naturalists outright reject any evidence that appeals to supernatural explanations.

2. *Nature is all there is*—Souls, minds, good, evil, emotions, and even the Mama Bear instinct are explained away in naturalistic terms: Love is just oxytocin in the brain; people are slaves to their genes; we can't blame them for acting the way nature made them.[18] The naturalistic terms are almost always evolutionary terms. Sexual attraction is just our evolutionary impulses picking the best mates to pass on our genes. Thoughts are just nerve impulses in the brain. (Ahem, so why are we trusting them?)

OFFER Discernment

It's important that we understand why people are drawn to naturalism, what good it has served, and where the lies have sneaked in.

Once upon a time, the supernatural was used as the explanation for *everything*. Thunder, lightning, crop yields, all of these were explained by appealing to gods, and if something was failing, well, sacrifice another virgin and hopefully things will calm down. Thank goodness we have moved past that!

Second, Scripture itself elevates creation as a testimony to who God is. Psalm 19:1-6 describes nature as *revealing knowledge without words*. Some theologians refer to God's two types of revelation: general revelation (nature) and special revelation (Scripture). God's attributes are "clearly seen from what has been made."[19]

Third, we cannot downplay the amount that nature *does* explain. Verses like Philippians 4:8 (which talks about our thought life) have commonly been considered good principles to live by, but not concrete solutions to serious problems. Now, thanks to neuroscience and epigenetic research, we realize that thoughts do in fact have a literal physiological effect on our genes (and thus brain chemistry) and our ability to respond to stress in healthy ways. Our stress response is both mental and physiological. Mess with the physiology, and the mental collapses as well. People who struggle with illnesses like clinical anxiety or depression no longer have to live with the "just turn that frown upside down" mentality that nonsufferers spout. They can seek mental, emotional, spiritual, *and* physical solutions as well!

My final point is a knock against the church's often simplistic "refutation" of evolution. During my graduate Evolution and Genetics class, I learned that evolution could do a lot more than I was originally taught. I *also* learned that the professor did not distinguish between what was observed and what was assumed or postulated. Conclusion: Evolution can do more than I originally thought but was still not sufficient to explain the jump from simple life to complex life (or even from nonlife to life).

To do that, you have to insert philosophy—namely that nature is capable of doing this all on its own. Most high school and college biology students do not understand enough to make this distinction. All they know is "My church lied about evolution." Let's not give the enemy that foothold, shall we?

So what are some of the lies packed within naturalism?

Lie #1: Science and Christianity Are at Odds

False. *Naturalism* and Christianity are at odds. Science and Christianity get along just fine. The belief that the universe is governed by natural laws that are testable, reliable, and which can be harnessed was originally a *Christian* idea grounded in the character and attributes of the Christian God. When you hear people make the claim that science and Christianity don't mix, ask them what they mean by "science." If they give you a naturalist definition, ask them what experiment they did to get that definition.

Lie #2: Science Uses Facts, Religion Uses Faith

False. Both science and Christianity are a mixture of facts and faith, as long as we are properly defining faith. Science relies more heavily on *repeatable observations*, but it is ultimately grounded on a philosophy that *interprets* all the data. Two scientists can look at the same data and come to different conclusions based on their starting philosophy. One *might* say that Christianity is heavier on faith, but so are all historical sciences. You can't repeat history like you can chemistry. Thankfully, Christianity is based on verifiable and supportable *facts* about Christ's life, death, and resurrection. From there, we have faith that what Christ said is true, but we can (or should) ground that faith in evidence. Blind faith is easy to lose. Faith grounded in evidence is harder to walk away from.

Lie #3: Non-Minds Can Produce Information

Information is transmitted when there is a sender, a receiver, and an agreed-upon means of communication. The only thing we have ever observed producing information is a mind. For the readers of this book, information is English. English did not produce English. It required a mind outside of English (that is, a person). A computer did not create computer language. A mind outside the computer created it (again, a person). Intelligent Design advocates say that nothing within DNA could have produced DNA, but rather, a mind outside of DNA produced it. The problem with *naturalism is that it does not have a category for a mind outside of DNA* (besides aliens), so it just sweeps the problem under the rug.[20]

> An important value in both science and Christianity is a spirit of humility, which should *not* be confused with the spirit of compromise.

ARGUE for a Healthier Approach

The main idea I would like you, as a Mama Bear, to remember is that science and Christianity are friends, and this can be shown by looking at the history of science. Copernicus, Kepler, Boyle, and Galileo—all of whom were major contributors to the Scientific Revolution—were men of faith. According to the book *100 Years of Nobel Prizes*, more than 65% of the winners had connections with a Christian denomination.[21] Atheist astronomer and physicist Robert Jastrow summarized the relationship between God and science in his *God and the Astronomers*:

> For the scientist who has lived by his faith in the power of reason, the story ends like a bad dream. He has scaled the mountains of ignorance, he is about to conquer the highest peak; as he pulls himself over the final rock, he is greeted by a band of theologians who have been sitting there for centuries.[22]

Furthermore, in the Women in Apologetics statement of faith, we say, "Properly understood, God's Word (Scripture) and God's world (nature)...will never contradict each other." It is not anti-Christian to admit that there are times when they *seem* to contradict. An important value in both science and Christianity is a spirit of humility, which should *not* be confused with the spirit of compromise. If they seem to contradict, it means that we are not properly understanding either general revelation (nature) or divine revelation (Scripture).

REINFORCE Through Discussion, Discipleship, and Prayer

1. Have your kids draw a picture. When they are done, ask them, "How did that picture get there? Was it you, or was it the crayon?" The answer is both! Nature is like the crayon, and God is like the artist. No amount of explaining the properties of the crayon can ever explain how the picture ended up on paper. That required a mind. Similarly, for science and God, no amount of explaining *how* things work will explain away *where* they came from. (See the "Explaining the Science vs. God" article on the Mama Bear blog.)

2. Talk with your kids about the correct definition of faith. Emphasize that faith is putting our trust in someone or something that has proven itself to be trustworthy. Bring this back to apologetics and Jesus, and show how God sent Jesus in the flesh, in history, to die and rise again with lots of witnesses who saw Jesus after the resurrection. Explain that we as Christians can feel secure knowing that we are placing our faith in something that really took place. Read 1 Corinthians 15, and show how, according to Paul, the evidence of the resurrection is the foundation of our faith.

PAWS for Prayer

Praise

Lord, I acknowledge You as supernatural. You are outside of nature, transcendent. Nature is not all there is; a mind was needed to create nature. You are the mind, the wisdom behind the universe. You have left Your thumbprint both in Your creation and in Your Word.

Admit

Science is not my Savior. Nature is not my Savior. Forgive me for the times when I dismiss Your Word as my ultimate authority and my source of truth.

Worship with Thanksgiving

Thank You for the role that Christianity has played in science. I thank You that You reveal Yourself through creation and that science allows us to "think Your thoughts after You." We proclaim that science and faith are friends! You created a finely tuned universe that speaks Your name with every constant and equation. I am grateful that You have given me more than a body; You have also given me a soul.

Supplication

May I and my kids proclaim that nature screams "creator" and that His name is Elohim. Lord, grant my children insight to not be fooled by things that sound smart and mysterious. Give them inquiring minds and wisdom to distinguish between truth and speculation. Protect our schools and churches from these lies. For those who are blinded to Your truth and who dismiss the supernatural from the start, lead them to honest inquiry and to follow the evidence where it leads—straight to You. Help my children understand science as a natural theology that helps them learn more about You.

In the name of my Creator. Amen.

Discussion Questions

1. **Icebreaker:** What is something in nature that has always left you amazed?

2. **Main theme:** *Science is a gift from God, but people have used it to replace Him.* What are some ways that people have tried to use science as a replacement for God?

3. **Self-evaluation:** It is tempting to think too high or too low of scientific discoveries. Which way do you tend to lean? Why? What is a healthy view of science?

4. **Brainstorm:** This one is hard, but look again at the differences between premodern, modern, and postmodern mindsets. Really dig into culture. Can you identify parts of culture that operate under premodern rules? Which ones are modern? Which ones are postmodern? How can you tell? (If this is too hard, save this question till you are done with chapter 10.) If this concept is still a little fuzzy, feel free to use outside sources.

5. **Release the bear:** Go on a nature walk with your kid(s). Find as many things as you can that are beautiful. Make a study of God's creation a part of your everyday life. Emphasize that science is a means to study what God made but could never explain the purpose of His creation.

Chapter 7

I'd Believe in God If There Were Any Shred of Evidence

Skepticism

HILLARY MORGAN FERRER AND REBEKAH VALERIUS

n 2012, Dr. Bart Ehrman and Dr. Daniel Wallace debated the topic "Is the Original New Testament Lost?" at Southern Methodist University in Dallas. They looked at the evidence for the New Testament documents and talked about whether we could know with any assurance that what we have in our Bibles reflects the original writings of the apostles.

Coincidentally, what was to become our entire Dallas apologetics group was in attendance—we just didn't know each other at the time. What triggered our awareness of this was a comment my friend Justin made about a question he had asked during the question-and-answer session of the debate. Every one of us remembered his question. That's when we started looked at each other and saying, "Wait…you were there? I was there too! We were *all* there? How cool!"

Years later, I discovered that a DVD of the debate had been released, but surprisingly, neither Justin's question nor Ehrman's answer were included. Every question and answer was featured on that DVD except his, so what I'm going to share with you is privileged, firsthand information to which only attendees at that debate are privy. (Rebekah and I suspect that Ehrman got such flack for his answer that he didn't want it circulating for posterity.)

Wallace presented evidence after evidence that he referred to as "an embarrassment of riches"—evidence that dwarfs the manuscripts available for all other ancient literature. Ehrman's response time and again was a nasal-sounding, "But how do we know for suuuuuuure?" (Remember our discussion about absolute certainty in chapter 6?)

Ehrman is a New Testament scholar and historian. He started out as a solid defender of the faith, though on the fundamentalist end of the spectrum in his Christian beliefs. He has degrees from both Wheaton College and Moody Bible Institute, but it wasn't until Princeton Seminary that his faith in the Bible's inerrancy was challenged. From his perspective, the historical evidence in support of the New Testament documents crumbled under the burden of absolute certainty. Disillusioned, Ehrman walked away from the faith for good. He went from being a fundamental Christian to a fundamental skeptic, a path taken by many contemporary atheists.

Though the question was scrubbed from the DVD, Wallace mentions the exchange in his book *A Defense of the Bible*:

> During the Q & A, a local pastor, Justin Bass, asked Ehrman what it would take for him to be convinced that the wording of Mark's Gospel was certain. Ehrman responded that it would require ten manuscripts all copied from the original of Mark's Gospel within one week of its composition…Ehrman later admitted on the Internet's *TC List* that he was exaggerating when answering Dr. Bass's question, in spite of the fact that Bass was [clearly] asking for the minimum amount of evidence required to convince Ehrman.[1]

The absurdity of Ehrman's answer may not make sense if you haven't studied ancient documents. (I mean, who *doesn't* study ancient documents between burpings and soccer practice?!) So let me put this in perspective: First, Ehrman demanded evidence that doesn't exist for *any* ancient literary work.[2] Not one. Second, historians determine authenticity by comparing two things: the number of manuscripts recovered, and the time gap between the original autographs and the copies. If you were to stack the ancient documents that have survived to this day for an average classical writer, it would stand about four feet high. If you were to stack the recovered manuscripts of the New Testament, it would stand about 5,280 feet high. *Quite a difference!* That's about 24,000 ancient New Testament documents. In second place is the Iliad, at 1,900 copies, and third place is Herodatus's History, at a whopping 106.[3] When it comes to the time gap between the original manuscripts and first known copies, the New Testament is measured in years or decades. All other ancient literature is measured in *hundreds of years.* Ehrman asked for *weeks.* If you dismiss the New Testament as being unreliable, you have to dismiss *all* ancient documents. As a professional historian of ancient literature, this should be a problem for Ehrman.

> **If you dismiss the New Testament as being unreliable, you have to dismiss all ancient documents.**

I wish it had occurred to me at the time to ask him, "Mr. Ehrman, if your criteria for reliability rules out *all ancient literary documents*, might your criteria be a little too stringent?" Given the standard he had set, the only lecture he could give from that moment on is to walk up to a podium and say, "We can't know *anything* for sure from the ancient world. Thank you for coming, and tip your waiter!" In essence, Ehrman really did answer Justin's question. His response essentially confirmed that there is no amount of evidence that would convince him because when it comes to radical skepticism, evidence isn't the real issue.

A Brief History of Skepticism

As we discussed in the previous chapter, naturalism leads people toward an unnatural confidence in the powers of science. As anyone who studies the history of ideas knows, societies rarely change their ideas moderately. Rather, we have the tendency to swing the pendulum from one end of the spectrum all the way to the other, giving us an entirely different set of problems to conquer. The modernists said, "If we can't be absolutely certain about everything, then by golly, we are going to *doubt everything.*" (I'm pretty sure they stuck their tongue out at something at that point. I'm not sure at what. Maybe at science?) At this point in philosophical history, the trend was that we could be absolutely certain that we could not know anything with absolute certainty.

Enter Hume.

> [If] we take in our hand any volume; of divinity or school of metaphysics for instance; let us ask: *Does it contain any abstract reasoning concerning quantity or number?* No. *Does it contain any experimental reasoning concerning matter of fact and existence?* No. Commit it then to the flames: for it can contain nothing but sophistry and illusion.[4]

In normal person language, Hume was basically saying that if you can't measure it, count it, experiment on it, or prove it true or false, then it's all just fancy words and it isn't real. To which we might ask, "Did you just use a bunch of fancy words to tell us how things with fancy words can't be proven to be real? Are you *absolutely sure?*" The irony was that he would probably say yes. We will get back to Hume in a moment. For now, we're going to introduce another "ism" that you've probably already heard of—atheism—because it is a kissing cousin to skepticism. Radical skepticism defines our modern atheists, and the best place to start our discussion is to explain *why* radical skepticism is so insidious.

Implications for Skepticism

As we are going to see in our ROAR section, a healthy dose of skepticism itself is not bad. As fellow Mama Bear Hillary Short said in her *Playground Apologetics* blog,

I want my churched-up, prayed-up, pre-school kid to be a skeptic too! Why? Because being a skeptic means that he will question what is presented to him. This is important because I will not always be the one presenting the ideas. A child who understands how to *discover* truth is primed for a faith that lasts much longer than that of a child who is merely *presented* with the truth.[5]

In this chapter, we are not talking about healthy skepticism, but rather a radical hyper-skepticism that borders on cynicism. It's the kind of skepticism that refuses reasonable evidence and demands proof beyond a *possible* doubt (kind of like Ehrman was requesting). Absolute certainty can only be achieved in math and logic. With everything else, there is room for uncertainty. If people are wanting reasons to doubt Christianity, they'll find them. You can always put another question between yourself and God. This is why it's so important to ask, "Why am I asking this question?" Sometimes doubting your doubts is the most rational thing you can do.

Go back to Hume's quote and ask yourself, "How much of the Bible includes things that cannot be measured, counted, or physically experimented on?" Probably a lot of it, if not all of it. How do we respond? Do we say, "Oh no—the Bible isn't true because I can't test it in a chemistry lab!"

Wait…huh? That's not how we test historical documents. There is *no* historical document that can be "proven" in the same way things are proven in physics or chemistry. Why do some people treat the Bible like it's the *one* historical document that has to bear this level of "proof"?

That's hyper-skepticism, and hyper-skeptics peddling hyper-skepticism to your kids often *sound* like the cool voice of reason, whispering in your child's ear the same words that Ehrman spoke at the conference. "How do you know for *suuuure?*"

What crucial area of theology does Ehrman's still, small (definitely not God) whisper affect? Miracles. If you want to know something with absolute certainty, miracles are the first thing to go. They aren't repeatable, and they don't make sense to someone who is already committed to naturalism, which says that everything happens by natural causes alone. Once miracles are dismissed, you've done away with Christ's resurrection, *the* miracle on which the entire gospel hangs. Sorry folks, you can't have Christianity without the resurrection of Jesus.

Read all the apologetics books you want. Answer every question perfectly. If our children swallow the whopper of radical skepticism, none of our answers will be considered valid. There is *no answer* that will satisfy someone who is determined to be skeptical. This is the unfortunate lesson we have learned from the new atheists.

Old Atheists vs. New Atheists (and the Importance of Knowing the Difference)

For our purposes, we will refer to the atheists prior to 2001 as the old atheists and the atheists from September 11, 2001 on as the new atheists. The difference between their arguments is huge, and they hinge on (1) the definition of atheism, and (2) how ready the atheists are to admit to the meaninglessness of life without God. The old atheists were unabashed about it, and I can respect their honesty. As atheist philosopher Bertrand Russell stated in his essay "A Free Man's Worship" (hint: this is most effective when read aloud with a British accent):

> [P]urposeless...is the world which Science presents for our belief...Man is the product of causes...his origin, his growth, his hopes and fears, his loves and his beliefs, are but the outcome of accidental collocations of atoms...destined to extinction in the vast death of the solar system...[N]o philosophy which rejects them can hope to stand...[O]nly on the firm foundation of *unyielding despair,* can the soul's habitation henceforth be safely built[6] (emphasis added).

I bet Bert was super fun at a party. Such despair was characteristic of the old atheists. However, after the events of 9/11, a new kid on the atheist block emerged. With people searching for answers to make sense of the radical religion on display with the Muslim extremists, bookstores were bursting with bestsellers bringing old ideas to the public in a new way. The most notable of these books were written by Richard Dawkins, Daniel Dennett, Sam Harris, and Christopher Hitchens, who were dubbed "the four horsemen of the nonapocalypse."

Dawkins, a biologist, not only revamped naturalism for a new audience but also expressed utter contempt for religion—so much so that it made him famous. He was here to free people from their infantile God delusion and to help them "leave the crybaby phase, and finally come of age."[7]

Dennett and Harris are both philosophers, though I use the word loosely when I speak of Harris. I'll never forget the moment when my husband (John Ferrer) finished Harris's book *Letter to a Christian Nation*, threw it on the ground, and proclaimed loudly, "*I* could argue for atheism better than this!" (It's true. I've seen him do it, right before he refutes all his own arguments.)

And then there's Hitchens. The loveable drunk who makes you laugh even while he insults you. His way with words helped cover a multitude of philosophical sins. His brilliance in connecting with audiences on an emotional level helped usher in a new demographic of non-God worshippers and equipped them to argue with conviction on the Internet with super savvy memes. Is it any indication of the depth of the new atheist arguments that one of their four horsemen actually coined the word *meme*? (Ahem…Dawkins.)

But we need to get serious because the new atheists are nothing to laugh at. While we can poke fun at their ideas and methods, they are people created in the image of God, and their souls are of infinite worth. Not to mention, their influence cannot be underestimated in contemporary online culture—*the culture your kids are immersed in as they do research for school papers, projects, and virtually any question that pops into their minds.*

The brute honesty of the old atheists is all but a memory. In their place, these new atheists have created a version of atheism that is not even debatable. No, I'm serious. To them, their kind of atheism is totally undebatable.

How *Not* to Debate a New Atheist

In every debate, there is a pro and a con position. I'm not talking about back-and-forths among friends on Facebook. I'm talking about formal debates, which are typically comprised of a representative from each side (usually professors or other influential voices within a given field), a moderator, a college campus, and an audience—often a standing-room-only crowd full of eager sophomores ready to try a new idea on for size. The pro position espoused by the old atheists (that is, the argument they tried to prove) was that God does not exist. A debate with an old atheist would look like this.

Pro (atheist)	Con (Christian)
There is *no* God.	There is *a* God.

No problems here. With these two opposing views, a debate was possible.

Enter the new atheists, who have redefined atheism as "lack of God belief." Let's diagram what *this* debate pro and con should theoretically look like.

Pro (new atheist)	Con (Christian)
I lack God belief.	You don't lack God belief.

As you can see, in this scenario, the opposite of "I lack God belief" is *not* "There is a God." Those are not opposite statements. The opposite of "I lack God belief" is "You *don't* lack God belief." Who could possibly argue that another person *doesn't* lack God belief?! It doesn't even make sense as a position. Our current Christian debaters have not quite caught up with this new atheist definition. So unfortunately, the debate I now constantly witness between Christians and new atheists is this:

Pro (new atheist)	Con (Christian)
I lack God belief.	There is a God.

Notice, these are two different debates! Never will their paths meet, and the two people will forevermore be talking past each other. It's like the Sisyphus of debates. (Sisyphus was the dude condemned to roll a stone up a hill only for it to keep rolling back down for all eternity.)

This reframing of the debate may or may not be intentional on the part of the atheist. It is (heartbreakingly) not noticed by most Christians. I just want to smack my forehead whenever I hear this fruitless debate taking place. Tip for the day: If a person is not offering a statement that has a con position, *don't debate that person.* Do not give him or her another con position. All that individual will do is keep repeating, "I'm not saying there's no God. All I'm saying is I lack God belief." And the Christian keeps giving that person evidences for God *ad nauseum.*

Remember when you were a kid and you played tag? The group would decide where "base" was—the spot where that someone could stand and be safe, untaggable. Usually "base" was some rock or a porch or something. With their new definition of atheism, the new atheists are essentially saying, "The soles of my shoes are base!" Thus, anywhere they stand, they are safe. The other person has the burden of proof.

This is not an honest position. Nobody writes books or accepts debate invitations to argue for things they "lack belief in." Why would we play this game with them? They have made themselves untouchable, and we keep falling for it. Channeling my inner Bob Newhart, "Just stop it!"[8]

ROAR Like a Mother!

RECOGNIZE the Message

I trust that you can now see the wedded bliss between skepticism and the new atheism. In our ROAR section here, we will be addressing both the *implications* of an unhealthy skepticism and the *message* that is peddled by the new atheists. As we do so, we'll use their own quotes as much as possible. This is not what message they are hypothetically peddling; this is what they are *openly* peddling.

1. ***If you can't know* everything *for sure, you can't know* anything *for sure***—Or, as Hitchens said, "we can't say…there is no god and there is no afterlife. We can say that there is no persuasive evidence for it."[9] By "persuasive," he means indisputable.

2. ***Religion is child abuse***—Just google this phrase and look at the number of websites that come up. On our Mama Bear Podcast #21, we discuss how a progressive children's pastor explained why she doesn't use the phrase "Jesus died for you/your sins." She says, "While I realize that statement won't psychologically damage every kid, if it damages one, it's not worth using."[10] (If you don't know what progressive Christianity is, see chapter 15.) Or, as Dawkins stated, "I think it can be plausibly argued that such a deeply held belief might cause a child more long-lasting mental trauma than the temporary embarrassment of mild physical abuse."[11] (The "deeply held belief" he is referring to here is the doctrine of hell.) Rebekah answered his accusation in her article titled *Is It Abusive to Teach Children About Hell?* She wrote, "One could say that more than ever our minds are on earthly things; we may preserve our mental health but lose our immortal souls."[12] If hell is a real place (as the Bible says that it is) then it is definitely *not* child abuse to make your kids aware of it. You don't have to describe it past what Scripture does, essentially trying to scare them toward salvation, but they should definitely know how miserable an eternity without God will be.

3. ***Man is not just equal to God; he's better***—From what I was taught growing up, Satan's original sin was his prideful desire to be like God. The sin of our modern culture—especially among those who profess hostility toward God—is not that they want to be like God, or even think they are as good as God. Rather, the going narrative

is that they are *better* than God—more compassionate and more loving. God is openly debased as a war criminal or moral monster. Our current temptation isn't to raise ourselves to His level; it is to lower Him below ours and look down in scorn.

4. ***Belief in God is some sort of wish-fulfillment, akin to believing in Santa Claus***—Richard Dawkins illustrates this point by saying, "People of a theological bent are often chronically incapable of distinguishing what is true from what they'd like to be true."[13] Dawkins begrudges people for not outgrowing God-belief once they've outgrown believing in Santa Claus.[14] But veteran debater Dr. John Ferrer states in his article *Rejecting a Rembrandt*, "Atheists, of this sort, reveal the shallow depths of their disbelief by the speed at which they mention Santa Claus."[15]

   Dawkins apparently thinks Christianity is all about living from one glory to the next. Ask those who have lost a child if they believe in Christ simply because "it's easy." Sometimes we believe things because we find them to be true. But we can't do that if we haven't examined the evidence (poke, poke).

5. ***Religion keeps people from asking questions***—As Dawkins states, "I am against religion because it teaches us to be satisfied with not understanding the world."[16] As Hitchens says, "What can be asserted without evidence can be dismissed without evidence."[17] Wait…I agree with that. Go Hitchens! Christians *should* have evidence for what they believe! As apologist Frank Turek says in the introduction to his CrossExamined.com podcast, "[People] don't think Christianity is true. They're talked out of it. You know why they're talked out of it? Because they've never been talked into it!" He's got a point, and Hitchens agrees.

OFFER Discernment

As previously mentioned, healthy skepticism is a good thing and should be encouraged. This entire book is based on the premise that we want our kids to be skeptical enough to see through the lies wrapped in partial truths. I can't say enough good things about healthy skepticism.

What *isn't* healthy is a demand to know everything. There are things in Scripture and in our world that we won't understand for numerous reasons. Some of them may be because they are beyond our capacity to comprehend. This is especially true when it comes to the problem of evil. We are not omniscient. We will never fully know the mind of God and why He allows certain things to happen. Sometimes He may withhold clarity from us until we learn a specific lesson first. What's more, if God were to unveil information to us all at once, we would crumble under the weight. Yet this is never an excuse for us to stop searching for answers. Rather, it is an invitation to look further.

I (Hillary) recently experienced this with my sister, Leslie. She was two years older than I. As Rebekah and I were writing this, I was constantly distracted by the fact that Leslie had only a few months left to live due to terminal cancer. In the face of leaving her husband and two young boys behind, she was searching for answers.

Several weeks before she died, we lay together in bed and I held Leslie as she cried out and asked God why He hadn't answered her prayers for healing. Her prayers were so beautiful, so real, so honest, and so pure. I'm sure I said something, but I can't remember what. Within a few days, she had placed a new video on her YouTube channel, describing how John the Baptist must have felt as he sat in prison and his disciples came to him with news about all the amazing miracles God was performing on behalf of other people, but not him. Leslie was feeling this same burden. It was the final words in Scripture's account of this event that troubled her the most. Matthew 11:6 says, "Blessed is anyone who does not stumble on account of me." Why would people fall away *because* of Jesus?

In her video, Leslie reminded us that it would be very easy to fall away from God when He does amazing things for others but not for us. All the questions that Leslie had the day before as we huddled in the storm of confusion were still there. However, her perspective had changed. She had answers. They weren't the ones she wanted, and she did not fully understand them, but she understood this much: God's grace is enough. Rather than point you to an endnote, I'm going to encourage you to watch Leslie's video at https://youtu.be/keR-ZYJobD8.

ARGUE for a Healthier Approach

One of Christianity's dirty little secrets that many inside (and outside) the church don't know is that Christianity invites skepticism! We *want* our kids to be skeptical when someone tries to feed them an idea. Out of all the world's religions, Christianity is the only one that has testable claims and invites rational inquiry. (Other religions consider it blasphemy to question their teachings.) First Thessalonians 5:21 says that we are to "test all things" (NKJV). And remember: The Bereans in Acts 17 were commended for being "noble" for fact-checking Paul. Healthy skepticism is also known as critical thinking.

Our children need to see that our faith can withstand questions. They need to see that when we adults have questions, we don't throw in the towel or stuff them within us. I can assure you that my nephews, Luke and Joe, watched my sister struggle *well*. Her example is one that they will carry with them forever in life.

Colossians 2:8 commands us to "see to it that no one takes you captive through hollow and deceptive philosophy." This is what a Mama Bear does—not only for herself, but also her cubs. Are there things we won't understand right now? Sure. (By the way, this is one reason we won't get bored in heaven!) However, when we are too quick to punt to "the mysteriousness of God," we can end up allowing ourselves to become intellectually lazy.

Before we tell our kids that "Only God knows" or "If we knew everything, we wouldn't need faith," let's make absolutely sure that their question doesn't have a good answer. The answer doesn't even need to be foolproof. It's not always possible to have ironclad answers for the "isms" we discuss in this book. What we want to do is give our kids tactics for how they can examine what's being told to them and to engage their critical thinking.

REINFORCE Through Discussion, Discipleship, and Prayer

Fuller Youth Institute found that when parents expressed doubts, that helped kids to know doubt isn't a bad thing because it can spur us to search for the answers. As we say at Mama Bear, "Questions are good. Enough unanswered or poorly answered questions leads to doubt. Doubt, when left to solidify, becomes unbelief which is really, really hard to reverse."

1. Encourage your kids to ask questions! Just as we can be certain about mathematics and logic, there is something else of which we can be absolutely certain. (Hume, are you taking notes?) Your kids *will* ask questions that scare the bejeebers out of you. (I remember a sixth grader once asking me the difference between Satanism and Gnosticism. Where did *that* come from?) Even if you can't answer a question right away, roll with it. Show your kids that you're not scared by tough inquiries. Have a pizza night while you scour the Web for answers. Make it a thing; do it together.

2. Introduce questions to your kids that you already have answers for. But don't share the answer too quickly. Let them squirm a little while they wrestle with the questions. I guarantee that you want this process to occur with *you*, and not with one of the street epistemologists. (If you've never heard of street epistemologists, look it up online.)

   Get one of Natasha Crain's books, write the questions within the books on little strips of paper, and put those strips in a fishbowl. Once a week during the family dinner, pull out a question that can serve as a conversation starter and talk about it as a family. (Keep her book close by for the answers, of course!)

We do not need to fear the new atheists. There is nothing new under the sun. There is no need to fear tough questions. We have an infinite God with tougher answers. And don't forget, Mama Bear: You are not alone in this journey.

PAWS for Prayer

Praise

Lord God, You are omniscient. You know all and see all. You are a God who grants us certainty of our relationship with You. There is no doubt through Your Word, Your ways, and Your worth that You are the one true God. You are trustworthy, the keeper of promises. You are the giver of hope and a sound mind.

Admit

Forgive my arrogance, pride, and self-congratulations when I demand certainty and feel entitled to all the answers I am seeking, when I think that to be skeptical is the highest value, or when I devalue the one thing I can know for sure—Christ and Him crucified. Our questions don't save us, Lord. Your answer saves us.

Worship with Thanksgiving

I thank You, Father, that my faith can withstand questions, that You give me reasonable and sufficient evidence. Your truths are testable and knowable. Thank You that the Christian faith is the assurance of things hoped for and the evidence of things not seen. Thank You for Your gifts of both evidence and faith.

Supplication

Oh God, help me train my children to be like the Bereans. Give me the ability to teach them how to search diligently, to be satisfied with enough yet never become lazy in their quest. Give them healthy skepticism so blind faith does not satisfy. Let us acknowledge and accept our limitations because You are God and we are not. Let my children squirm and wrestle with their doubts, and help me be their cheerleader. And may I never give them simplistic answers because it is easier.

In the sure name of Jesus, amen.

Discussion Questions

1. **Icebreaker:** If you were to ask God one question, what would it be, and why?

2. **Main theme:** *There is healthy skepticism and there is unhealthy skepticism.* Describe the differences between healthy and unhealthy skepticism. Why should we encourage our kids to have healthy skepticism? How can we tell when skepticism has turned unhealthy?

3. **Self-evaluation:** People often fall into the trap of either answering every question with "Only God knows—just have faith," or responding to every answer with "But what about…?" In other words, some people don't seek answers to any of the tough questions, and others are never satisfied no matter how good the answers. Draw a horizontal line on a piece of paper with "Blind-Faith Betty" on one end and "Never-Satisfied Nancy" on the other. Where do you think you fall on the spectrum, and why?

4. **Brainstorm:** Compile a list of questions your kids have asked that you didn't know how to answer. If you're part of a group, create this list together. Keep this list somewhere that allows you to easily access it, or add to it, like on your phone or in your purse.

5. **Release the bear:** Ask your kids what questions they have for God. If they can't think of any, pick one that your group put on their master list. Have a family night to research the answer. (Obviously, don't pick questions you can't answer like, "Did Jesus ever have head lice?"—an actual question asked by one of our Mama Bear's kids recently.)

Chapter 8

The Truth Is, There Is No Truth

Postmodernism

REBEKAH VALERIUS AND HILLARY MORGAN FERRER

After a full day of managing your home, chauffeuring children from activity to activity, going to work, and generally keeping your head above water, you barely have enough mental energy left to use the right toothbrush (oops, sorry Hon!), much less understand some abstract philosophy from who knows where that believes who knows what because who knows why. But we truly hope you're beginning to see how powerful (and sneaky) ideas can be, ideas that are shaping our world even as we sleep.

We Mama Bears have noticed how much kids' questions have changed since we were young. Back then, children asked questions like, "What was it like to walk on dry land after Moses parted the Red Sea?" But when Alisa read through Exodus with her daughter, Dyllan's first question was, "Mom, did those miracles *really* happen?"

Are our kids like 1,000% smarter than us? Maybe, but intelligence probably isn't the issue here. Rather, the philosophy *de jour* has changed. Our respective cultures influence what questions we ask and why we ask them. As G.K. Chesterton observed, people usually have "one of two things: either a complete and conscious philosophy or the unconscious acceptance of the broken bits of some incomplete and shattered and often discredited philosophy."[1] He went on to note that it's these broken bits of ideas that, when uncritically absorbed, do the most damage.

When we were kids, people still generally assumed that both morality and truth existed and could be known. It didn't occur to us to question the supernatural events of the Bible (at least not as children). But with the dawning of postmodernism, even our kids' questions are changing, and we might be tempted to think it's just a weird phase. It's not. These questions are important, and unless we learn how to address them in a way that makes sense to the next generation, our kids will stop asking. And trust me, you *don't* want them to stop asking you questions. (As much as you might think you do.) For them to stop inquiring usually means one of three things: (1) they have disengaged completely, (2) they have made up their mind in a direction they know you won't like, or (3) they've given up on you and will pose their questions to someone else or the all-knowing Google.

We all have a philosophy, whether we realize it or not. Even saying, "I don't have a philosophy" is a philosophy. In other words, we all live our lives by certain assumptions, by basic beliefs about how the world operates: Is there a God? Are good and evil real? What is truth? Is there an afterlife?

These are life's ultimate questions, and we should make sure our answers are rooted in truth—not cultural trends. How we answer these questions will determine what foundation we build our lives on. Unfortunately, every single one of these is up for grabs in our postmodern culture.

Remember the parable Jesus taught about the wise and foolish builders? (Matthew 7:24-26). The wise man built his house upon the rock of Jesus's teachings, and when the storms came, his house stood firm. The foolish man, the one who disregarded Jesus's teachings, built his house on the sand. Many of the philosophies you are learning about in this book are like the sand in that parable. They make for shaky foundations.

Postmodernism is one such philosophy, and our world is desperately trying to build upon it. The problem? It doesn't even try to build on sand—postmodernism builds on thin air. Postmodernists simply do not trust foundations, even sandy ones. In fact, the more solid or fundamental a belief, the more skeptical they become. They want to tear such beliefs apart through what is called *deconstructionism*. When they are finished, there is nothing left to support the world they are building, and the walls are crumbling fast into a heap of confusion. Keep that picture in mind as you read along.

What is it about postmodernism that's important for Mama Bears to know? If you plan on sending your kids to college, and especially if they major in a field of humanities (like history, English, or philosophy), they will be steeped in postmodern assumptions from the get-go. Some in the sciences proudly proclaim that the humanities are dead. To this we cry foul; the humanities are not dead. They are just really, really sick, and post-modernism is the disease.

A Brief History of Postmodernism

Remember from our naturalism chapter that premodernists viewed God (or gods) as the ultimate source of meaning and knowledge. This doesn't mean that they ignored common sense or observations. They just didn't have the scientific prowess to understand things like seasons, storms, or other "acts of God." Ancient cultures understood nature as personifications of their deities. If it rained, Zeus was happy. If there was lightning? Oops. He was mad. After the Scientific Revolution, man realized that he was, in fact, capable of understanding nature, and even harnessing it for his own purposes. But he went further—he also became arrogant in his use of science to discover the laws of the universe and assumed that the same process could be used to discover *immaterial* truths as well. Purpose, meaning, ethics, morality—man boldly declared that these mysteries were discoverable through logic and the scientific method. No God/gods/Zeus needed! Granted, people had legitimate reasons for being skeptical of religion. As Nancy Pearcey notes in her book *Total Truth,*

> During the religious wars of the sixteenth century, Christians actually fought and killed one another over religious differences—and the fierce conflicts led many to conclude that

universal truths were simply not knowable in religion. The
route to unity lay not in religion but in science.[2]

The modernists were convinced that by pooling their collective common sense, logic, reason, and science, an objective standard of truth, morals, and meaning would organically emerge. Did they deliver? Spoiler alert:
not even close. As mentioned in the naturalism chapter, science proved
to be just as dogmatic and dangerous as religion. The split was inevitable.
Ask any mom how easy it is to get the whole family to agree on what to
eat for dinner. How could modernists possibly think that people would
unite on something as important as the meaning of life?

Enter postmodernism. Disenchanted with the failings of modernism, the postmodernists did what all disillusioned young lovers do and
started racking up a list of their former beloved's flaws, starting with
the inconsistencies. On one hand, modernists held unquestioning confidence in materialist naturalism—belief that truth could only be found
through what we are able to study with our five senses. But they also had
an unwavering conviction that human reason—something that cannot
be studied with the five senses—was also trustworthy. Remember "my
brain is trustworthy, according to my brain" in chapter 6? Let's think this
through: The modernists denied that any transcendent source created
our minds. Mind, brain, it's all the same, they said. It's just conglomer-
ations of nerve impulses. The nerve impulses that are best fitted for survival are the ones that…well…survive. And now we're trusting these
nerve impulses to tell us the meaning of life? *Why?* That doesn't even
make sense! If purely materialist evolution is true, my brain evolved to
give me survival, not truth.

The postmodernists were at a crossroad. They could either question
the dogma of naturalism (but in doing so, allow a divine foot back in
the door), or they could deny that absolute truth existed or was knowable. Unfortunately, instead of questioning the dogma of naturalism, they
rejected the idea of truth. (Talk about cutting off your nose to spite your
face!)

Postmodernism did (and still does) *feel* like a liberation of sorts. With all the battles fought over truth, society saw *truth* as the bully, not the people supposedly wielding it. It makes me think of that scene in *The Wizard of Oz* where everyone is singing "Ding, dong, the witch is dead," only this song was more like "Ding dong, truth is dead!"

In fact, truth had become synonymous with power and oppression. This is what psychologists might call "a conditioned response." Like Pavlov's dogs, which salivated at the sound of a bell, people bristled upon hearing the word *truth*. It sounded like one more bully technique.

Like emancipated minors, the postmodernists proudly proclaimed to God, science, and authority, "You can't tell us what to do anymore!" But as we all know, real life is more difficult to navigate without the safety of structure. Rules can be used to oppress, but they are also useful for establishing order.

In their efforts to prevent *false* ideas from slipping into society, postmodernists made it impossible for *true* ideas to take root. Postmodernists rejoiced that nobody could declare that sex outside of marriage, abortion, or homosexuality were objectively immoral. However, what they didn't realize was that they *also* now prevented society from saying that unprovoked murder, torture, and sex slavery were objectively wrong. If there is no objective, absolute right or wrong, then no one can criticize or condemn *any* moral choices, no matter how evil. You can't even call it evil!

What does a society like that look like? Philosopher Stephen Hicks observes that given this state of affairs, "there is nothing to guide or constrain our thoughts and feelings. So, we can do or say whatever we feel like."[3] Yup. That's what it looks like.

Postmodernism and Truth

As you can see from the history above, postmodernism is inextricably tied to truth: Does it exist? And if so, how can it be known? (Refer back to the chart on page 102 if needed.) As we explore this, let's talk a little bit about the differences between objective truth and subjective truth.

Objective truth is another way of saying *absolute truth*. Absolute truths are statements or beliefs that are true for all people, at all times, and in all situations. They are based on an object outside of our own opinions, feelings, or preferences. (Think "based on object = objective truth.") For example, Rebekah and I are looking at my purplish computer case right now. The purplish color is not determined by our perception of color, but rather on the wavelength of light emitted from my computer case.[4] That wavelength doesn't change based on our perception of it. Whether we like it or not is subjective. The color is objective. Most people intuitively understand this, which is why the gold/white/black/brown dress debacle made such a splash. It messed with our sense of objectivity.

On the other hand, subjective truth is based on a person—the subject. I can claim that turtle sundaes are the best sundaes in the world, but that is based on my taste palate—my personal preference (me, the subject). Subjective truths are often qualified by an adjective that is debatable, like best. Personally, I don't even like to put these types of statements into the realm of truth because it's more accurate to describe them as opinions.

Up until recently, our postmodern culture said that *all* truth statements were in the subjective realm. We can't say, "Abortion is wrong." Rather, we can only say, "Abortion is wrong *for me*." However, there is a world of difference between those statements.

Friend, as you talk with your children about important issues, you *must* understand this difference. When you tell them "Christianity is true," their postmodern mindset might be tacking on a silent *"for you"* at the end of that statement. When you say that something is true or right or wrong, they may agree *for now*. You might even see them dutifully nodding in agreement. However, if you don't get a handle on this postmodernism thing early, you might end up with a teenager or twenty-something who is completely respectful of all your "views." They are fine with those things being true *for you*, and not *for them*. If they have uncritically absorbed the lies of postmodernism, they will enter their young adult years trying to figure out "their truth" to build on, all the while being totally respectful of yours (until you try to claim that your truth should be theirs—then you'll have pushback).

For parents whose children have been obedient all through their growing-up years, this can come as a shock. These parents *thought* they were helping their children build on a foundation of truth and were completely unaware that, with postmodernism, their children would later reinterpret this activity as what developmental psychologists call "parallel play." You do your thing, I'll do mine. They reinterpret all your teachings as you showing them *your* foundation and *your* truth—not *the* truth. Postmodern principles are insidious in that way. They are like viruses that lay dormant for years. We may not even know our kids are infected until it is too late. That is why we need to expose the lies early and show how a postmodern mindset leads to chaos, not freedom.

Postmodernism and the University

In premodern times, universities were founded for the purpose of teaching students objective truths about the world. Remember when I said in the naturalism chapter that we are sort of in a post-postmodern era? Schools nowadays have a new truth that they are promoting: Objective truths are just power plays. Tolerance, diversity, autonomy, and fairness are the highest virtues to which all others must bow. According to philosopher Stephen Hicks, "postmodern professors' primary role is to now teach students to identify political oppression, particularly those of their own Western culture where the primary perpetrators are males, whites, and the rich; who have used power cruelly at the expense of women, racial minorities, and the poor."[5] (We will discuss the consequences of this approach in our chapter on feminism.)

So when your child comes home from his or her first semester at college and proudly proclaims that your Christian beliefs are merely a social construct used by white, Anglo-Saxon, Protestant men to exert control over women and minorities, you can thank postmodernism.[6]

In many ways, our educational system is split along the lines of modernism in the sciences and business schools and postmodernism in the humanities. Let's be honest: Even in our own minds, we tend to unknowingly flip between these two views of the truth. We unquestioningly swallow anything said in an article that starts with "scientific studies show," but begin our Bible studies with "What does that verse mean *to you?*" Not even the church has escaped the lies of postmodernism.

ROAR Like a Mother!

RECOGNIZE the Message

1. *Deconstructing any "truth claim" to show bias*—A truth claim isn't necessarily true. Like the phrase suggests, it is just something that someone *claims* is true. It is very easy to be sucked into truth claims that aren't actually true. The postmodern way of dealing with such claims is to deconstruct the statement, starting with the person who says it. A postmodern who is trying to dismiss a truth claim will do so by figuring out the supposedly hidden biases of the person making the claim. This is done to show that this truth is really just "*that* person's version of truth."

2. *Use "I feel" instead of "I think"*—There are times when this is necessary, but postmodernists have demanded that *all truth statements* start this way. Consider this: How many times have you heard someone say, "Use your *feelings* language?" We cannot say, "You acted disrespectfully when you spit in my face." No. Rather, we must say, "I *felt* disrespected when you spit in my face." That's an extreme example, but it should get the point across, because I truly *think* (not *feel*) that, in this culture, it is objectively disrespectful to spit in someone's face on purpose. That's not just my opinion.

3. *Nobody knows for sure*—The main thesis of postmodernism is that because we all have slightly different perspectives, we can't trust any one perspective. Who knows whose perspective aligns closest to reality? Is it the white, middle class Protestants in America? The ancient Incan sun worshippers from Peru? It reminds me

of the rare occasions that my sister and I would fight over a toy, and our mom would take it away. Postmodernism treats us all like naughty schoolchildren who can't play nicely with truth. Everyone was fighting over whose truth was truest, so postmodernism came along and said, "Because you can't play nice with your truth claims, *nobody* gets to play with them. Nobody gets to claim to know the truth. There. Now you can all get along."

4. ***You have to figure it out for yourself***—According to postmodernism, the meaning of life ultimately comes down to one thing, and like the grizzled cowboy Curly said in the movie *City Slickers*, everyone has to figure it out for themselves. This of course sounds appealing to many young people because it feels like a grand adventure. For much of their lives, they've been told what to do and what not to do (see the first paragraph of chapter 1), and now they have a dreamy philosophy that tells them, "It's all up to you. You can decide for yourself!" Who wouldn't want to hear that? Truth is whatever we want it to be? What an ear-tickling philosophy!

OFFER Discernment

So far, we've mostly highlighted the negative aspects of postmodernism. Before we talk about the lies, let's first tip our hats to some of the good that postmodernism has brought.

First, postmodern ideas influenced the church to give up on some of the negative effects of modernism. Modernists assumed that all people would see things the same way if they just used their reasoning abilities. What a sad, monochromatic-looking church *that* must have produced, denying our individual perceptions and perspectives.

Second, postmodernists placed a practical limit on what human reason was capable of. Reason can be used to argue for God's existence or to question it. But reason alone can't be used to paint a complete picture of God and of salvation.

Finally, postmodernism has revealed to us the rich diversity that God delights in, especially through worship. Back when I (Hillary) was at the

Village Church in Dallas, we would have an all-campus worship service once a year. We would borrow a building at one of the nearby mega-churches, and our Dallas, Plano, Fort Worth, Denton, and Flower Mound Village Church campuses would all get together for a night of diverse praise. I remember a bump-on-a-log man sitting next to me who looked like he wanted to be anywhere but there. He was older and rather large. As the night progressed and he remained seated, I wondered if he was capable of standing without assistance. The worship team went through their contemporary set, and then the bluegrass numbers, and then urban spoken word, and finally traditional hymns. When the traditional hymn band got up, my rotund neighbor leapt to his feet and sang those hymns with his hands held high and with all the gusto he could muster. It was one of the Best. Moments. Ever. I immediately confessed my judgmental thoughts and thanked the Lord for the privilege of worshipping next to such a beautiful soul.

I'd been dancing in the pews during one of the contemporary music sets. There was a group of guys downstairs from me who were going full groove during the bluegrass set, and this large, elderly man next to me poured his heart out during the hymns. What a lesson I learned that day! We were all worshiping the same Jesus. We were all agreeing to the lyrics of the songs and speaking millennia-old creeds together, yet the ways we related to God were unique. Without such variety, our brothers and sisters in Christ would be the worse for it. *That* is the redeeming aspect of postmodernism. More than the movements that preceded it, postmodernism has likely paved the way for artists, dancers, and nonconformists to sup together at the table of our Father and has shown us a fuller spectrum of what worship can look like.

But back to reality and time for the inevitable buzzkill. That's about all the good we can say about postmodernism. The damage that postmodernism has wrought cannot be overstated. Like most philosophical corrections, it swung way too far in the opposite direction. What are some of the lies it smuggles into our way of thinking?

Lie #1: Our Perceptions Determine Reality

The basic definition of truth is "that which corresponds to reality." In other words, truth is telling it like it is. So if our perceptions determine reality, and truth is that which *corresponds* to reality, then we are essentially saying that our perceptions determine truth. (This is one of those "if A = B and B = C, then A = C" situations.) Think about all the implications of this. All determinations of right and wrong are based on people's subjective experiences. What used to be innocent Freudian slips are now microaggressions. If you approach a girl who feels like a boy and say *she*, you can be charged with a hate crime. (At least you can in Canada, and it's not far off for us. That way of thinking is becoming more common in the United States as well.) No one is safe. There is no room for misunderstandings. Ultimately, this is the world that postmodernism gives us.

Lie #2: All Truth Claims Are Power Plays

In debates, there is a logical fallacy called "poisoning the well." To poison the well is to attack someone's character by pointing out that person's alleged flaw, and this flaw is so egregious that no one would trust anything else that person says. For example, what if someone you really trusted said, "Be careful with Bob. He is a master manipulator. There's always an agenda with him." How difficult would it be for you to trust anything Bob said after that? Taking it to the real world, what if a teacher or professor made you *really* believe that "all truth claims are power plays"? What is your kneejerk reaction when a pastor says that Jesus is "the way, *the truth*, and the life"? Think about it. For the postmodernist, those are threatening words. But Christianity is ultimately about truth: the truth of Jesus's life, death, and resurrection—and the moral truths that He taught. If it all gets reduced to power plays, then we have no basis for determining right or wrong.

Lie #3: All Truth Is Subjective

This is the thesis of postmodern thought: Even if there is such a thing as truth, there is no way to know it for sure. (Fun experiment: When people say, "All truth is subjective," ask them, "Is *that* truth subjective?" If they says yes, then their statement is false. If they say no, their statement is still false. Not that our goal is to win arguments. But if we can keep bad ideas from spreading, I'll call that a win.)

ARGUE for a Healthier Approach

Do not despair! I know this chapter may have you feeling like there is no hope for the next generation, but there is. When it comes to teaching our children, we can counteract these lies by pointing out the inconsistencies. Remember what we learned in chapter 6 about self-defeating statements? Luckily, most of postmodern thought is self-defeating, and it isn't hard to demonstrate that—even to kids. Alisa has a fabulous story about a conversation she had with her daughter Dyllan:

> One day, Dyllan was mad at me for making her follow certain rules. She announced, "When I grow up, I'm going to have NO RULES." I told her that if she wanted to change or get rid of rules, that was fine. But would she allow everyone to kill each other? She said, "Well, okay. That would be the ONLY rule." Then I said, "Would you let people punch each other for no reason?" She said, "Okay. But only those two rules." Then I said, "What about stealing? Would you allow that too?" Exasperated, she replied, "Okay. But only those three rules!" The conversation went on like this for a few more minutes, and she ended up basically agreeing to all the rules I already had expected her to follow. Then I pointed out, "It sounds like you would make the rules to be quite a bit like they already are. Maybe rules are a good thing?" She had no choice but to agree.

Most of postmodernism's claims can be turned on themselves: Truth claims are power plays. Are you *claiming* that to be *true*? What kind of power do you get from such a statement? (Quite a lot, actually.) Are you saying that it is objectively true that all truth is subjective? Does perception define reality, or is that just your perception?

Helping our kids to understand the difference between absolute and subjective truths is key to helping them avoid the traps of postmodernism. The claims of Jesus's life, death, and resurrection are absolute because they are based on real historical events. Your children's favorite color, flavor of ice cream, or chosen profession are subjective because they are based on your kids' preferences.

When it comes to matters that are not absolute (preferred dress, customs, worship styles), ask your kids why they think God created almost 200 different varieties of roses. Maybe He likes diversity more than we thought? We can praise the Lord in diverse ways without relegating ancient creeds and doctrines to the dustbins of archaic opinion. There is a difference between core truths and peripheral truths, and it's important that we know how to tell the difference between the two.

REINFORCE Through Discussion, Discipleship, and Prayer

1. *Find examples in culture*—One way that I (Rebekah) show my children the consequences of postmodernism is by finding examples in the culture—for example, postmodern artists tend to revel in meaninglessness, divorcing their art from any deliberate meaning. If the art is asking the viewer to ask questions and figure out what it means *to them*, there's a good chance you're looking at postmodern art. Scope out examples of postmodern architecture on Pinterest sometime. Those buildings can have all sorts of wild configurations above ground, signifying absurdity, rebellion, and irreverence—all common themes in postmodernism. Point out to your kids that, underground, these supposedly "postmodern" buildings have the same traditional foundations every other building needs to be able to stand upright. We can also find many examples of postmodern assumptions in popular culture, especially children's programming. "Live your truth!" and "Follow your heart!" are the epitome of postmodern messages.

2. *Teach your children to recognize these messages* and see them for what they are, critically and compassionately, because the people pushing them are confused. Such messages *sound* empowering because they allow the subject (them!) to create meaning. Ask them: Who gets to decide which meaning is correct? Isn't it more fun (and useful) to find the *real* meaning of an idea, a word, a concept, or a belief rather than declaring that all answers are correct regardless of their differences or whether they contradict one another?

3. *Help your little bears see that truth is not a power play, threat, or hate crime*—Ultimately, truth is a *Person*. Jesus said, "I am the way and the *truth* and the life. No one comes to the Father except through me" (John 14:6). He also said, "You will know the truth, and the truth will set you free" (John 8:32). This is *good news* to share with the world.

4. *Discern the difference between objective and subjective truth*—When you read the Bible with your kids, let your first question be "What was the author trying to say to his audience?" instead of "What does this passage mean *to you*?" Yes, the Word is living and active, and it speaks to us today. However, our first goal in understanding the Bible should be to discover what it meant to the people *for whom it was originally written*. Make sure your children understand and value this message first before they move on to application.

PAWS for Prayer

Praise

Lord, I praise You that all truth is weighted and measured by Your Word. You are the giver of wisdom when I lack it. You are the rock upon which I can build my thoughts. You are a sure foundation, not shifting sand.

Admit

Lord, forgive us for falling prey to the lies of postmodernism. Forgive those who deconstruct what You have purposely and sovereignly constructed. Create a repentant heart in those who reject the goodness of authority and the wisdom of rules that establish order. Forgive those who don't worship the great "I AM" because they idolize subjectivity by saying "I am" the subject of my own truth. Deliver us from the deception of our perceptions.

Worship with Thanksgiving

Thank You that absolute truth is true at all times, for all people, in all situations, and not just "true for you" or "true for me." Thank You that truth, goodness, beauty, and morality are real and can be known. We celebrate that Your church is richer for the good in postmodernism, which recognizes a diversity of perspectives on expressions of worship.

Supplication

Help me teach my children that truth is not burdensome or tyrannical, but rather, that it is liberating and instructive. Let Your truth be our strong foundation that no one can tear down. Give me the courage and wisdom to teach my children to think with their minds and feel with their hearts and to never confuse the two. Help us discern the difference between truth and truth claims, and to not fear standing for the assurance of truth and "telling it like it is." We pray for those, especially college professors, who teach a postmodernist worldview and relate everything to political oppression. Release them from walking in the futility of their minds, darkened in their understanding, alienated from You because of the ignorance that is in them due to the hardness of their heart (Ephesians 4:17-18).

In the name of Jehovah Nissi, the Lord our banner, You are victorious over false ideologies. Amen.

Discussion Questions

1. **Icebreaker:** The history of advertisements shows our culture's descent from objective claims (modernism) to emotional claims (postmodernism). What are some of the most ridiculous ads or commercials you have ever seen? Given postmodern assumptions, why do you think the company advertised the way they did? How does this reflect our culture? Here's one to get you started: "Your way, right away" (Burger King).

2. **Main theme:** *Truth is real and can be known.* Discuss the differences between objective and subjective claims. Why do you think postmodernists have concluded that truth cannot be known?

3. **Self-evaluation:** How often do you go to the Bible and ask, "What does this mean to me?" before researching what the passage meant to the people for whom it was written? Why is it important to first know the original meaning of the message?

4. **Brainstorm:** What are some truths that culture has decided are subjective (that is, a matter of personal preference) that the Bible says are objectively true? List as many as you can think of.

5. **Release the bear:** Talk to your kids about the differences between objective and subjective truth. As you go through your week, pay close attention to truth claims in advertising or the media. Ask your children, "Is that a subjective claim or an objective claim? How do you know?"

Chapter 9

You're Wrong to Tell Me that I'm Wrong!

Moral Relativism

HILLARY MORGAN FERRER AND REBEKAH VALERIUS

I (Hillary) love playing card games with my nephews. There is one game that I learned in high school that apparently the kids are still playing. However, when my nephews taught me how to play it, it had a *lot* more rules than when I was a teen. The goal of the game is to get all the cards. One way is to win little battles, and the other way is to slap the pile of cards when you see doubles, thus picking up the whole pile. The slapping rules have expanded considerably since I was young. No longer is it just doubles. Now you can slap for all sorts of hard-to-remember combinations.

The way my nephews treat the rules of the game is a perfect analogy of what our modern society has done with morals. Each boy has his own favorite rules—namely, the ones that he can best remember. So naturally they each keep trying to convince the rest of us to play by the set of rules that give them the competitive advantage. Why not? *If you can make the rules, you can unmake them.*

This is basically how our society treats morality these days. Instead of viewing morality as a reflection of deeper truths, people treat morals as cultural norms that can be revised without consequence—much like the rules of the card game. And like the card game, everyone in society is vying for a different set of rules that they think the rest of us should abide by.

Before we start explaining moral relativism, though, let's first explain what we mean by relativism. The word *relative* means "in relation to." *The irony of relativism is that in order for something to be relative, there has to be something else that is absolute.* For instance, directions to Dallas are *relative* depending on where you are coming from. But they are all based on the *absolute* fact that Dallas will never be south of Houston, and is in Texas, not California. People often think that the debate is between relative truth or absolute truth, but it's not. The debate is really about which absolute we are starting from. As Christians, we believe that everything is relative to God's moral law. C.S. Lewis said in *Mere Christianity,*

> My argument against God was that the universe seemed so cruel and unjust. But how had I got this idea of just and unjust? A man does not call a line crooked unless he has some idea of a straight line. What was I comparing this universe with when I called it unjust?[1]

Our world is trying to tell our kids that all morals are relative to the individual, but that's like trying to get directions to a moving target. All you can do is wander aimlessly and hope you hit it. To say that all morals are relative to the individual is to essentially say that there are no absolute morals—things that are right or wrong for all people, at all times, in all places.

Moral Relativism and Postmodernism

Moral relativism is the logical outworking of postmodernism. If absolute truth can't be known and all we can do is "live our truth," then we must figure out a way to get along when our truths inevitably conflict (because they will!). Moral relativism's solution? Tolerance. Remember our self-defeating statements from the naturalism chapter? Moral relativism is ultimately self-defeating because on one hand, it demands that everybody tolerate each other. On the other hand, it is very intolerant of those who are seen as intolerant. As our chapter subtitle says, "You're wrong to tell me that I'm wrong!" (To which we could reply, "No, *you're* wrong to tell me that I'm wrong for telling you that you're wrong!") It reduces to the "Nuh uh!" "Yeah huh!" arguments between kids, but on a whole new level because we are dealing with adults doing this, and they are *super* convinced that they are right.

If this sounds irrational to you, it is. So why can't people see how irrational this is? Simple answer: Their logical reasoning is not engaged. Emotions are now the main arbiters of moral truth. The *strength* of one's emotions determines exactly *how* right or wrong something is. If you are debating a moral relativist on Facebook and try to engage in discussion, you may see him or her go into ALL CAPS MODE. ALL CAPS MODE IS LIKE YELLING, AND IF THEIR REASONING DIDN'T PER-SUADE YOU BEFORE, MAYBE YOU'LL CAVE WHEN YOU SEE HOW MUCH THEY REALLY, REALLY MEAN WHATEVER IT IS THEY ARE SAYING IN ALL CAPS.

Emotion and reason *should* work hand in hand. Once upon a time, counseling was centered upon helping someone's emotions to match reality. Now people are more concerned with crafting reality to either match emotions or alleviate bad emotions. Even science must bend the knee. (That's not a human baby. It's just a fetus, and not even DNA can inform you of the gender.) As we said in the linguistic theft chapter, emotions are great followers but horrible leaders. Our society is currently living out the grand experiment of what happens when you put emotions in charge all the time. It's not pretty—more on this in chapter 10.

Moral relativism has invaded our culture because people have rejected any real-world objective grounding for morality. The moral law is called the moral *law* for a reason. It isn't our preference and it isn't our opinion any more than is the law of gravity. In his book *The Reason for God*, Tim Keller notes that the ancients believed that "if you violated that metaphysical order there were consequences just as severe as if you violated physical reality by placing your hand in a fire."[2] (The metaphysical order was the moral law.)

A vivid picture of this appears in Oscar Wilde's book *The Portrait of Dorian Grey*, where a wealthy socialite has his portrait painted and then wishes for the portrait to age in his place. The book details the various moral depravities Dorian Grey indulges in, and after each incident, it describes the physical change that takes place to the painting—visual consequences for breaking what the reader intuitively knows is the moral law. At the end, Dorian is so disgusted by what the portrait has become that he can no longer abide its ugliness and he slashes it to bits.

When we break the moral law, our souls are changed. We can't see it like in *The Portrait of Dorian Grey*. Breaking the spiritual law has spiritual consequences. Is it any wonder that our morally relative society has an epidemic of depression, anxiety, and panic attacks? I'm not saying there's a one-to-one correlation, like you sin and boom—depression sets in. Rather, our society is setting spiritual fires all over the place and wondering why our world is going up in flames. We not only reap the spiritual consequences of our own sin, but we are also subject to the effects of the sin of others. Ask any person who grew up with an alcoholic parent or who was the victim of sexual abuse, and you'll have a very clear picture of the ramifications of disobeying the moral law—the consequences are not limited to the soul of the transgressor. There is a school of thought called "moral and ethical realism" that emphasizes the objective nature of certain "values" so strongly that they call the moral law "moral facts" instead of moral values. Values may change depending on the person, but facts are true for everyone—for all people at all times.

The Right and Wrong Ways to Frame Moral Relativism

Moral relativism is a huge problem in our society right now. Nobody knows which way is up, or who decides what is right. One of the biggest challenges we face as parents is wanting to have simple answers for our kids. And let's face it: We would all love simple answers.

The easiest (but least effective) way to get a simple answer is to over-simplify a problem. Unfortunately, moral problems do not leave us with this luxury. What often happens is we give platitudes, standalone Bible verses, or what I lovingly call "bumper sticker wisdom." We coldly state, "The Bible says it, I believe it, that settles it," and go no further. While this might work for some people (usually the ones already on board with God and Christianity), this kind of "reasoning" assumes a premodern mindset, and we are in post-postmodern times. Appealing to authority does nothing to convince people of truth. We can try, and we might even be heard. But we won't be understood and persuasive.

Scripture is vital for our understanding of truth, but it is more like a manual than a single tool. We shouldn't whip out Scripture and just start banging things with it. We should use it to guide our interactions. Scripture shows us how to use the multiple tools that God has given us.

Values, truths, moral principles, and the fruit of the Spirit are all like tools in a toolbox. Thank You, Jesus, for giving us so many tools! Imagine trying to work on a car engine with only a hammer or a lug wrench. (That's a thing, right?) There are many problems you can fix with each of these tools, but armed only with a single tool, we can do more harm than good. We need lots of different tools, and we need the manual (Scripture) to show us how to use them.

Unfortunately, our society has thrown out many of the tools that used to be in the toolbox. Moral facts, objective truth, God, and even the manual (Scripture) have been tossed to the wayside. People have opted out of toolboxes, and instead settled for their favorite tool, maybe two. One person values compassion, attempts to solve all problems with compassion, and prioritizes problems requiring compassion. Another person has tolerance and attempts to use tolerance alone to resolve all issues. Another uses Scripture and ignores mercy and relationship, lobbing truth bombs and letting the pieces fall where they may, declaring to their victim "The word of God will not return void!" There is a time and a place for each of these, but usually the best results are achieved by using them all together. And there's no single rule that can replace the guidance and tools of Scripture and the Holy Spirit, and there is no easy way to navigate the moral landscape. The truth does not change, but people do, and the way we approach them is vital. We all need humility and discernment.

A Brief History of Moral Relativism

Moral relativism is what happens when you take postmodernism to its logical conclusion. (Although we should clarify that moral relativism has always been around because people have always tried to justify their sin.) For our purposes, we'll just focus on the most recent wave. Not to keep harping on the whole premodern/modern/postmodern thing, but society really has been shaped by these ideas. Whereas the premodernists used reason, revelation, and authority to determine truth, the modernists decided that human reason was sufficient. However, their assumption was based on the idea that by using our collective human reason, we would all come to the same conclusions—that is, 2 + 2 = 4, so unprovoked fist + face = bad, right? It's all just math.

The postmodernists questioned the contradictory conclusions of modernism that (1) humans could construct their own truth, and (2) this truth would be objective and binding for everyone. The postmodernists said, "Hold on, everyone is disagreeing. Either there is no objective truth, or we keep messing it up." (Helllllooooo—original sin!) In other words, it's either our fault, or truth's fault. They voted truth off the island.

Part of the postmodernists' rejection of truth was motivated by a commitment to naturalism. As (atheist) biologist Richard Lewontin famously summarized,

> Our willingness to accept scientific claims that are against common sense is the key to an understanding of the real struggle between science and the supernatural. We take the side of science *in spite* of the patent absurdity of some of its constructs…*in spite* of the tolerance of the scientific community for unsubstantiated just-so stories, because we

have a prior commitment, a commitment to materialism…
[M]aterialism is absolute, for we cannot allow a Divine Foot
in the door.[3] (And remember from chapter 6 that materialism is almost interchangeable with naturalism.)

The *imago dei* is woven into our moral fabric. A person can say, "We can't
judge other people's truths" all day long, but will get visibly uncomfortable when you ask if that applies to a hypothetical society that tortures
babies for fun or believes that sex slavery is a solid business investment.
Psychopaths aside, we *all* know that some things are wrong—for everyone, at all times, and in all cultures. The moral law is written on our hearts
(Romans 2:15).

There are certain parts of humanity that, if removed, create a vacuum.
Whatever fills the void ultimately becomes a monster because we are being
ruled by something that was never meant to rule. The moderns rejected
God, which created a vacuum of worship that reason and science then
tried to fill. When the postmodernists rejected objective truth, emotions
were next in line for the throne.

Moral relativism says, "What's true for you may not be true for me.
Nobody can tell me what is true. Let's all hold hands and sing 'Kumbaya.'
Nobody is wrong—what's not to celebrate?" The *functional* conclusion,
however, is just a new objective standard: Nobody can say that anybody
else is wrong. If you do, you've broken the cardinal rule of moral relativism, and you will be publicly shamed for it. As Jonathan Merritt says in
The Atlantic,

> [A] "shame culture" has now taken [moral relativism's]
> place…that, if violated, results in unmerciful moral crusades
> on social media…This system is not a reversion to the val-
> ues that conservatives may wish for…Instead of being cen-
> tered on gender roles, family values, respect for institutions
> and religious piety, it orbits around values like tolerance and
> inclusion. (This new code has created a paradoxical moment

in which all is tolerated except the intolerant and all included except the exclusive).[4]

Mama Bears, just to be clear, as Christians, *we* are part of the intolerant and exclusive club; Christianity is intolerant of sin, and Jesus's claims to lordship are exclusive. Think back to how many things you got shamed for in middle school and high school. The wrong haircut, the wrong clothes, the wrong Trapper Keeper. If that weren't enough, our kids are now being bullied for having the wrong beliefs! We cannot underestimate the extreme pressure to fit in. To survive the junior-high jungle, our Christian kids often disconnect their public beliefs from their private beliefs. The soul, however, cannot abide a ruptured worldview for long. It seeks to patch it back together, but it can't do it correctly if it never knew how it fit together in the first place. The result? Basically, the Frankenstein of religion. Create a new faith, a new Christianity, and put it all together in a new way so that one can hold the tolerant values demanded in public (tolerance of sin, inclusion of all beliefs) and still embrace all the *Christian words* of traditional faith. In case you are wondering what this looks like in practice, see Alisa's chapters titled *New Spirituality* and *Progressive Christianity*.

ROAR Like a Mother!

RECOGNIZE the Message

Moral relativism isn't very difficult to see in our culture. Here are a few statements your kids will probably hear or read.

1. ***What is true for you may not be true for me***—The word *true* has been hijacked. People still want truth; they just don't want to define it as truth. What if it's true for me that your statement is not true? Whose truth wins?

2. ***I am the only one who can determine my truth***—This is radical individualism. We turn into wandering stars instead of living in community.

3. *Making my own choices (personal autonomy) is the highest priority*—If there is anything that gets in the way of me doing what I want to do, vilify or dehumanize it. It is obviously waging a war on me or is oppressing me in some way.

4. *Don't force your truth on me*—According to postmodernism, all truth claims are repressive attempts to control others. Claiming that something is truly true, like *for reals* true, is a microagression at best, and forceful oppression at worst.

5. *Love is love*—Nowhere is moral relativism more obvious than within the realms of sex, gender, and everything related. Contraception, divorce, cohabitation, abortion, gay marriage, and gender identity—the whole landscape is a mess. (You had no idea, right?) And in this area, even Christians feel motivated to find wiggle room.

OFFER Discernment

So why is moral relativism so attractive, and what problems is it attempting to solve? At first glance, it should be obvious: Nobody wants to be told what to do. But let's go a bit deeper than that. Why would society be struggling so much under the burden of being told what to do by authority figures?

First, we must acknowledge how many times we Christians have abused moral authority and taken our personal *convictions* and made them moral *absolutes*. For example, the book *I Kissed Dating Goodbye* came out during my (Hillary's) senior year of high school. I saw some in the Christian community turn dating into the unpardonable sin. One guy—Joshua Harris—was convicted to not date, and youth groups across the nation turned it into gospel truth. Harris actually apologized years later for the book because he saw what it did to so many young people. (Personally, I wanted to just give him a hug and tell him it was not his fault that Christians turned his book into the sixty-seventh book of the Bible.)

Romans 14 makes it clear that there is a spectrum of Christian convictions. When people deny legitimate Christian freedom, they tread on dangerous ground. Hyperfundamentalism and moral relativism are both errors of extreme that will forever react to one other. Some moral relativists really do have noble intentions and are trying to reestablish peace and resolve conflict among inhouse disagreements. Or they are just so worn out from seeing the Bible being used as a hammer. None of these are necessarily bad motivations. It's moral relativism's *solution* that is the problem.

What are some of the lies within moral relativism that we need to acknowledge?

Lie #1: Total Moral Relativism Is Possible

False. It's not even *logically* possible. It's a self-defeating statement. To say that nothing is true is to claim to know the truth about truth. For moral relativism to work, nobody can have strong convictions. You are allowed to believe whatever you like, unless you think your beliefs are *actually* true. Then moral relativism has a problem with you because in and of itself, truth is exclusive. It excludes falsehood.

Lie #2: Everyone Embracing Moral Relativism Will End All Conflicts

False. All we do is change who is oppressed. When people's "truths" ultimately conflict (and they will), then it is the squeaky wheel that wins the argument, usually bullying everyone else into silence. As parents, how often can you get your kids to agree on anything? And yet we think we can get the whole world to agree? If it doesn't work on a small scale, it won't work on a large scale.

Lie #3: Truth and Compassion Are Diametrically Opposed

Few moral relativists will come right out and say it like this, but it's pretty heavily implied. This is what's known as a false dichotomy. It's true that people will usually gravitate toward truth or compassion. (The Myers-Briggs Type Indicator calls this dichotomy the "thinkers" and "feelers.") But guess what? Thinkers can feel, and feelers can think. We *can* do both. Do not concede to this lie that you have to pick between truth and compassion. People who think they have to choose between the two often turn into one of two caricatures that my childhood pastor called the "compassionate compromisers" and "terrifying truth tellers." Our goal should be both truth and love.

Lie #4: The Person Expressing Compassion Automatically Has the Moral (Relativist) High Ground

This lie is tricky to discern. Often the compassionate language of tolerance *sounds* so close to the heart of Christ that we can't quite remember (or articulate) why certain sins are wrong. As I've said before, the proverbial road to hell is paved with good intentions. Nowhere is that more apparent than with misplaced compassion. Compassion rarely looks down the road. Compassion only wants to make things better *now*. It doesn't anticipate unintended consequences. Misplaced compassion might tell us to never discipline our children because it causes them distress. Anyone who's watched *Charlie and the Chocolate Factory* knows what kind of brat that approach to parenting will ultimately produce. My (Hillary's) husband often says that some of the greatest atrocities foisted on mankind have been done in the name of compassion.

ARGUE for a Healthier Approach

So how do we prevent our kids from getting sucked into moral relativism?

1. *Emphasize that nobody is a complete moral relativist*—As soon as a moral relativists's wallet is stolen, he isn't going to think, *Oh well, the thieves are just living their truth…with my money.* Neither will he blame the thieves' upbringing or economic factors. (His defense lawyer might, though.) Most people are objectivists as soon as their own comfort is violated. Similarly, if you hear your children making comments like "I wouldn't do that, but I wouldn't tell someone else not to," identify what they are talking about and establish if this is a legitimate moral fact that Scripture has addressed, or if it is an area of Christian freedom. (Or if they are referring to a non-Christian, someone whom we *shouldn't* be telling what to do.)

2. *Acknowledge moral facts*—Your kids will be told one of two lies: (1) all religions are completely different, or (2) all religions are basically the same (pluralism—see chapter 11). Both of these statements are false. Most religions differ in their fundamental doctrines yet acknowledge similar moral facts, like the facts that murder, lying, cowardice, and stealing are wrong, and altruism, love, honesty and mercy are good. For more on this, see C.S. Lewis's appendix in *Abolition of Man*, where he compares law codes from various times and cultures.

3. *Acknowledge the consequences of disobeying the moral law*—If you have a compassion-driven child on your hands, rejoice! What a beautiful soul. However, the compassionate child is tempted to do or say whatever will cause the least amount of immediate pain to another person. This instinct that can cause him or her to affirm things that shouldn't be affirmed. We need to emphasize that God is not a cosmic killjoy. He did not create moral laws to squash freedom and hurt people. As the architect of our souls, He knows what will harm us. The true act of compassion will encourage people *toward that which is good for their souls*. Granted, the manner in which we do this will either be the aroma of Christ or the stench of condemnation. Be perfume, not sulfur.

4. *Emphasize legitimate Christian freedom and gray areas*—Kids who think the world is black and white will feel embittered and lied to when they discover the gray. All too often, they end up interpreting gray areas as being closer to black than white, and then defect to the proverbial dark side. I can't tell you how many atheists John, Rebekah, and I have interacted with who were raised in a hyper-fundamentalist environment, and this very scenario is their story.

5. *Be discerning with Christian celebrities*—We sometimes turn off our brain as soon as we see the word *Christian* in a famous person's bio. This is unwise. One of the biggest problems right now is the number of high-profile Christian figures who have decided

to embrace the tools of compassion and tolerance to the exclusion of biblical guidance, especially with regard to sexuality, gender, and the exclusivity of Christian claims. Why are celebrities prone to this? They realize that conflict will reduce their audience. Also, nobody wants to hurt people, and when culture tells us we are "hurting others" with our Christian truths, our tendency is to stop talking. The compassion in us wants to alleviate the pain, even if that leads to doctrinal compromise.

6. *Just because there is Christian freedom does not mean there are no absolutes*—Why do we keep bouncing between extremes, between legalism versus lawlessness? Why do we keep making it all or nothing? It's lazy. We have *both* Christian freedom *and* Christian absolutes. It's not either/or. If morality is grounded in God, then we can bet that it'll be both absolute and complicated at the same time. Christian living has laws and guidelines like a mountain path has guardrails—a world of adventure awaits, but safeguards are in place to help guide our growth and exploration and to keep us from rolling down the mountain.

REINFORCE Through Discussion, Discipleship, and Prayer

1. Younger children are still in the black-and-white stage of thinking; we are still trying to teach them right and wrong. Make it a point to not only provide your children with the rules, but the *reasons* behind the rules. Help them understand how rules are created for our benefit, out of love or for structure. Help them to recognize the natural consequences of breaking the rules (like hurting their foot when you told them to wear shoes!). This will prepare them to understand the idea of moral consequences as they get older (as opposed to just physical consequences).

2. As your children grow older, they will encounter things that are sometimes right and sometimes wrong. For example, consider the matter of keeping secrets. In general, our kids should keep their

promise not to tell a secret. It is different, however, if keeping the secret could cause someone harm or involves something that an adult needs to know about. As soon as your children are able to understand the concept of moral dilemmas, discuss how to navigate them, and keep your instructions at age-appropriate levels.

3. As you talk with your children about consequences, be honest about your own sinful past in age-appropriate ways. How has your sin affected your soul? How has your sin affected someone else? Reinforce to your children the concept that the moral law is based on moral facts, and disobeying has moral consequences (like how disobeying the law of gravity has physical consequences).

The following are for older children, if and when you deem it appropriate.

4. Talk to kids about all the tools God has given us in our toolbox. A good place to start is Galatians 5, the fruit of the Spirit, and the passages addressing spiritual gifts (Romans 12:6-8; 1 Corinthians 12:8-10; 1 Peter 4:11). Create hypothetical moral dilemmas and discuss how each of these tools is important for addressing the dilemma. For example, consider abortion. We have an epidemic of single motherhood. We need *compassion* when talking to a struggling young mother who is terrified. She needs *service* to lighten her load. She needs to know the *truth* of how abortion can damage her soul. She needs *grace* if she has already made the wrong decision.

5. Pay attention to media headlines that report on protests. (These shouldn't be too hard to find these days.) Practice the ROAR steps by helping your little bears to recognize what message is being preached, what value the protestors are upholding, and what legitimate concerns are being addressed. What lies are sneaking in? How can Scripture better address the values that the protestors hold so dear? What can your children do to be part of the solution?

For example, there are true stories of homosexuals being brutalized and treated as subhuman. Is this how God would have us treat them? Acknowledge the pain they have experienced. How do the protestors see themselves as "championing the cause of the oppressed"? What does Scripture have to say about sexuality and marriage (Matthew 19:1-4)? What does Scripture have to say about love (1 John 4:8; Romans 5:8; 1 Corinthians 13)? What is our duty in response to this movement? (Hint: We are not called to judge those outside the church, but those inside [1 Corinthians 5:12-13]. We are also called to judge what is true—see John 7:24 and 1 Thessalonians 5:21. Judging rightly is a confusing concept for kids to grasp because all they hear from others is "Don't judge.")

Talk with your kids about how we can best love people while still embracing biblical truths. Look at how Jesus treated sins stemming from a person being fallen, weak, and subject to temptation, like the woman at the well and the woman caught in adultery. Compare these examples to how Jesus treated the sins of pride and rebellion, as exhibited by people like the Pharisees. How did Jesus show compassion without condoning sin?

PAWS for Prayer

Praise

You are the moral lawgiver. You give us our rights, and therefore only You can take them away. We are indeed endowed by You, our Creator, with inalienable rights. You are the moral order creator, the chaos eraser. You are the God of the universe, and there are universal rules that apply to everyone, at all times, and in all places. Who are we to think that we can dismiss or ignore these rules? You, God, are the definition of what is good.

Admit

Forgive me, forgive us, for letting the strength of an emotion or personal preference become our god, for rejecting that morality is grounded in reality. We are ashamed that we have allowed the thread of truth to be

ripped out of the moral fabric of our religion, our politics, and our pleasure. I admit that I often value pleasing man instead of God, not rock-
ing the boat under the guise of tolerance rather than standing on the rock.
Forgive us for empowering others in their sin when we esteem fake compassion over truth. It's *not* "all relative." We are objectively sinners in need
of a Savior.

Worship with Thanksgiving

I thank You that breaking spiritual laws has spiritual consequences that
serve to reprove me. Thank You that Your holy Scripture is the seamstress
of our moral fabric and we are made in the *imago dei*. We are grateful for
"oughts" planted inside of us that ought to be obeyed and not dismissed.

Supplication

Show me where I have adopted moral relativism. Help me show compassion to those with muddled thinking and incoherent thoughts about
truth. Help Your church repair the moral fabric by weaving compassionate
truth into our conversations. May we remain intolerant of sin, embrace
the exclusive claims of Jesus, yet include everyone in the message. Don't
let us be swayed by the compassionate language that confuses truth. Oh
Lord, this is hard. We need Your help. Make us the aroma of Christ to a
world starving for the bread of life. May we watch our method as much as
our message as we call sin for what it is, and not by any other name.

In the name of Jesus our rock. Amen.

Discussion Questions

1. **Icebreaker:** Name something you did where nobody had to punish
   you, but because breaking the moral law has moral consequences,
   you ended up reaping the consequences of your own actions.
2. **Main theme:** *Moral facts exist, and there are spiritual (and sometimes
   physical) consequences for breaking them.* What are some things that
   everyone considered wrong when you were growing up, but that

society is now embracing? In what ways have you seen societal morals change? What effects has this had on our culture?

3. **Self-evaluation:** Are there any morals that you've held to for the most part, yet you wiggled out of when they became inconvenient? This could be a very personal question, so only share what you feel comfortable saying. Why do you think that you changed your mind on the issue? Were there any spiritual, physical, or emotional consequences for going against what you knew to be true?

4. **Brainstorm:** Three of the main reasons God created rules is (1) to protect us, (2) to create an orderly society, and (3) to give us true freedom. Choose a few areas where the Bible and our culture radically disagree. What are the individual and societal consequences (psychological, physical, emotional, economic, etc.) that occur when biblical principles are ignored? How does following these principles actually free us? How does disobeying them bring bondage?

5. **Release the bear:** Pick one of the moral principles discussed—for example, lying—and create a fictitious world with your kids in which lying is okay. In what ways will people be affected? In what ways would a society that accepts lying become chaotic? Show how consequences don't always mean being punished by mommy or daddy. Some consequences occur naturally because we have disobeyed God's moral law. Emphasize how this law—that is, do not lie—is God's way of protecting us, freeing us from lies, and creating an orderly society in which we can thrive.

Chapter 10

Follow Your Heart—It Never Lies!
Emotionalism

Teasi Cannon, Hillary Morgan Ferrer, and Hillary Short

Do you ever look back on the things you did as a child and cringe with embarrassment? I (Teasi) do, especially when I think back to my middle school years. You see, I was a dramatic child—not theater dramatic, but emotional. It was not uncommon to find me standing in front of my bedroom mirror and listening to sad music just to make myself cry so I could enjoy watching each tear travel down my cheeks (I stopped doing this sometime in my early twenties, so no worries). For the longest time, the most effective song for this was "Hopelessly Devoted" from the *Grease* soundtrack. I would play this song ad nauseum, stare into my own sad eyes, contemplate how desperately lonely I was, and dream of a day when I'd be rescued from the drudgery that was my average middle-class life.

Believe it or not, I loved feeling sad.

But I also loved feeling happy. I simply loved *feeling*, and thinking about feelings, and talking about feelings. I have always been comfortable in the realm of feelings, or, as we're discussing in this chapter, emotions. And I believe there isn't anything wrong with that. Emotions are a gift from God. He uses them to touch us and to teach us. But I'm pretty sure He never meant for them to lead us, as our discussion on emotionalism will reveal. I once heard someone say, "Emotions are like toddlers. They are fun, but you'd never put one in charge."

The Difference Between Emotions and Passions

My (Hillary's) husband once observed that getting emotions under control is different for everybody. For some people, it's like wrestling a bear, and for others it's like shuttling a mouse into a cage. Emotions can be powerful little beasts and are often immune to the various methods of truth seeking, like science, divine revelation, authority, and even logical reasoning. However, as we will see, emotions *can* be valuable for discovering truth, as long as they are informed by Scripture, reason, and reality. Like our physical bodies, our emotions need to be shaped by discipline—otherwise they're not a pretty sight. To understand what it means to discipline our emotions, we must first understand the difference between *emotions* and *passions*.

As far as we can tell, there are many physical and nonphysical parallels within the human body. For example, what's the difference between the brain and the mind? Naturalists believe they are essentially the same. The Christian, who acknowledges both body and soul, can distinguish between the two. The brain is the physical component of our thoughts while the mind is the nonphysical part that sends out commands. Play a game with your kids where you both strike a pose or make a face. You'll have a fun time with laughter and silliness. Ask them, "What made you strike that pose, or make that face?" They probably won't know. There is something mysterious built into us that enables us to immediately come up with ideas and execute them. The materialist would say it's the chemicals in our brains that generate the ideas for faces or poses, but that's a slippery slope to go down. If we are merely slaves to what the chemicals in our brains do, then we're not responsible for our thoughts or actions.

But according to God's Word, we are *not* just chemicals. We are volitional beings who can make good decisions, bad decisions, or funny faces (if that's what we so choose). The chemicals in our brains may help or hinder our ability to make good decisions, but we still have the ability to make choices. There is something about the idea of *self* or *me* that is not reducible to chemicals or neurons. Scientists have barely begun to scratch the surface when it comes to understanding the difference between the brain (physical) and the mind (nonphysical), and there's still a lot to learn.

Now, to draw the parallel with regard to emotions, we have physical and nonphysical components to our feelings. In the book *Not Passion's Slave: Emotions and Choice,* Robert Solomon distinguishes between passions and emotions. Passions are the chemical (physical) part of our feelings over which we have little control. These are the primitive, physical components of our feelings, such as fear, arousal, or anger. On the other hand, Solomon identifies *emotions* as a kind of *judgment.* Emotions can change quickly regardless of what is going on in the body. Let's unpack that for a moment.

Say you are a peevish preteen and you are waiting for your mom to pick you up from school. Ten minutes go by, then half an hour, then a full hour. You are probably fuming by this time. Suddenly a car comes screeching up, and it's your dad. He says, "Quick—get in. Mom has been in an accident, and we're going to the hospital." I wager that your anger toward your mom would disappear immediately. Why? Because your emotion of anger was based on your *judgment* that she had forgotten you. (How dare she!) But with the new information you've received from your dad, your emotional judgment has changed and now you're worried about your mom. You're probably feeling panicky, which is understandable given the circumstance. At first you were upset because of what you *thought* was true (mom forgot me), but your emotions changed immediately once you discovered the facts. *Well-informed emotions can strengthen your grasp on truth.*

When disciplined by Scripture, reason, and reality, emotions are powerful reinforcers. When I become aware of an injustice, I might feel angry and be motivated to act. When I as a Mama Bear see truth compromised, I can get very indignant, and this might motivate me to write a book to help other Mama Bears wade through the lies. (Wink!) When I watch a documentary on children being sold into sex slavery, I will feel compassion and be motivated to contribute to an organization that's working to end human trafficking. When I experience a powerful worship service, I can be overcome with love for my God and all that He has done for me. In each of these situations, emotions are pointing me not only toward truth, but actions as well. It's wonderful how God has wired us, but sin has twisted us in ways that we no longer work according to manufacturer's specifications.

A Brief History of Emotionalism

Emotionalism basically refers to replacing our God-given reasoning faculties with emotion. Is something right or wrong? I'm not sure. Hold on a sec, let me see how I feel about it…Where are you leading me, heart?

We've seen more detailed explanations of the historical journey toward emotionalism in our previous chapters, but let's review some of it again here. Remember that naturalism says the only things that are knowable are what we can experience through our five senses—in other words, the material world. The problem is, naturalism has no category for aspects of life that are undeniably real yet cannot be defined or experienced by our five senses—things like love, morals, or even God. Material naturalism relegates these into the realm of useful fictions at best, or tyrannical bullies at worst. The moderns expected that science would provide them irrefutable answers to all life's questions. When this didn't happen, radical skepticism set in, which paved the way for postmodernism.

When postmodernism took the stage, the disillusioned masses said, "If we can't know everything, then we can't know anything." The modernists had thrown out authority and divine revelation as sources of knowledge. Postmodernists went one step further and threw out human reason as well and claimed that all truth is ultimately subjective—a product of perceptions that have been shaped by culture and society. At this point, we suspect they had an "Oh crap" moment when they realized they had just thrown out *all* means of knowing truth. Maybe there was something they had overlooked?

Consider this illustration: I (Hillary F.) love chocolate. Occasionally

I'll get a bag of chocolate and go through it slowly. When it's all gone, I'll feel sad. Sometimes, even when I know I've run out of chocolate, I'll check the bag *just in case* there's one more piece. Occasionally there is! Oh, the elation of finding that *one last M&M* in the package! I wager that's how mankind felt after tossing out all the methods available for truth-finding. People went back to their toolbox to see if there was anything left to help them find truth, and yes, there was—emotions. Woo-hoo!

As we have discussed above, emotions *can* be a valuable means of reinforcing truth, but the caveat is absolutely imperative, and I have no problem repeating myself: Our emotions *must* be disciplined according to Scripture, reason, and reality. If they are not, then who knows what our emotions will churn out as "truth"? Jeremiah 17:9 says, "The heart is deceitful above all things and beyond cure. Who can understand it?" Even though I try desperately to control and inform my emotions with truth, I still have irrational feelings. I can feel worthless (not true), I can feel unloved (not true), I can feel like I am all alone (not true!).

The problem with using our emotions for determining truth is that they have to first be *conformed to truth* in order to tell us anything useful. For a compass to work, it must first be magnetized. Otherwise, it won't point to true north. Disciplining our emotions with truth is like magnetizing our emotional compass. We can follow our emotions, but only *after* we have made sure our emotional compass is pointing in the right direction.

Too many people today determine truth by their emotions yet have not bothered to magnetize their emotional compasses. They say, "Let's go north!" and proceed to walk in all different directions, trying to convince everyone else to follow them. Instead of disciplining their emotions to match reality, they are trying to make reality match their emotions. When they feel scared, they *assume* that they are in danger—instead of perceiving real danger and then feeling scared. In this way, emotionalism mistakes feelings for facts. But there's little assurance that those emotion-loaded opinions are indeed *facts* unless Scripture, reason, and reality are fact-checking those feelings. And when people have already bought into postmodernism, they don't even believe that they *can* know objective truth. One person's feelings can be just as "factual" as the next—which is to say, none of us have the facts and we're all wandering lost in a maze of wrong. The only way your feelings can be a trustworthy guide is if you don't need to get anywhere anytime soon.

Friend, this is not a healthy situation. Emotionalism has left reality completely out of the equation. Here are more examples: Does hell make you uncomfortable? Don't worry; we'll just turn it into a metaphor. And by all means, don't use DNA or body parts to determine your children's gender. First they have to tell you what they "feel like." Sound familiar? These all start with an emotion, and then make conclusions about reality instead of starting with reality and disciplining the emotions so that they follow. *Emotions* now determine truth and reality. (For all you mothers of teenage girls, *that's* a scary thought!)

ROAR Like a Mother!

RECOGNIZE the Message

This part of the ROAR section will be slightly different than in previous chapters because there are two aspects to emotionalism: the *assumptions* that are built in, and the way that it is *packaged*. Knowing both facets is important for recognizing the message of emotionalism.

The Assumptions of Emotionalism

Today's postmodern society has tossed out any truly useful standard for judging the truthfulness of our emotions. So that we can more readily recognize when emotionalism is at play, let's look at some of its built-in assumptions.

1. *I cannot choose or control my emotions*—This is partly true and partly false. We cannot control our *passions*—our body's physiological response to situations. We might, however, be the first generation that has broadly accepted the idea that emotions *can't* be controlled. All civilized societies are built on the assumption that

people can and should control themselves, including their emotions. Civilization depends on it. We expect different behavior from adults than from children because children are still learning how to control their emotions. We even have clinical diagnoses for people who experience difficulties in this area (that is, bipolar, OCD, etc.).

2. *Negative emotions are harmful*—There is limited truth to this. There is very little good that will ever come from things like verbal abuse or clinical depression, but negative emotions are a part of life. Things get weird when you try to eliminate negative emotions from a person's life. The belief that negative emotions are harmful has led to two recent phenomena: (1) the tremendous emphasis on the importance of self-esteem (not entirely bad), and (2) the removal of competition from many children's activities. In an effort to prevent kids from interpreting the loss of a competition or game as rejection, we removed competition altogether. Everyone gets a trophy! Everyone is special! Unfortunately, while our kids' self-esteem may have soared, their self-control plummeted. Many lost their ability to handle competition, setbacks, rejection, and negative emotions. Enter the snowflake generation—those whose sense of balance in life is as volatile as fresh snow on a sunny day.

3. *We must change reality to protect emotions*—This is the logical conclusion of the preceding two assumptions. If (1) we can't change our emotions and (2) negative emotions are harmful, then we *must* (3) change whatever is causing negative emotions so that we can live healthy lives. It is an inescapable conclusion of the first two assumptions.

I cannot even begin to explain how many ways this assumption has infiltrated society. We see it in our educational system (with the failure to hold back struggling students), our judicial system (like the Stanford rape case, where the judge didn't want to "ruin the rapist's life"), our political system (where colleges shut down, cancelled exams, and passed out puppies and Play-Doh to help students deal with the results of the 2016 election), and I don't even need to mention how this has affected sex and gender issues. Now Canada is enacting public policies that dictate what words people must use based on how those words make others feel. And we aren't just talking about words that legitimately should be avoided. Now we're to the point that society is frowning on use of the *m* and *f* words (male and female).

The Packaging of Emotionalism

Now that we understand the basic *assumptions* of emotionalism, let's take a look at how we see emotionalism packaged.

1. *Trigger warnings*—Trigger warnings are statements that alert people, in advance, to topics or words that might cause someone distress. The term was originally applied to warnings directed at trauma victims who would need to know that an upcoming discussion could cause flashbacks, panic, or anxiety. Now the term is used much more loosely to refer to material that might cause *any* kind of uncomfortable feeling—all because of the assumption that negative feelings are supposedly harmful and must be avoided at all costs. (Side note: One of the messages I [Hillary F.] loved from the Pixar movie *Inside Out* was when the character Joy realized how important Sadness had been, and how valuable negative emotions can be.)

2. *Follow your heart*—How many times have you heard that one? My husband and I like to whip out this little nugget of awesomeness whenever one of us needs directions to get somewhere. "Which way am I going?" "I don't know. Just follow your heart." According to the wisdom of the age, our hearts are the barometers of truth, and it's our pesky minds that get in the way! If we can just turn off our minds so that we can clearly hear what our hearts are saying, then the road will be clear. (Do an Internet search on "regrettable tattoos," and you'll find a lot of evidence that "Follow your heart" is not the best way to make decisions.)

3. ***I'm offended***—More and more, we are seeing our world ruled by whether or not someone is offended. (Except for when it comes to Christians—nobody cares when we are offended.) Not only will people speak up for their own offense, but they will try to predict what will offend someone else and speak up for that person. A few years ago, one of our local banks removed a Christmas tree from their lobby because a customer claimed that it was offensive. All I have to say is that if you live in the United States and you can't handle the sight of a Christmas tree, then don't leave your house from about November to January first. Don't risk it, friend!

OFFER Discernment

I (Teasi) mentioned at the beginning of the chapter that emotions are God-given. We cannot throw out the truths that emotions are real, important, and aren't going away. Nor should we underestimate the ways they can reinforce truth.

One of the best analogies I've heard for understanding the true purpose of our emotions is by comparing them to the warning lights in a car. The lights are there to alert you that something is going on and deeper investigation is needed. A car owner has several options when the "check engine" light turns on. She can put duct tape over it (denial), she can smash it (lash out at reality), or she can take the car to a mechanic to find out the truth about what's going on under the hood. Obviously, the third option takes time, requires reliance upon an expert, and can be costly, which is why many people delay facing the facts.

And there are times when emotions can clue us in to deeper realities that we have forgotten. In the article "I was an Atheist Until I Read *Lord of the Rings*," author Fredric Heidemann recounts how his upbringing in an atheist family led him to reject God on an intellectual level. (Human reason can be just as misused as emotion.) It wasn't until he read the classic Tolkien novel that he noticed longings in himself that could not be explained by his naturalistic assumptions.

In my narrow confines of scientism, I had no way of processing what made Tolkien's masterpiece so profound. How could a made-up fantasy world reveal anything about the "truth"…Why am I relating to ridiculous things like talking trees and corrupted wraiths? Why was I so captivated by this story that made fighting evil against all odds so profound? Why did it instill in me a longing for an adventure of the arduous good? And how does the story make sacrifice so appealing? *The Lord of the Rings* showed me a world where things seemed more "real" than the world I lived in…The beautiful struggle and self-sacrificial glory permeating *The Lord of the Rings* struck a chord in my soul and filled me with longing that I couldn't easily dismiss. My attempts to explain these problems in my naturalistic, atheistic worldview fell flat.[1]

Emotions don't just clue us to problems, they can also help us see good things. I find it interesting that the fruit of the Spirit, as described in Galatians 5:22-23, includes emotion-laden terms like *love, joy,* and *peace.* These feelings are indicators of the Holy Spirit's ministry in our personal lives. Emotions can move us to worthy endeavors.

As we affirm the place emotions can have in our lives, it's important to equip ourselves to discern the lies promoted by emotionalism.

Lie #1: If I Feel It, It's True

Again, mothers of teenage girls have seen this lie up close. Probably daily. We need to remind our kids that, yes, emotions *can* lead us to truth, but not always. Consider, for example, world-famous artists and musicians who struggled with feelings of worthlessness to the point that they took their own lives. They let their feelings dictate their perception of their worth, and sadly, they acted upon those feelings even though many others looked upon them and their skills as having great value.

Sometimes our feelings lie to us, and other times they accurately reflect reality. But how can we know the difference? It's important for us to turn to an *outside* standard that helps ensure we assess our feelings correctly. Are we truly not good at anything, or do we just *feel* that way right now?

I (Hillary F.) have a joke with my husband over what I call "I'm worthless-o'clock." I'm guessing it has something to do with my circadian rhythm. Every night by a certain time, I feel very tired, and this feeling is often interpreted by my mind as a sense of worthlessness. I'm now at the point where I've learned to expect this, but it took me a long time (and many pep talks from John) to realize that I wasn't duped all day into a feeling of achievement only to arrive at the truth of my abject failure, usually between nine to twelve o'clock in the evening. Something else is going on in my body, and rather than trust it, we just make a joke out of it.

Lie #2: My Feelings Are Your Responsibility

Earlier we looked at the "I'm offended" phenomenon that is widespread today. People have swallowed the lie that because they can't control their feelings, then the outside world must conform to their feelings—ideally in ways that avoid the possibility of negative emotions. One of the first lessons we learn in kindergarten is that everyone can't have exactly what they want all the time. We must take turns. We must share. We must follow the rules, and often we don't get to make them. We don't get to be a butterfly flying around the classroom when it's time for human kindergarteners to take a nap. In a world where no two people think or feel exactly alike, we can expect ideas to conflict, collide, and cause bad feelings.

Lie #2 does not give us permission to be jerks and say, "Your bad feelings are on you! Too bad, so sad." Yes, your actions can cause negative feelings in others. But good grief, we can't orchestrate the world so that nobody ever experiences bad emotions! Sadly, legislators in North America are under this delusion and are trying to engrave this aspect of political correctness into law. That they are attempting to do this should scare us, for there are far-reaching implications for us as Christians if this trend continues.

Lie #3: To Endure Emotional Distress Is to Endure Injustice

This is the going narrative right now, and it incorporates one of our linguistically hijacked words: *injustice*. We will see this lie explored in the chapter on feminism, but let's get one thing clear now: Outside of coercive or traumatic abuse, nobody can *force* you to feel anything. Can they *influence* how you feel? Absolutely, but we really need to find the sweet spot in between not being jerks and developing thicker skin. Somewhere in between those two is a reasonable expectation for society.

ARGUE for a Healthier Approach

So how can we dignify all the good that emotions do without falling into the lies discussed above? I have read in several places that we make approximately 35,000 conscious decisions a day. I'll be the first to admit that at least a few of mine are made based on emotions. I'm thankful for the grace that God and my family show me in the times I don't make the best decisions (my husband has special "putting-up-with-Teasi rewards" awaiting him in heaven, for sure!).

As we become more consciously aware of our tendency to jump to emotion-based conclusions, we will find ourselves on the road to change. The most important first step we can take in the right direction is to become aware of the difference between truth and a truth claim. As we've said in previous chapters, truth is whatever corresponds to reality. A truth claim is something that someone *claims* corresponds with reality, whether or not it actually does, and regardless of how you feel about it. It's testable. Truth claims don't earn the right to be truth unless they actually correspond with reality. Often, we react emotionally to claims that, with just a tiny bit of thought, could be logically dismissed.

The Bible instructs us to exercise this kind of discernment. In 2 Corinthians 10:5, we are told to "take captive every thought." As we mentioned, emotions are a kind of judgment, and can often be expressed as a claim. For example, "My teacher hates me," "This relationship feels so right," "Dirty dishes make me angry." Usually when someone feels angry, she can point to something that she believes is the cause—that's a thought and an emotional judgment. Our emotions and thoughts can interact like that. As we examine our emotions, we examine our thoughts.

This may sound weird, but I like to imagine literally putting my thoughts and feelings in a jar like I used to do with bugs when I was a child. Stare that thought down. Turn the jar around. What kind of thought or feeling is it? Does it line up with the teachings of Christ? Is that claim that I picked up from a popular Christian teacher anywhere in the Bible, or at least biblically sound? Does this thought or feeling align with reality, or only my perception?

Recently I saw a tweet from a Christian organization that said, "God is about to take every tear you've cried and turn them into a 100-fold blessing." There were several people who liked that statement (the online version of "amen!"). While this message sounded very appealing to me, especially because I was going through a difficult season in my life, I still took the thought captive and asked myself, "How do they know that? This tweet is going out to everyone in the world. Are they saying that even someone in war-torn parts of the Middle East can claim this *today*? Do they have the biblical authority to proclaim that?"

While I'm sure the motivation for writing and sending that tweet was innocent, this truth claim isn't true. It may cause people to feel good, but does it align with the reality they're facing in their lives? How many more claims like this are being fed to us every day? We've got to put those bugs— I mean truth claims—in a jar, tighten the lid, and look them over.

When it comes to our kids, here are a few important messages we need to get through to them:

1. ***We have some control over our emotions***—Because the Bible tells us we can take thoughts captive and instructs us to renew our minds (Romans 12:2), we can be certain it is possible to change what we think and how we feel. Here's a little test for you: Think about a hamburger. Are you envisioning a hamburger in your mind? Now think about a hot dog. Were you able to switch the image in your mind when I asked you to? Then I have great news for you: You're

able to change your thoughts (but you're probably hungry now…). Because our emotions flow from our thoughts and beliefs, when we change our thoughts, we are able to take great strides toward transforming our emotions. We can *be transformed by the renewing of our minds.* This means that even when we are experiencing a *passion* that we cannot control (like anger), we *can* control our actions. The more we teach our kids the cultural mantra that they are helpless slaves to their emotions, the more their emotions will become ruthless tyrants over them. Trust me, that is not the legacy you want to impart to your kids.

2. ***Praise emotions when they do align with truth***—We don't want to raise little robots who are terrified of emotions. That's why it's essential to help our kids discipline their emotions. Untrained emotions can be like dogs that run around and pee on everything, or worse, attack unprovoked. A well-trained dog, on the other hand, can charge into a burning building and drag a person to safety. The effects of trained and untrained emotions are just as dramatic.

   Revel in your love for other people. Drink deep from the fountain of praise during a worship service. Get angry when you see true injustice. Vehemently protect those who need it. Give generously to those in need. Allow your emotions to reinforce what God has said is good, evil, shameful, praiseworthy, and beautiful. But do not let your emotions *dictate* what is good, evil, shameful, praiseworthy or beautiful.

REINFORCE Through Discussion, Discipleship, and Prayer

1. ***Teach your kids about emotions***—When I (Hillary S.) found myself in the throes (and throws) of a strong-willed toddler, I bought a set of "feelings flashcards" on the advice of an incredible parenting coach. My husband and I would read through these flashcards with our son at bedtime, just as if we were reading a story.

On the front of each card was an emotion, and the opposite emotion was stated on the back side. "Excited" could be flipped over to then read and illustrate "Disappointed." It was important to read these cards in times of calm and reinforce the learning by simply saying to our son what he was feeling in times of crazy (for example, "You are so mad right now. You are so, so mad.") Eventually he gained enough "feelings vocabulary" to tell me "I'm fwustwated!" instead of angrily grabbing at my earrings. Buying or making feelings flashcards is a great foundation for the little ones.

2. *Teach your kids to identify their emotions*—As kids grow older, they need to be taught to *identify* their feelings. All too frequently we assume that children know what's going on within themselves emotionally when, in fact, that may not be the case. That's why it's important for you to model emotional identification for them. Let them hear you examine and name your own emotions, the positive and the negative, and teach them to do the same. Asking "How did that make you feel?" is a great way to communicate compassion and attentiveness, and to create a space ripe for hearing more details of the story.

3. *Equip your kids to make right decisions*—After children are able to describe and identify their emotions, they are then ready to learn how to properly integrate emotions into their decision-making process. Feelings should never be the sole decider, but neither should they be left out of the equation. The Myers-Briggs Type Indicator uses the Z-model of decision making, utilizing four main facets of how people process information. The Z-Model is an excellent tool for teaching kids who are ready for this stage. The diagram below shows the four-part process: (1) Look at the facts, (2) use the facts to form a big-picture of the issue, (3) identify possible courses of action and their outcomes, and (4) evaluate how each outcome affects everyone else, not just yourself. From there, choose the best course of action.

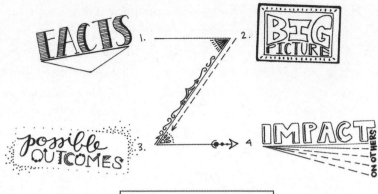

Z-Model for Decision Making

Illustrated by Rachel Forrest

After your kids work through the four parts of the Z, have them reevaluate the emotion. More often than not, a new perspective steeped in truth will put that emotion into focus, transforming anger into compassion, loneliness into security, or fear into bravery. Of course sometimes this process will affirm a negative emotion like indignation, which, as mentioned in this chapter, can lead to action that spurs positive change. Either way, the process serves as a good way to merge emotions with careful thinking. And that, my friend, is what it looks like to rock as a human.

PAWS for Prayer

Praise

Lord, You are the creator of my mind, will, and emotions; You are my reason and intellect. Though my feelings fluctuate, You are unchanging, the lover of my soul, longsuffering toward my self-centered emotions, and patient with my sinful ways. In Your wisdom as a God of discipline You lovingly correct me. In the same way that You have given the earth's waters their boundaries, You can bring boundaries to the habits of my mind, rescuing me from waves of emotionalism that would crash upon my God-given reason.

Admit

Forgive me for not realizing how deceptive my heart can be, for letting emotion rule over reason. Forgive me when I allow feelings, rather than your Word, to determine truth. For idolizing feelings and expecting others to conform to them.

Worship with Thanksgiving

I thank You, Lord, that my emotions are a gift from You and that You help me discipline them using Scripture, reason, and reality. You grant the ability to balance heart *and* mind and use them both as catalysts for action. You have given me the mind of Christ, not faulty perceptions, to evaluate truth claims against reality and your Word.

Supplication

Help me recognize the difference between my passions and emotions and to use them according to Your will. Grant that I may accurately analyze my own thoughts, emotions, and uncover truth claims that masquerade as truth. Lord, magnetize my emotional compass to point to objective truths. Help me teach my children to navigate cultural lies by upholding your Word as their compass. May they learn to appropriately control their emotions, properly harness negative emotions, and deal with reality as I model that for them.

In the name of Jesus, the Shepherd of my mind. Amen.

Discussion Questions

1. **Icebreaker:** Describe a time when you "followed your heart" and ended up doing something really stupid. Be honest—every person has at least a one of those stories.

2. **Main theme:** *Emotions can be helpful as long as they are disciplined*

with Scripture, reason, and truth. How has our society confused facts and feelings? Based on what you learned in the chapter, what are the differences between *passions* and *emotions*? Can you think of a time when you felt strongly one way, received new information, and had your emotions change? How does this show that emotions can be judgments? (Or at least reactions to faulty judgments?)

3. **Self-evaluation:** How often do you allow emotions to dictate your decisions? Have your kids seen you make emotionally based decisions on the spur of the moment? In hindsight, did you regret those emotion-based decisions, and why? How might renewing your mind (Romans 12:2) aid in sanctifying your emotions?

4. **Brainstorm:** Why are you a Christian? (As you answer, don't leave out the Holy Spirit's role in your salvation.) Draw a line down the middle of a piece of paper and label one side "Emotional Reasons" and the other side "Factual Reasons." How many of your reasons fall under the factual category? How many under the emotional category? If your primary reasons for being a Christian are emotional, how might the enemy come in and steal away your foundation? What are some ways that you can integrate factual reasons for belief into the mix? Emotions can change, facts don't. How might incorporating unchanging facts make your faith stronger, especially in light of Hebrews 11:1?

5. **Release the bear:** Next time you are faced with a strong, unpleasant emotion, don't let it overtake you. Take that emotion captive and ask yourself, "What judgment is this emotion making? Is that judgment true?"

Chapter 11

Just Worship Something

Pluralism

CATHRYN S. BUSE

I recently changed careers from being an engineer at NASA to teaching AP calculus and apologetics at a small Christian high school. It was as odd a transition as it sounds! I have a lot of experience with calculus, but teaching it was much different than using it in a work setting.

Imagine the following scenario: One day as we are reviewing homework during a class session, it appears that each student had come up with a different answer on the same problem. All the students were sincere about their answers. Most of them had worked hard to arrive at their solution and felt good about it. Some of them hadn't given the problem much thought but figured their answer was close enough. And a few were unsure, but didn't know how else to think about the problem. As the teacher, I decide to give all of them a score of 100% and tell them they were all correct—as long as they were sincere or tried hard. I also gave 100% to those who hadn't tried hard, as long as their answer made them feel good.

Would that have made me a good math teacher? Absolutely not! Why? Because regardless of how many different sincere answers they came up with, there was still only one correct solution (which is one of the things I love about math).

What does that have to do with this chapter's topic of pluralism? *Pluralism*, by definition, refers to a society with ethnic, racial, religious, social, and ideological diversity. But for our purposes, we want to discuss *religious* pluralism, the idea that all religions offer legitimate paths to God. It's not just that many people have different religious ideas, but that they make truth claims (even contradicting ones) and assert they are *equally valid*. How did we get to that determination?

A Brief History of Religious Pluralism

When settlers first came to the United States, it was to find a place where they could worship freely (think Pilgrims). It was freedom of worship that became the bedrock of American society and the First Amendment. The United States government cannot forbid you from practicing whatever religion you want so long as you don't impose in some way on other people, meaning you probably wouldn't be allowed to practice a religion that sacrifices young virgins to a volcano god. Otherwise, you can worship as you please.

In the United States' formative years, the Christian worldview was the predominant religious belief. There was a general like-mindedness, and thus no real conflicts, about *who* people were worshiping. As this nation continued to be a beacon of religious and economic freedom to the world, a plethora of others who held to differing religious beliefs arrived on our shores. Today, only 46% of Americans claim to be Christian, and only 10% of American adults say they hold to a biblical worldview.[1] We live in a truly pluralistic society.

Pluralism isn't the problem, though. The fact that there are multiple religions all around us simply tells us there is ample opportunity for sharing the Christian faith with others! So what's the problem? Many people have come to conclude that all those different beliefs are equally valid and thus must be true. But as you'll remember from previous chapters, just because an opinion is sincere or popular does not mean it is true. It's common to hear people say, "Your religion is true for you; my religion is true for me." How exactly did society reach that conclusion?

Contemporary views of secularism and tolerance have played a big role in getting us to this point. Secularism says that church and state should be separated and it pushes to remove all discussion and expression of religion from the public arena, making religion a private matter. Believe and practice what you like, as long as you don't talk about it. *Tolerance*, under society's new definition of the term, insists that no one's ideas be treated as inferior (even though there are still bad ideas out there). In a society where multiple religious beliefs coexist, *secularism, colored with tolerance, leads to the false dichotomy that either (1) all religions are equally valid, or (2) no religion should be discussed.* There is no middle ground. You must either affirm all religions or acknowledge none of them. As Christians, we certainly want our religion to be acknowledged, so does that mean we have to accept other religions as true too? How do we approach this dilemma?

ROAR Like a Mother!

RECOGNIZE the Message

Culture says we should be tolerant of people of all religious beliefs. And we Mama Bears agree, as long as we are using the correct definition of *tolerance*. (Remember the linguistic theft chapter?) We should treat the followers of other religions with respect and dignity, which includes extending to them their right to worship as they choose. We should desire peace with one another regardless of our backgrounds or beliefs. Scripture tells us to pursue peace with all people (Hebrews 12:14) so that unbelievers may be drawn to the peace and holiness of the gospel. In fact, the second greatest commandment is to love your neighbor—therefore, we should be tolerant in the sense of being genuinely respectful of other people's viewpoints, perspectives, and religions.

Respectfully ask questions of people who have different religious beliefs. Learn why they believe as they do. Show them that you love them as a person, even though they follow a different religion. In these ways you can better understand how to meet them in their life with the gospel. We should be welcoming, peaceable, loving, and helpful to those who believe differently. *This* kind of tolerance and acceptance is biblical.

Our innate desire to have peace with our neighbor is a good thing—until that alters how we view truth. We deny truth when we say things like, "It doesn't matter what you believe as long as you're sincere." Or when we praise another religion because we think it makes its followers good, moral people, whereas Scripture says that without Christ we are all sinners separated from a perfect and holy God. Can we accurately say that all paths to God are equally valid, or that we are all praying to the same God? Does God accept all forms of worship? Can we accept other religions as valid paths to reach God just so we can all get along? Perhaps you've seen the bumper sticker COEXIST, which advocates such thinking. But we cannot focus on the second greatest commandment—loving our neighbor—while ignoring the first! The new definitions of *tolerance* and *acceptance* are not biblical. True tolerance does not require that we consider other religions to be true alongside Christianity.

In today's culture, the problem goes even deeper than that. We are told that in the pursuit of peace, we should remain silent about the gospel so that we don't offend people. Some church groups now do mission work that focuses solely only on loving other people without speaking the truth of the gospel. There are pastors and teachers who refuse to preach on difficult passages of Scripture because they don't want to make people uncomfortable. They rarely discuss sin, judgment, or hell because they fear those topics may offend others and cause attendance to drop. The focus has shifted to using the gospel for social engineering and peace instead of sharing it to bring salvation to those who are spiritually separated from God.

With the combined pressures of a pluralistic society and political correctness, Christians have become silent, neglecting the command to go and *tell* the gospel to others. This flies in the face of the oft-quoted statement, "Preach the gospel at all times. When necessary, use words," which is wrongly attributed to St. Francis of Assisi.[2] One statement we do know he said is this: "It is no use walking anywhere to preach unless our walking is our preaching." St. Francis was telling those who call themselves Christians to fully embody it in their lives. He wanted people to not just proclaim the gospel but live it out as an example of Christ to others. His exhortation would be more accurately summed up, "Practice what you preach." And notice that his point had to do with *preaching*. That was what St. Francis devoted his life to: preaching the gospel at all times *with words*. He preached in the church, in the public square, and in the farmlands because he knew words were necessary for others to know Jesus, and he knew his life must show Jesus too.

OFFER Discernment

So how do we show tolerance without accepting as valid those ideas "raised against the knowledge of God"?[3] We can accept an invitation to dinner and enjoy a nice meal with someone while not accepting (or agreeing with) his or her opinion on how to best discipline children. Likewise, we can show Christian love to our neighbors and surrounding community, accepting them as humans worthy of love and dignity without agreeing with their beliefs. As in the Mama Bear tagline, we love *people* but demolish their *ideas*.

Therefore, we need to demonstrate to our kids a loving spirit toward all people, not just those with whom we agree. Our intrinsic worth is not based on our doctrine. We are to love and respect all people because they are made in the image of God. However, the way God says to love and respect them is different from the way the world insists we do that. Here are some lies we need to recognize in order to keep the right perspective.

Lie #1: Sincere Belief Makes Something True

One can sincerely believe something yet be sincerely wrong about it—even if it is believed with all his or her heart. My child sincerely believes he deserves a cookie even when he doesn't eat all his supper, but he is sincerely wrong. And as sincerely as my math students may believe the answer is 19 when it is 53, they are still wrong. Sincere belief does not make something true.

The same principle applies to religion and philosophy. In fact, one of the laws of logic is the law of non-contradiction. That is, two conflicting statements cannot both be true at the same time and in the same way. If I say a table is a rectangle and you say the same table is a triangle, by definition, we cannot both be right. Likewise, if Becky says there is no god, I say there is one God in three persons, Jane says that there is a God but there is no Trinity (no Son of God and no Holy Spirit), and Mary says there are 19 gods, we are all defining the essence of God differently and in ways that contradict. God cannot be three persons in one yet also exist as 19 separate gods. God cannot consist of the Father, Son, and Holy Spirit (the Christian definition) and at the same time be one God with no Son of God and Holy Spirit (as taught in Islam).

We cannot all be worshiping the same God if we define God in conflicting ways. Though different beliefs may be sincere, if they are contradictory, it means one of us is right and the rest are sincerely wrong, or all of us are wrong. The only nonviable option is that we are all correct.

It doesn't matter how sincerely we believe, how devoted we may be, or how good our religion may make us feel. If there are fundamental differences at the core of our beliefs, they cannot all be right.[4] When Jesus said, "I am the way and the truth and the life,"[5] He was making a truth claim. By the very definition of truth, Jesus was excluding all other ways to heaven.

Can we coexist with people of other religious beliefs in a peaceable fashion? Absolutely, as long as we recognize that we contradict each other on fundamental points of doctrine. We disagree, and that's okay! We cannot force everyone to believe the same things. Would life be easier if we all agreed? Sure, but that is not going to happen. That is why we need to learn how to get along in spite of our disagreements. As we learned in chapter 4, to be tolerant assumes people will have differing viewpoints—otherwise, there is nothing to tolerate.

Lie #2: It Doesn't Matter Who You Worship, Just That You Worship

Not all worship is created equal. Just worshiping *something* doesn't make what you're worshiping true. Our desire to worship simply shows that we are doing what we were created to do—worship. But it is the *object* of our worship that matters. What's more, worship isn't always religious in nature. People worship sports teams, celebrities, hobbies, and more.

There is nothing redeeming about worship if it's directed toward the wrong object. That is why Jesus said we are to worship in spirit and in *truth* (John 4:24). That goes back to the greatest commandment He gave us: to love the Lord your God with your whole being—and Him only (Matthew 22:37). Worship without sound doctrine is idolatry and is like inventing a god and deciding to worship *that* instead of worshiping the one true God.

It's somewhat like when you drop your two kids off at childcare. Upon your return, you don't retrieve just any two kids. You want *your* two kids, even if they've been driving you crazy. And the truth of who your two children are excludes all the other children. Is that being intolerant, unloving, and unaccepting of the other children? Not at all! It's just that those other kids aren't yours. You wouldn't just grab any two kids and say, "Well, at least I'm going home with two." Likewise, God doesn't say, "They're not worshiping Me, but hey, at least they're worshiping something." No—He wants worship to be given *to Him* and Him alone. After all, He is the one who created us, loves us, and died for us. When people worship the sun god instead of the God who made the sun, God isn't pleased. When the Israelites molded the golden calf and danced around it, they dishonored God. It is the heart *and* doctrine behind our worship that makes it either honoring or dishonoring to God.

That is the danger in validating other religions simply because their followers are sincere and devoted in their worship. Look at how God responded to the Old Testament people groups who worshiped anything or anyone other than Him. God wanted the pagan, false religions driven out from the land He was giving to the Israelites. He commanded that the Canaanites and the Amalekites be destroyed because of their pagan religious practices, including child sacrifice. He prohibited the Israelites from intermarrying with people who followed a different religion (the New

Testament equivalent appears in 2 Corinthians 6:14—"Do not be yoked together with unbelievers"). That may sound harsh, but God knew the effect those pagan religions would have on the nation of Israel, the nation from whom the Savior of mankind would come.

God would not specify the destruction of false religions if all religious worship was equally pleasing and acceptable to Him (Deuteronomy 12:29-31). He made it clear He didn't want the people of Israel dabbling in those false religions because doing so would open them to accepting their teachings and adopting their practices. *God is serious about the influence and danger of worshiping false gods.*

Lie #3: All Paths Lead to God

Not only does it matter who we worship, but it matters who—or what—we trust for our eternity. Jesus said that He is the way, the truth, and the life, and *no one* comes to the Father but through Him (John 14:6). This means people cannot get to God through Hinduism, Buddhism, or any other religion. Just because another belief system offers sincere worship doesn't mean that system honors God or its path leads to Him. Worship must be done in spirit and in truth, and this means worshiping God alone and having faith in Jesus alone.[6]

Lie #4: The True Gospel Unites All People

False. The gospel can be divisive! When Jesus said that He brought peace on earth, He wasn't talking about peace between people, but peace between people and God. Only through the sacrifice of Jesus on the cross can sinful, depraved mankind experience peace with a perfect, holy God. Unfortunately, our Lord predicted quite the opposite—in Luke 12, He said, "Do you think I came to bring peace on earth? No, I tell you, but division."[7] Yet shortly after this statement Jesus commanded us to live at peace with one another. That seems contradictory, doesn't it? But think about what He was saying: *The gospel will divide people, but we are to live at peace with them.* That is how we are to approach this pluralistic society in which we live.

Speaking the gospel will create division between people. After all, you are either for God or against Him. Jesus said that you either go through the narrow gate to heaven or you walk on the wide path to destruction (Matthew 7:13-14). You either love the light or the darkness (John 3:19). The name of Jesus will divide people, and the world will hate us for bearing His name. But when the world hates us, it's because it hated Him first. It is not *us* whom they reject and are divided against, it is Jesus.

Does that mean we should remain silent so we can avoid that division? Goodness no! We are commanded to go into the world to tell others about Jesus and what He has done for us. Paul said in Romans 10:14, "How, then, can they call on the one they have not believed in? And how can they believe in the one of whom they have not heard? And how can they hear without someone preaching to them?" One way for others to come to know Jesus is by hearing us speak about Him and His truth. We can't afford to remain silent. God uses His own people to reach the lost. What a privilege it is to take part in His plan to change someone's eternal destiny by speaking truth!

ARGUE for a Healthier Approach

We are surrounded by the followers of multiple religious belief systems. We want to live at peace with them, yet we also want to share the gospel. The problem is, the gospel creates division. What are we to do? We aren't the nation of Israel taking the Promised Land, so we must deal with the matter of religious pluralism in a significantly different way. Thankfully, we can still look back to the Old Testament for some great examples of what to do.

Daniel, along with other preeminent young Jews, was taken out of Jerusalem and into captivity by the Babylonians. King Nebuchadnezzar wanted to reeducate these Jews to think and act like Babylonians, and he instructed them in the Babylonian way of life—with regard to education, laws, religion, and diet. Because the Babylonian diet was very different from that prescribed by the Levitical law for Jews, Daniel and his three friends stood up for what was right by God. They politely declined the king's food and asked if they could eat vegetables and drink water.

They didn't stage a protest and announce that the king would burn in hell. Rather, they asked if they could obey the laws of God.

Keep in mind that thousands of other Jews were taken into captivity as well. What were they doing? Chowing down the king's food! They fell right in line with the ways of the Babylonians and embraced the religious practices of their captors. They exchanged the God who led them out of Egyptian slavery for the false gods of the Babylonians. So when the king called on the Jews to worship his golden statue, what did the majority of them do? They bowed down! What did Shadrach, Meshach, and Abednego do? They stood their ground and refused to bow. They were surrounded by pagan worshippers but knew their devotion was not acceptable to the one true God. When a later king, Darius of the Medo-Persian Empire, passed a law forbidding prayer to anyone but himself, what did Daniel do? He opened his window and prayed to God—just like he had always done. He didn't even hide himself!

Despite living a life of exile among people with beliefs contradictory to their own, Daniel and his friends continued to worship the one true God. They loved their neighbors by living at peace among them and were rewarded for serving as top advisers to the king. But they did not adopt the religion practiced around them simply because of the peer pressure. Nor did they think, *Everyone else believes something other than the God of Abraham; I guess I can too. This religion must be equally valid—I mean, look at how many of them worship like this!* No, they knew that their God was the one true God, which excludes all other objects of worship. Even if everyone else rejected the one true God, they would not. By living their faith in truth, they ended up having a significant impact on King Nebuchadnezzar. In fact, you could make a case that Nebuchadnezzar himself became a believer (see Daniel 4). In the book of Daniel, we see that it is possible for believers to worship God in the midst of an entirely pagan culture under a pagan ruler.

We want to raise our kids so they can be like Daniel. Odds are wherever they go in life, they and others who hold to a biblical worldview will be outnumbered by those who are in alternate belief systems. So we must teach our children how to live as exiles: (1) Be respectful to those around you, and (2) don't cave in to other beliefs, no matter how popular they are or how unpopular Christianity may be. Doing that is no easy task! By analogy, it's hard enough to stick to a diet when all your friends are eating chocolate cake in front of you. How can we as Christians stand firm in our faith when everyone around us believes differently? I believe it's possible when we—and our children—know the truths of Christianity. Our kids won't be motivated to withstand peer pressure simply because mom and dad told them to. Rather, they must know, in their own minds, the truthfulness of Christianity. Then they can stand for their faith with the boldness Daniel showed.

For a New Testament example of holding to the truth of Christianity while being surrounded by others of a different belief, let's look at Peter. While in Jerusalem, where Jewish people vastly outnumbered the Christians, he did not hold back from preaching the gospel. How was he able to remain bold? He and the other early believers asked God to grant them the courage to speak God's Word. They said, "We cannot help speaking about what we have seen and heard."[8]

We should pray for the same every day—that God would give us the boldness to speak the things that we have seen and heard in Christ Jesus. We probably won't be called to speak before kings as Daniel did, on the temple steps as Peter did, or even in the city square of the Areopagus as Paul did. But if they can speak before kings and scoffers, we can certainly speak truth over coffee with a friend who doesn't believe in Jesus.

Yes, we are to live at peace with our neighbors and to love them as ourselves, whether they are Hindus, Muslims, or atheists. We are to care for them, help them, and pray for them. At the same time, we cannot remain silent about the truth. Because *when we know the true way of salvation, withholding that truth from others is not loving at all.*

Nabeel Qureshi—a former Muslim who came to Christ after many years of interacting with Christian friends—commented about other believers in his life who never asked him whether he knew Jesus. He said, "Why had other Christians never asked me this question? They did think I needed Jesus to go to heaven, right? Were they content with letting me go to hell, or did they not really believe their faith?"[9] We must love others enough to speak the truth, even when it's unpopular. In our pluralistic society, the harvest is plentiful, but the workers are few. Be loving and be bold in your faith!

REINFORCE Through Discussion, Discipleship, and Prayer

Young Children

Give some examples of opposites and explain why both cannot be true at the same time and in the same way. Relate that to the differing beliefs found in other religions (such as one person who believes God exists and another who doesn't). Explain why contradictory beliefs can't all be right. Be sure your children understand that not everyone believes in the God of the Bible—and this is why we are called to tell them about Jesus. Discuss ways you can still show love to someone who holds to different beliefs, interests, and convictions.

Middle and High School

Discuss ways that your tweens and teens can show love and kindness to someone of a different faith. Identify respectful ways they can ask questions and build bridges. Do some role-playing that teaches your kids how to listen to someone else's viewpoint before countering it with their own. Pick a different religion each week and discuss the core doctrines of that religion and how it differs from Christianity (for help, see the world religions blog series by Lindsey Medenwalt at mamabearapologetics.com). Most importantly, make sure your children understand why Christianity is true (for help, see my book *Teaching Others to Defend Christianity*).

PAWS for Prayer

Praise

Jesus, You are supreme, highest in rank, sovereign, reigning above all others. I praise You because You—without question or confusion—are the one true way to reconciliation between God and man. I proclaim what

You said: "I am the [only] Way [to God] and the [real] Truth and the [real] Life; no one comes to the Father but through Me" (John 14:6 AMP).

Admit

Forgive our world for valuing tolerance over truth. Forgive those who call You a liar and cheapen Your sacrifice by declaring that all paths to You are equally valid. Forgive us for our silence due to the fear of offending others.

Worship with Thanksgiving

Thank You that despite the perils of pluralism we have opportunities to share that there is "no other name under heaven that has been given among people by which we must be saved [for God has provided the world no alternative for salvation]" (Acts 4:12 AMP). Thank You for Your laws of logic, which help reveal contradictions, and for the ability to discerningly love a person who is made in Your image even when his or her beliefs do not correspond to Your truth.

Supplication

Lord, I need Your power to help me teach my children to respect and love our neighbors and speak the truth even when it is uncomfortable or unpopular to do so, especially when the convictions we hold so dear feel threatened. Help me model to my children how to not sacrifice truth on the altar of peace or popularity. Teach us to not confuse sincerity of belief with the truthfulness of a belief. Help me demonstrate that Christians can love others despite disagreeing with them on core beliefs. Strike down the lie that disagreement is synonymous with hate. Show me how to teach my kids that there is a plurality of ideas but not a plurality of truth. Inform my worship with Spirit, truth, and sound doctrine. Empower me to recognize and reject all beliefs raised up against the knowledge of You while still affirming the person who is made in Your image.

In the name above all names, Jesus. Amen.

Discussion Questions

1. **Icebreaker:** How many people of different religions have you interacted with? What was your interaction like?

2. **Main theme:** *You can seek peace with all people without having to regard all ideas as equally true.* At Mama Bear Apologetics, we say to demolish arguments, not people. What is the difference between the two? How have you seen this done well? How have you seen this done poorly?

3. **Self-evaluation:** Are you comfortable interacting with people who are different from you—whether because of race, income, religion, sense of humor, or…? How well do you know what other religions teach?

4. **Brainstorm:** What are some ways that you and other Mama Bears can practice being loving to people who hold to different beliefs?

5. **Release the bear:** More than likely, there are other moms at your child's school who are very different from you and have different beliefs. Pick just one and invite her to a lunch date. Start out by listening to her and asking questions. Get to know her as a person. Find out why she believes what she does. For helpful tips, see Hillary Short's *Playground Apologetics* series on the Mama Bear website.

Chapter 12

I'm Not Religious; I'm Spiritual!

New Spirituality

ALISA CHILDERS

"Ommmmmmmmmmmmm." I walked into my living room one night to discover my seven-year-old daughter sitting criss-cross applesauce with her eyes closed, arms slightly bent, and thumbs and index fingers pinched together.

"Um. Honey, what are you doing?" I asked in the most nonchalant tone I could muster. For an instant I imagined my sweet, Jesus-loving daughter going off to college one day, converting to Buddhism, and running off with the first angsty hipster to quote Deepak Chopra. Back to earth. She's seven. We have time.

"I learned it in school!" she replied innocently as if she had no idea what she was doing. Because she didn't. She had been taught Transcendental Meditation in a PE class at her private Christian school. Let that sink in for a moment. This may seem shocking to some, but to others, it may seem like a typical Tuesday—even for a Christian school. What's the big deal? (Turns out it was a rogue PE teacher who hadn't cleared the idea with the administration, but still...)

This is because our culture has been inundated with New Age mysticism over the past few decades, and most people, including Christians, aren't aware of how it permeates everything from the way we eat to the way we talk to the way we think about the world—and in some cases, the way we do church and worship God.

For some of us, the mere mention of the phrase *New Age* conjures images of drug-induced hippies meditating in flower fields, or some wacky crystal-toting holistic healer handing out vitamin samples at a local health-food store. As out of touch as these images may seem, New Age beliefs are incredibly popular in our culture—and they are almost always promoted as being Christian in some way or other.

To understand this new spirituality, we must understand New Age mysticism (NAM).

A Brief History of New Age Mysticism

Finding its roots in ancient occult practices, Eastern religions, and the transcendentalism of the early 1800s, NAM began to blossom in America during the tumultuous sixties. In the midst of war, nuclear threats, the sexual revolution, second-wave feminism, and the civil-rights movement, tensions were high, and people were looking for spiritual answers.

In 1987, *Time* magazine published a story on the growing trend of NAM, featuring Shirley MacLaine on the cover. The issue reported that the movement was growing steadily in the United States, with New Age titles at Bantam Books increasing tenfold in the eighties alone.[1]

But almost no one can claim more responsibility for catapulting NAM into the mainstream of American consciousness than daytime talk show queen Oprah Winfrey. In the early nineties, she started discussing New Age books such as *Return to Love* on her number one daytime talk show, establishing its author, Marianne Williamson, as a prominent voice in the New Age movement and propelling her book to the *New York Times* best-seller list. If Oprah endorses a book, it will most likely become a best-seller—a phenomenon known as "the Oprah effect."

This is just one example, but Oprah's influence in bringing New Age thought (often delivered in Christian language) into the hearts and homes of millions of Americans is incalculable. Through her many media outlets, she has peddled and promoted New Age thought leaders such as

Deepak Chopra, Eckhart Tolle, Rhonda Byrne, Gary Zukav, Elizabeth Lesser, Michael A. Singer, Mark Nepo, and Rob Bell. (Yes, that's *pastor* Rob Bell, and we'll get to him in a moment.)

By 2012, Pew Research Center reported that one-third of millennials don't ascribe to any particular religion, with 37% of that group describing themselves as "spiritual but not religious," and 58% feeling "a deep connection with nature and the earth."[2] Combine that with major celebrities telling them to "live their truth," and you've got fertile soil for New Age doctrines to take root under the guise of what's now called the new spirituality.

This new spirituality is just good ol' New Age with a modern makeover. It has shed the image of a fortune teller wielding a crystal ball and has now been refashioned in the image of a hipster wearing skinny jeans…wielding a latte…and often wearing a cross. Same message, different branding.

In this chapter, we will focus on four of the most common and culturally popular lies of the new spirituality, which have to do with meditation, pantheism, the divinity of all mankind, and relativism.

ROAR Like a Mother!

RECOGNIZE the Message

NAM is typically a hodgepodge of Eastern religious ideas, psychology, modern philosophy, pseudoscience, and Christianity. Let's zoom in to see a practical example of NAM teachings in action.

In January 2008, the "Oprah & Friends" satellite radio channel launched a year-long class with daily lessons and affirmations from the book *A Course in Miracles*. The teacher of the class, Marianne Williamson, described it as a "self-study program of spiritual psychotherapy"[3] that seeks to take certain "principles" and apply them in practical ways.

The book upon which the class is based, *A Course in Miracles*, was published in 1975, and is a collection of spiritual revelations recorded by Columbia University professor Helen Schucman. Schucman received these messages from an entity she called "the Voice," which she later identified as "Jesus Christ."[4] If you are wondering what kind of "dicta-tions" she received from this supposed "Jesus," here are a few examples. They sum up the ideas of the new spirituality perfectly:

- "Do not make the pathetic error of 'clinging to the old rug-ged cross.' The only message of the crucifixion is that you can overcome the cross."[5]

- "The name of Jesus Christ as such is but a symbol. But it stands for love that is not of this world. It is a symbol that is safely used as a replacement for the many names of all the gods to which you pray."[6]

- "The Atonement is the final lesson he need learn, for it teaches him that, never having sinned, he has no need of salvation."[7]

- Lesson 61 asks the reader to affirm "I am the light of the world."[8]

- Lesson 259 asks the reader to affirm "there is no sin."[9]

- Lesson 70 asks the reader to affirm "my salvation comes from me."[10]

Schucman effectively declared humans to be their own gods and sources of truth by removing all the parts of Christianity that are perceived as unsa-vory, such as sin, the blood atonement, and separation from God; cob-bling together "wisdom" from different religions; and turning Jesus into a generic symbol of love.

Lie #1—God Is All, and All Are One

One of the core principles of the new spirituality is that everything in the universe (including you and me) is made up of the same substance and reality. In other words, there is no separation between you, your dog, and the tree outside that your dog just peed on. This worldview is called *pan-theism* and believes that "God" is a type of divine consciousness or energy that is one and the same with the universe, something we can tap into as we become more "enlightened."

Remember James Cameron's blockbuster movie *Avatar*? This is a prime example of works that promote a pantheistic worldview. But nothing illustrates pantheism better than the much-beloved Star Wars movies.

Star Wars fans will remember the famous scene in *The Empire Strikes Back* in which Buddha...I mean Yoda (did I say Buddha?! Ahem...) is in a swamp training the young Jedi Luke Skywalker. He is teaching Luke to move inanimate objects by accessing "the force" with the power of his mind. Yoda explained the force like this: "Life creates it, makes it grow. Its energy surrounds us and binds us. Luminous beings are we, not this crude matter. You must feel the Force around you; here, between you, me, the tree, the rock, everywhere, yes. Even between the land and the ship."[11]

Interestingly, the creator of the Star Wars movie franchise, George Lucas, confirmed in a *Time* magazine interview in 1999 that he indeed intended to present the force as a religious symbol: "I put the force into the movies in order to try to awaken a certain kind of spirituality in young people...more a belief in God than any religious system." (Sounds a lot like the "spiritual but not religious" motto that 37% of young people now identify with, doesn't it?) When the interviewer pointed out that the force strongly echoes notions of God that are found in Eastern systems like Buddhism, Lucas replied, "I guess it's more specific in Buddhism...I wanted to try to explain in a different way the religions that have already existed. I wanted to express it all."[12]

You might be surprised to learn how many supposedly Christian thinkers teach something very similar to what Yoda taught Luke. For example, many Christians are aware of the firestorm of controversy that was lit when a pastor from Michigan, Rob Bell, released his book *Love Wins*. Bell's insinuation that there *might* not be a literal hell was received by some Christians as a revolutionary fresh look at an archaic doctrine, while provoking others to cry "Heresy!" In response, conservative theologian John Piper famously tweeted, "Farewell, Rob Bell."

But Bell's treatise on hell was just the beginning. He went on to write a book titled *What We Talk About When We Talk About God*, in which he described God in New Age terms such as a "life force," and "creative energy," and an "unending divine vitality,"[13] Although Rob did make a passing comment about God's transcendence, he went on to echo many a New Age guru as he described how this "energy" connects everything in the universe: "When we talk about God, we're talking about the straightforward affirmation that everything has a singular, common source and is infinitely, endlessly, deeply connected."[14]

This isn't some hippie guru sitting on a mountaintop in India meditating himself into nirvana. This is a well-known and beloved Christian pastor marketing these ideas as Christianity and tying them up in a slick, modern bow. Interestingly, Bell ended up going on tour with Oprah and Deepak Chopra. Full circle achieved.

If you think these ideas would never find their way into otherwise solid biblical churches, consider this: I was so excited last summer when I found an evening vacation Bible school for my kids (five whole evenings to myself in the middle of summer? Sign me up!) and the theme was Star Wars. I picked my children up at the end of the first session just in time to catch the closing skit, in which the children were being taught to understand the work of the Holy Spirit—by comparing Him with the Force in Star Wars. "It's a feeling that starts in your belly and moves its way up into your heart. That's how you know you are called." What? My husband turned to me and said, "Well, there went your free nights this week." Losing my evenings was a small price to pay for truth.

Lie #2—Congratulations, You Are God!

If we are all truly one, a natural progression in thought will take place. Let's follow that down the rabbit hole, shall we? If we are all made up of the same substance or reality, then there is no separation between us and God. Therefore, we and God are one—we are all divine. We just need to achieve "higher consciousness" or a higher state of being to fully realize it—just like Jesus did! In fact, there's a term used in New Age circles called "Christ consciousness," which is described as the "awakening" Jesus had when He finally realized His own divinity, His connectedness with the universe.

This is incredibly deceptive because of its obvious appeal. If we can just recognize the divinity in ourselves, we can rid ourselves of old-fashioned and pesky little things like sin and human depravity. In other words, stop seeing yourself as something negative, like a sinner. You are awesome just as you are! Sounds great doesn't it?

These messages aren't always marketed to our kids in obvious ways. Your children aren't going to turn on the latest Netflix show and hear their favorite character say, "Hey kids…guess what? You are god!" But there are incredibly subtle and persuasive forms in which this message permeates children's media and entertainment.

For example, the 2018 Disney movie based on the popular novel by Madeleine L'Engle, *A Wrinkle in Time* (ironically starring Oprah Winfrey), depicts a young girl, Meg, who travels across the universe to save her father. She meets three beings who recruit her for this mission and endow her with wisdom and encouragement. After being told that her father has been trapped by an evil "energy" that is too strong for their "light," Meg is advised by Mrs. Which (Oprah), "You're going to be tested every step of the way. Have faith in who *you* are." In the theatrical trailer, the message "The only way to defeat the darkness is to *become* the light" appears on the screen in bold letters as powerful music is played.

Notice that the emphasis is put on the self. *You* become the light. Have faith in *yourself.* There is no need to reach out to anything outside yourself for help or salvation. *You* are enough. It's all inside of *you* already. This echoes the affirmations listed above from the Oprah master class: "There is no sin. My salvation comes from me." (And if you are god, that makes perfect sense!)

Lie #3—It's All Relative

Today's new spirituality embraces the "freedom" of letting go of the ideas of absolute truth and objective morality. In fact, it teaches that you can create your own reality. If you feel that something is real, it is. If you believe something is right, it is. If you think something is true, it is! Of course, it doesn't take a brain surgeon to see that this way of thinking is a hot mess—riddled with contradictions. In an interesting twist, the new spirituality teaches that contradictions are a good thing, and that logic is less reliable than the "truth" gained through meditation and personal intuition. Deepak Chopra, quoting a famous Indian spiritual teacher, wrote, "The measurement of enlightenment is how comfortable you feel with your own contradictions."[15] (For more on this, see chapter 9, on moral relativism.)

Lie #4—Meditation Is the Answer to All Your Problems

Aside from the various *beliefs* that make up new spirituality, different *practices* such as meditation have become popular ways to de-stress and connect with the divine. Proponents tout scientific studies to back up its benefits, and usually market meditation as nonreligious—merely psychological in nature.

A few years ago, Oprah was a guest on *The Dr. Oz Show* to talk about her discovery of Transcendental Meditation (TM). She enthusiastically sang the praises of the practice and was so impressed with its results that she paid for hundreds of her staff members to be trained in TM. She explained that stopping twice a day as a staff to meditate at the same time helped improve people's relationships, sleep patterns, and overall job performances.

TM has become very popular in the West with celebrities like Katy Perry, Jerry Seinfeld, Russell Brand, David Lynch, and Clint Eastwood crediting it with improving their lives.

Some types of meditation involve clearing the mind completely of thoughts, but TM involves focusing intently on a mostly meaningless word (a mantra) and then letting that word morph and change into whatever it wants. As practitioners follow the sound wherever it leads, they can sometimes achieve no thought at all. TM expert Bob Roth explained, "TM allows the active thinking mind, all of it, to just settle down and experience quieter levels of thought, and then experience what has been called the source of thought, the unified field of consciousness or transcendent level of the mind."[16] Notice the focus on the self—that is, connecting with what's already inside of you.

Another popular form of meditation in the West is "mindfulness." Former New Age enthusiast and mindfulness devotee turned Christian educator Marcia Montenegro defines it as "a technique of sitting still (though there is also a walking meditation), observing the breath, being aware solely of the present moment, and learning to let thoughts pass by without entertaining them."[17] Although often presented as a secular method founded on science, mindfulness is deeply rooted in the Buddhist teaching of detachment—disconnecting from desire, which keeps people from achieving nirvana.

OFFER Discernment

Proponents of the new spirituality are often sincere seekers who are looking for spiritual answers. They comprehend the emptiness of atheism and the bankruptcy of naturalism. As commendable as these traits are, they fall into an age-old trap that the apostle Paul laid out in Romans 1.

1. Pantheism

Christianity is unique among most other religions in that it teaches that God is personal and entirely distinct from His creation. He is not the rocks, the trees, or the ocean; He created those things and is separated from them. This is referred to as God's *transcendence*. God is also not a force or an energy field or some type of cosmic glue—He is a Person.

In Romans 1, Paul explained where pantheism came from. He started off by saying that all people can know certain things about God just by observing nature. (Isn't that cool?) In other words, we can look at the trees, the sky, and the world around us and know that God exists and that He is powerful. Paul went on to describe certain people's minds becoming dark and confused to the point that they began to think they were smart when, instead, they were utter fools.

Paul said it this way: "They exchanged the truth about God for a lie, and worshiped and served created things rather than the Creator—who is forever praised" (verse 25). That's pantheism in a nutshell—instead of worshipping an all-powerful Creator, people worshipped the *things* He created.

2. Divinity of All Mankind

The Bible clearly states that human beings are flawed (that's putting it lightly). It teaches that our hearts are wicked, and that we have all sinned to the point that we cannot approach God on our own. In the Old Testament, the prophet Jeremiah described the human heart as "desperately sick" (Jeremiah 17:9), and in the New Testament, the apostle Paul described us as being "dead in our sin" (Ephesians 2:1). In fact, Mark 7:21-23 lists all the evil things that flow out of our hearts (evil thoughts, deceit, and murder, oh my!). That's a far cry from being divine. That actually puts us in the position of needing a Savior.

What about that "Christ consciousness"? The Bible describes Jesus as the resurrected Christ—the anointed One, *not* as some type of symbol of divine love or a representative of any other god you might choose to pray to. Jesus wasn't just a regular guy who achieved some type of enlightenment or divine status. Rather, He claimed to exist eternally with God before He took on human flesh and came to earth (John 8:58; 17:5). In fact, a careful reading of the Gospels shows that He displayed all the same attributes as God Himself. He didn't just come to invite us all to have some sort of epiphany and realize that we are all united as humankind. He came to save us from our sin.

3. Relativism

Before we get into what the Bible says, can we talk some common sense? Put on your thinking cap and come on a journey with me.

Let's start by talking about truth. Truth is when you believe or say something that lines up with reality. We all want what we believe about the world to line up with reality, right? (You're likely to be diagnosed with some kind of disorder otherwise.)

Instinctually, we all know that two contradictory statements can't both be true at the same time and in the same sense. For example, if I hold up an apple and say, "This is an apple," and then say, "This is not an apple," one of those statements is incorrect. Clearly, the apple can't both *be* an apple and *not be* an apple at the same time and in the same sense. So if *I* say it's an apple, and *you* say it's not an apple, one of us is wrong—one of us has a belief that doesn't reflect reality. This makes that belief, by definition, *not true.*

There is no such thing as *your* truth or *my* truth. "My truth" is a myth. There is only *the* truth. Imagine you are helping your daughter with her math homework, and she solves a problem by coming up with a random number. When she turns in her homework the next day, what do you think her teacher will say when she explains that she was just "living her truth"?

Or imagine your teenager sneaking into your purse and stealing a $20 bill. When you confront him about it, he says, "I'm just living my truth, mom." It wouldn't fly—not for a second.

Or imagine you sincerely believe you are capable of flying. What would it mean to "live your truth" when you decide to test your theory for the first time by jumping off a skyscraper? Yikes. (If this is you, please do NOT follow your heart. If you've been told to never give up on your dreams, please—give up on this dream immediately.)

I could go on, but you get the point. It's a nice enough idea to *say* that contradictions are a good thing, but when played out in reality, it just doesn't work.

The Bible has a lot to say about the nature of truth. In fact, it teaches that Truth is a *Person.* Jesus said, "I am the way, the *truth,* and the life" (John 14:6). At His trial before Pilate, He said, "Everyone on the side of truth listens to me." That is the opposite of "live your truth." We are supposed to live *His* truth—the truth.

4. Meditation

Some Christians might say, "Meditation is biblical, right?" They are correct, but it depends on what type of meditation they're talking about. There are many Bible verses that speak positively of meditation—as long as the focus is God's Word. In fact, the word *meditation*, when used in the Old Testament, means to think deeply, ponder, or reflect on something. Psalm 119:15 says, "I will meditate on your precepts." and verse 148 says,

"My eyes stay open through the watches of the night, that I may meditate on your promises." We are commanded in Scripture to meditate on what God has to say. Simply put, this is an intense focus and study on the meaning and application of Scripture.

Are there some studies that show supposed health "benefits" of meditation? Sure, but we are not just aiming at physical health. Spiritual health is just as important, and most types of meditation being taught are based on blatantly New Age and antibiblical principles, opening your mind to who knows what.

Bottom line: Biblical meditation leads you to focus on something outside of yourself, to focus on God's truth. Thus it *engages* the logic/thinking part of your brain. New Age meditation, on the other hand, forces you inward and *disengages* the logic/thinking part of your brain—supposedly connecting you with the "oneness" of everything.

ARGUE for a Healthier Approach

The main thrust of this chapter is to help you recognize that the key teachings of the new spirituality culminate in a total dependence upon and worship of yourself. Have you ever heard the mantra "You are enough"? Actually, Scripture tells us the opposite. You are absolutely, most definitely *not* enough. You are so desperately not enough that it would be impossible to even calculate your not-enoughness.

This is actually good news! In fact, it's the whole point of Christianity: We are all sinners in desperate need of a Savior. We can strive all we want, try all we want, meditate all we want, center ourselves all we want, but doing these things will never make us good. Apart from Christ, there is nothing that can save us, redeem us, cleanse us, or make us worthy. That's why the new spirituality is a sham. It seeks to convince you that you are already good—but a quick skim through the history of human behavior will paint quite a different picture.[19]

This realization is what prompted New Age enthusiast Mary Poplin to surrender her life to Christ. She wrote,

I remembered a popular New Age teacher I had once seen
holding court in a California restaurant, aglow with light
and love. Afterward, this woman had gotten into an alterca-
tion with the owner of a car she had backed into accidentally.
Amid her angry shrieking, the man kept telling her, calmly
but firmly, "This is who you really are." When I heard this,
I knew I was just like her: pretending to be good, yet filled
with bile.[20]

Mary came to realize what Christianity has taught all along. No matter
how hard we try, how often we meditate, and how much we practice certain principles, we can never make ourselves good. Our hearts are desperately sick, and only the blood of Jesus can make them clean and whole.

REINFORCE Through Discussion, Discipleship, and Prayer

One of the main strategies of the enemy is to normalize and desensitize
our kids to the new spirituality. Watching their favorite cartoon character "live her truth" or "follow her heart," can seem so positive and beneficial. Take, for example, the popular Disney Junior television show *Mickey
and the Roadster Racers*, and an episode entitled "Guru Goofy." According to the episode's description, "Goofy tries to teach Donald mindfulness
in order to calm down for the Roadster Games." Hey, if Goofy is practicing mindfulness, it must be harmless and even helpful for anxiety, right?

It's fairly easy to spot doctrines of the new spirituality in "Guru Goofy,"
but how can we learn to recognize these ideas when they are more carefully camouflaged? Three words: practice, practice, practice. Be on the
lookout for the message espoused by the new spirituality on TV, in commercials, movies, apps, online games, social media, and billboards. Make
a game out of this, make it a fun activity with your kids. Teach them to be
like detectives looking for clues.

When they hear a phrase like "follow your heart," ask them practical
questions like, "What if someone's heart is telling them to do something
bad?" and "What does the Bible say about our hearts?" Injecting humor

can help as well. Simply lean over and whisper, "What if my heart tells me to take a nap in the middle of a busy street?" Or, "What if I get mad at your dad and my heart tells me to kick him in the shins?"

If a commercial on TV communicates, "You are enough," you might say, "Hey, can you go pick up that car with your bare hands? No? You mean you actually *aren't* enough?" Or in response to "The answers you seek are inside yourself," you might say, "Really? Even the answer to how to fix the broken dishwasher?" Your kids may roll their eyes, but these kinds of questions will train them to think critically as they engage with their culture.

When our kids witness us interacting with new spirituality calmly, without fear, and even with a bit of humor, it will show them that we are a safe place to help them process what they are hearing and will open the lines of communication for years to come.

PAWS for Prayer

Praise

God, I praise You as the Rock of Ages, the Ancient of Days. You are the voice of truth that projects across all time and eternity. You alone are the light of the world. You are transcendent, the creator who is distinct from His creation. You show us Yourself through Your creation and its "magnificence enlightens us" to Your nature (Romans 1:20 THE VOICE).

Admit

Lord, forgive Your church, whether in ignorance or with awareness, when we have tread in areas contrary to Your truth. Forgive all who have traded "the splendor and beauty of the immortal God to worship images of the common man or woman, bird or reptile, or the next beast that tromps along" (Romans 1:23 THE VOICE), and who "gave their lives and devotion to the creature rather than to the Creator Himself" (Romans 1:25 THE VOICE).

Worship with Thanksgiving

Thank You that I am not able to bring about my own salvation. Absolute truth and objective morality exist because they are rooted in Your nature. As Your child, I connect with the divine through prayer and Your Word. I do not need to "detach" from anything because I am attached to the family of God; I don't have to disconnect from desire; rather, You give me the desires of my heart.

Supplication

Lord, open my family's eyes to the different types of new spirituality that are being taught in our children's schools, even Christian ones. Give us eyes to see, ears to hear, and minds to recognize disguised language, beliefs, and practices, and then obedience to expose the subtle and seductive deceptions. May I boldly show my children that the only enlightenment we need comes from Your Scripture, authored by You, the light of the world. May our only meditation be on Scripture, its meaning, and its application. Please remove from us any fear of engaging logic and thinking minds. Please protect us against normalizing and desensitizing our kids to the teachings of this new spirituality. Give me the skills and persistence to train my children to think critically about what they hear and give them eyes to see through the lies disguised as truth. In the name of Elohim, the triune God, Creator. Amen.

Discussion Questions

1. **Icebreaker:** Did you or anyone you know ever play with a Ouiji board, tarot cards, or read their horoscope? Why do you think these things are so attractive to people, including kids?

2. **Main theme:** *New Age principles have been repackaged, but they are just as dangerous as ever.* Of the four main themes of new spirituality, which one have you noticed most frequently in popular culture?

3. **Self-evaluation:** There are aspects of the new spirituality that sound attractive. If you were honest with yourself, which parts attract you? Why do you think that is? Is there a biblical truth that has been distorted? Why do you think you—and people in general—are drawn to the distorted version?

4. **Brainstorm:** In what ways has culture used Jesus as a generic stamp to turn anything into a Christian message? Has there been a time when you bought into New Age principles and mixed them in with your Christian beliefs? Have you seen this occur in any popular Christian books? How should you respond when that happens?

5. **Release the bear:** One of the problems with the new spirituality is that it tries to add to the Bible—crystals, meditation, chanting, etc. Emphasize to your kids that if we needed crystals (or whatever), God would have told us.

Chapter 13

Communism Failed Because Nobody Did It Right

Marxism

Hillary Morgan Ferrer

arxism? As in communism Marxism? In a book for moms? Yeah, that's what I thought too. It never entered my mind to include Marxism in this book until it became clear that it would be negligent not to. It's that pervasive.

Up until recently, my thoughts were, *Isn't communism a thing of the past? USSR? Berlin wall? Have we learned nothing about the errors and evils of Marxism? And isn't Venezuela learning this lesson, like, right now?* Spoiler alert: No, apparently we have *not* learned this lesson.

My nephew went through a phase of jumping off the back of the couch. For weeks, my sister and her husband kept telling him, "You're going to hurt yourself," which of course, he did. After getting stitches on his lip, my sister asked him, "What did you learn?"

"To not jump off the couch," he replied.

"What about jumping off other things," she asked. "Is that okay?"

"Yeah, that's okay."

That's kid logic for you!

Evidently a lot of people are the same way when it comes to Marxist policies—and that includes both socialism and communism. Talk to any Marxist and point out all the failed communist regimes of the past and present, and they'll say, "None of those countries did it right. If we can just do it right, it'll work." In some ways, they are correct. When you read Marxist literature, you'll notice it completely ignores original sin and human nature. Marxism could theoretically work as long as you don't have those two little factors at play. Good luck with that.

Those who are ignorant of history are doomed to repeat it, and friend, fair warning: We are on the path toward repeating ourselves. Don't believe me? Just look at the May 2018 issue of *Teen Vogue* and you'll see a feature article on Karl Marx and his ideas, all of which are painted in a very favorable light.[1] At the end of the article is a link to an article on capitalism that helps your teen daughter understand capitalist philosophy ("greed is good") and individual capitalists (wealthy people who have a large amount of capital…and who benefit from the system).[2] That's in *Teen Vogue*! Back in my day, we learned about the latest lip gloss colors and laughed over reader-submitted most embarrassing moments.

Bottom line is that if Marxism isn't on your radar, it should be.

The history your kids are learning in school is *not* the history that you and I learned. The pilgrim's search for religious freedom has been replaced by horrible stories of Native American slaughters, conquest, and generally racist examples of founding fathers. I'm not saying that this stuff isn't true, but there *is* an agenda here: America is bad. America is capitalist. Therefore, capitalism is bad.

Why Are We Talking About Failed Economic Policies in a Book for Moms?

Just so no one misunderstands me, I want to say right now that *the Bible is not pro-capitalism and America is not God's chosen nation.* I am not trying to make a statement on political parties here. Rather, my goal is to expose the lies that are being smuggled into our children's minds through Marxism. Marxist ideas in the form of socialism and communism can *sound* completely reasonable, and even gospel-driven. But make no mistake: The end goal is the dissolution of all hierarchies. And yes, that includes the family unit, religion, and morality. Marx says in *The Communist Manifesto*, "Communism is that stage of historical development which makes all existing religions superfluous and supersedes them"[3] and that "Communism abolishes eternal truths, it abolishes all religion, and all morality."[4] He even refers to the sacredness of the relationship between parent and child as "disgusting."[5]

Marxism is more than just a failed economic policy—it is essentially a religion, one that touches on every facet of life from church to family to morality. As Bruce Mazlisch said in his book *The Meaning of Karl Marx*, "Naturally, so defined, Marxism cannot be considered a religion. If, however, one looks at the functions of religion, especially its psychological functions, its offer of a total explanation of history, its messianic sense of time, its eschatological vision of a conflict between the forces of good and evil, and its hope for a complete regeneration of man, then Marxism can indeed qualify as a religion."[6]

Marx was very open about how Christianity and his philosophy could *not* coexist. As Marxist disciple William Z. Foster said in his 1932 book *Towards Soviet America*, "Not Christianity but Communism will bring peace on earth."[7] Marxism essentially takes the story of sin and redemption and reinterprets it into capitalism and communism.

As I've studied Marxism, here's what I've come to realize: (1) It's worse than I suspected, and (2) I'm sorry to report that it isn't only college students who are exposed to it. Although, to be clear, if you plan to send your little darlings to college, you will most likely need to understand what is being taught, if for no other reason than to pick up on hints from your budding comrade during Thanksgiving break.

What's the Difference Between Marxism, Socialism, and Communism?

Before we embark on the history of Marxism, we must first clarify some terms. First, Marxism is a broad field of thought, not a single monolithic belief system. There are so many brands of Marxism that wars have been fought over the various offshoots. Not even Marx's own writings are considered consistent.[8]

Second, Marxism, socialism, and communism are often (mistakenly) used interchangeably because they are in the same family. But there are subtle differences. Socialism has been around longer than either Marxism or communism. Socialism, like Marxism, has many different flavors, but the general idea is that the state (that is, centralized government) is in control of all production and distribution of goods and makes all decisions regarding commerce. Socialism *can* coexist with freedom of religion, but it generally promotes secularism—a radical separation of church and state where religious ideas are welcome only in the private realm of hearth and home. Communism, on the other hand, is unapologetically atheistic.

The Marxist version of socialism is a stepping stone to communism.[9,10] Communism is the utopian belief that all power can be put back into the hands of the working class and they will govern themselves—no gods, no masters. The "people" would collectively own all manufacturing, all commodities, and there would be no more "classes" of people, meaning that everyone would be perfectly equal. Sounds great doesn't it? Unless you are like me, and you remember how well this worked with high school group projects. I was the one who cared the most, so I ended up doing all the work. The *idea* of equality is great, until you remember that it doesn't guarantee equality of *motivation*. But I digress.

In this chapter, we are addressing Marxism because it is the seed that is being planted in universities across the country. You generally won't hear professors say, "Now I'm going to convert you to Marxism." Parents would riot. However, after years of university ministry, I can assure you that Marx's ideas are being promoted like crazy. And in case you are still unconvinced, think of the sheer number of young supporters for Bernie Sanders, who openly ran for president on a socialist platform.

So, while we use all three terms in this chapter—*Marxism, socialism,* and *communism*—keep these differences in mind. And remember that while Marxism ultimately failed, it keeps crawling back into the popular eye under new management, hoping to beguile a new, dewy-eyed generation who, very likely, has the most noble of intentions (that is, equality and care for minorities and the oppressed).

A Brief History of Marxism

Marxism is a philosophical and economic theory espoused by Karl Marx in the 1850s. According to Marx, all human history can be understood in terms of a civilization's "mode of production." In other words, how do humans harness nature and technology to meet their needs? While various philosophical systems were intended to explain individual aspects of human existence, Marxism was intended to be an overarching principle, a worldview.

> If a theory doesn't account for the evil within
> our own souls, then it cannot account for
> the evil in the world. Period.

Think back to our chapter on naturalism. According to Marx, humans are predominantly biological beings with no immaterial soul (materialist naturalism). That alone should clue you in to why his theory will never work. If a theory doesn't account for the evil within our own souls, then it cannot account for the evil in the world. Period. And any solution it proposes will ultimately end with evil people in power, which has *always* been the case when a country goes communist. It starts all dreamy-eyed and utopian, and then bam—Lenin, Stalin, Mao, and Castro.

If humans are just biological machines without a sin nature, then we cannot account for why they do bad things apart from genes and environment. Marxism says, "Change the environment, give people everything they need, and they'll all be noble and will work hard for the benefit of society." (Because that's what you witness with your kids, right? Ha!) Is a person genetically defective? Time to remove him or her from the gene pool. (Hint: There is a reason communist dictators have a history of killing their own people in unprecedented numbers.)

> Do not underestimate how much evil can be rationalized
> when one is convinced that they are "acting for the
> greater good."

So What Do the Marxists *Think* They Are Doing?

The dedicated Marxist is fully convinced that our society just needs the right environment whereby evil people will become good and inequality between classes of people will be abolished. They are so convinced that their solution will solve the world's problems that they justify the "by any means necessary" approach: "Trust us! You will thank us later when you see how much better things are!" Or, as Robert Harvey summarizes, "Implicit in the whole structure was the belief…that the end justifies the means, that…anything done in the name of progress is essentially good, no matter what the cost."[11] Do not underestimate how much evil can be rationalized when one is convinced that they are "acting for the greater good."

Philosophers like Plato and Aristotle taught that humans needed truth, goodness, and virtue to flourish. Along came Marx, and all of a sudden humans could only flourish by getting rid of classes of people. Personal choices do not make us who we are. Beliefs, religion, gender, philosophy, family, sin, human nature—none of these could adequately explain human beings for Marx. "Modes of production" (that is, economic interactions) were his ultimate explanation for all human behavior.

What Is Meant by "Modes of Production"?

In the late 1700s, a new development arose that forever changed the way people made, bought, and sold goods—factories. Before that, people made their own clothes, grew their own food, and built their own houses. Or they were skilled craftsmen and produced the goods from start to finish and traded their wares for someone else's. I remember watching *Little House on the Prairie* as a kid. Everyone in the community had a trade, except the Olsens, who basically represented evil, greedy, capitalism that nobody liked.

The industrial revolution came about because factories were more efficient than individuals at making wares. Craftsmen were removed from the home and put into sweatshops of mass production, which meant goods could be produced and sold for a fraction of the cost. The workers no longer owned the goods, but rather, traded their time for money. These laborers were treated as expendable and lost their independence and their creative input. As Marx rightly pointed out, the worker became "an appendage to the machine."[12]

To play devil's advocate, Marx made some legitimate points in *The Communist Manifesto* about the abuses that occurred to workers during the industrial revolution—like how industrialization commoditized children for cheap labor.[13] Unfortunately, despite improved work standards and government regulations that have significantly reduced workplace abuse (like workers getting fired when they were injured by machines), modern Marxists (socialists and communists) still portray *all* capitalism as evil (and usually personified as "the man").

But let's ask ourselves: *Is building a business bad?* Say a person starts a business and eventually becomes successful enough to hire workers. These workers do not own the business; rather, they work for the owner, whose goal is not merely to create and sell at cost, but to create and sell for a profit. When that happens, the workers have job stability and the owner can expand the business—and hire more workers. This is Capitalism 101.

Marx considered this process to be exploitation of the workers because their efforts were not being equally traded for product. An equal trade would result in no surplus, and thus no profit. According to capitalism, profit is good. Profit means that the owner can reinvest the money, grow the business, and ultimately hire more workers. More workers create more product, which then creates more profits. This is how one builds a business. That, in turn, enables people to make a living and communities to grow.

According to Marx, however, profit concentrates the power in the hands of the owner while the workers remain disadvantaged and are thus exploited. The rich stay rich, and the poor stay poor. The workers may not even realize they are being exploited, a concept that will take on a new significance when we talk about feminism (see chapter 14).

The aforementioned power and profit differentials play out in what Marx calls "class struggle." So central is this theme that he opens part 1 of *The Communist Manifesto* with the declaration that "history of all hitherto existing society is the history of class struggles."[14]

Not sin. Class struggles.

The ruling class (which he called the *bourgeoisie*) makes decisions for the sole purpose of maintaining its power. Any talk of virtue, common sense, religion, ethics, values, or humanity is a clever ruse to reinforce the ruling class's power and subjugate the lower class (the proletariat). To translate this into twenty-first century "Occupy Wall Street" language, the proletariat are the 99 percenters and the bourgeoisie are the 1 percenters. We see this same type of thinking in feminism, except it refers to the ruling class as "the patriarchy."

Marx believed that in order to create a just society, power must be put back into the hands of the working class. Revolution would come not from the elite intellectuals, but rather from laborers. (But don't misunderstand: The intellectual elite were required to awaken the working class and mobilize them politically—a strong theme for contemporary Marxist intelligentsia.)[15]

Marx also viewed capitalism as fundamentally unstable because workers would not put up with exploitation forever. Because Marx predicted economic implosion as a result of capitalism, those who follow his teachings believe that by hastening this economic collapse, they are doing the nation a service. Ripping the Band-Aid off quickly, so to speak. Expedite the revolution, and you can expedite progress. (If you've ever wondered why it seems like some politicians are trying to destroy the foundation and fabric of America, this is the reason. For our society to be "fundamentally transformed," one must first demolish the old guard who is currently "oppressing the workers" through capitalism.)

Our initial response to the overall message of Marxism might be, "What is the problem? Shouldn't we be against the exploitation of workers? Shouldn't we want to defend the cause of the downtrodden? Aren't these the orphans and widows whom the apostle James talks about that we are supposed to protect?" It's time to put on our thinking caps and break down this philosophy the ROAR way.

ROAR Like a Mother!

RECOGNIZE the Message

Now that we have a rudimentary understanding of Marxism, we must look at how it has integrated itself into contemporary society and how we can recognize its message when we hear it.

1. *Rejecting innate sin*—According to Marxism, we have both an enemy and original sin, but it's spelled C-A-P-I-T-A-L-I-S-M, and capitalism is synonymous with oppression. Because evil is supposedly a product of one's economic environment, Marxists use a person's environment to not only explain bad behavior but excuse it. (There is *some* truth to this, which we will discuss in the "Offer Discernment" section.) People act the way they do because of oppressive forces outside their control. Remove these toxic forces, and their greed, selfishness, and violence will go away. Getting our country to adopt these "fair and just" conditions will be difficult, according to Marxists, but ultimately worth it.

2. *Recognizing oppression*—Marxists believe that the history of man is the history of oppressors who are protected by "the system," whether that be capitalism, religion, or the traditional family. According to Marxism, the oppressed play a role too, in that they don't realize they are being oppressed (which they call "false consciousness"). If people don't realize that they are oppressed, then

they won't join forces to overthrow the oppressors. So the job of a good Marxist is to help people recognize all the ways they have been wronged and to properly identify the class that has wronged them. This is called "identity politics," and it is a *strong* theme in the political sphere, and now in the educational sphere, from kindergarten to university students.

3. ***Demonizing the wealthy***—It is assumed that wealthy people could achieve their stature only by exploiting the workers beneath them and unfairly passing down the wealth of previous generations to their kids. Marx believed that a true revolution could only come from a working-class rebellion, so the goal of Marxists is to portray the upper class as inhumanly as possible. Anger against the "fat cats" is aimed toward effective political activism. In the words of Jack Black from *School of Rock,* Marxists have a bad case of "stick-it-to-the-man-itis."

4. ***Emphasizing "justice" and "equality"***—Any perceived differences between people are deemed to be inequalities or injustices. To rectify the situation, we need to fight for equality and justice, right? (But don't ask too many questions, they say. If you're not for us, you're against us.)

   When Marxists talk about injustice, however, what they really mean is "differences." (Have you ever noticed how futuristic movies often portray people as all wearing identical jumpsuits? Dissolution of differences supposedly equals dissolution of inequality.) The traditional understanding of justice is "a fair and reasonable treatment of individuals." For a Marxist, *justice* means equality of *outcome*, not equal access, equal opportunity, or equal treatment. (Remember our linguistic theft chapter?) If there are any differences between male and female, there is gender injustice. If a man can walk away from a pregnancy but a woman can't, then we must call for reproductive justice. If there are any differences between the black, white, Latino, Asian, or Native American cultures, these are deemed to be racial injustices. To a Marxist, justice leaves no room for legitimate differences. Differences—even valid ones—are injustice, and we should fight to remove them.

5. ***Obscuring the goals***—According to Marx's writings, settling for smaller goals can be counterproductive because when people have some of their demands met, they are inclined to become content with their present situation. Contentment is the enemy of revolution, and revolution is the goal. Saul Alinsky wrote in *Rules for Radicals* that "goals must be phrased in general terms like 'Liberty, Equality, Fraternity'...not in concrete terms of dollars and hours but psychological and constantly changing."[16] When you ask an Occupy Wall Street protester or a women's march protester what his or her demands are, you probably won't get a clear answer that can be objectively measured. (How do we measure whether "the patriarchy" is gone?) Measurable goals are bad because they can be met. With Marxism, the objective is to bring large-scale change that helps to establish communism, which, according to Marx, must be preceded by revolution. In case you were wondering, the first step toward revolution is to create enough chaos so that the ruling class is easier to overthrow. Upon realizing this, the protests that we see taking place at college campuses start to make more sense. If you think I'm making this up, read Alinsky's *Rules for Radicals*. It's an eye-opener.

OFFER Discernment

Very few people openly identify themselves as a Marxist (although that is starting to change). Despite *Teen Vogue's* efforts, Marxism—and the communist political and economical policies that emanate from it—is still viewed negatively by many people. But the ideas Marxists espouse do not go away; they are like the bad ex-boyfriend we keep crawling back to. After all, he looks so different! (He got a makeover and goes by "social justice" now.) He says everything we want to hear ("Come on, baby—I can give you heaven on earth!") Deep down we know that he can't keep his promises, but maybe he's changed. It'll be different this time!

Communism is bad, but social justice sounds good, right? Marx's new followers often call themselves social justice warriors, or SJWs for short. SJWs tend to be young and idealistic. They rightly identify areas in which we as a nation need to change, but they don't understand that the solutions they offer are grounded in Marxism. In their zeal for justice, they may not realize that they are being used to further an unbiblical agenda. This is where parental guidance is crucial. When children hear Marxist rhetoric disguised as social justice and other seemingly noble goals, it can be difficult for them to see the evil that lurks beneath.

Discerning the good and bad of social justice takes a lot of chewing and spitting. We need to make sure that we aren't rejecting the entire message simply because we know it leads to communism. When our young people hear us critique social justice without affirming the good, they lose faith that we are objective. In their eyes, we appear as clueless drones who are perpetuating the problems that they desperately want to solve. They need to know that we, too, see the problems, and that we, too, care about them. So what can we affirm?

First, a social justice warrior is concerned for the marginalized, much as Jesus was. If we are not deeply compassionate toward the poor and the marginalized, then we don't understand the heart of God (see Deuteronomy 10:18; Psalm 140:12; James 1:27).

Second, SJWs legitimately desire to remove racism and sexism from today's society. As much as we would like to think that racism is in our rearview mirror, it is still alive and kicking. I have friends of color who have told me stories that make me furious. They are not race baiters, and they haven't bought into identity politics. Likewise, the Me Too movement has shown us just how pervasive the mistreatment of women still is, especially within the church! I am saddened that it has taken a secular movement to urge Christians to clean their own houses. An abuser is allowed to maintain spiritual authority because "he's got such a powerful ministry" or "he's such an amazing teacher." Meanwhile, victims are told to forgive their abusers and place their trust in the church's "internal review" process. This unbiblical response further traumatizes the victims and enables the abusers. This is *not* what proper biblical leadership looks like.

Third, we need to recognize that a person's environment does affect his or her behavior. If a child is more worried about where the next meal will come from or getting jumped by a neighborhood gang, studying for an English midterm is probably going to be seen as a lesser priority. When children do not feel safe in their own homes, they often cannot mature emotionally and psychologically. Where I differ is that I don't think all these problems will go away by throwing money at them. Money alone cannot replace the stability and security provided by intact, healthy families.

Fourth, are there legitimate abuses of capitalism? Absolutely! There are unscrupulous business owners who take advantage of their workers. There are people who exploit the cheap labor of illegal immigrants and undocumented workers because they have no protection. There are people who work three jobs, yet still can't seem to make ends meet.

If all we do is counter SJWs arguments with examples of all the good aspects of America and capitalism, they will leave the conversation thinking, *She wasn't listening to me. Maybe I need to shout louder?*

Acknowledge. Grieve. Work for reform. Godly conviction is good. Let true injustices spur your heart to action. But stay alert for the lies in the social justice movement that we need to spit out. Our kids need to hear us both affirm the truths and reject the lies. Biblical justice will always line up with the nature and character of God, but that won't always be true about social justice.

Lie #1: To Love a Person, You Must Love Their Beliefs

There is a huge lie that is currently permeating every area of our society: A person and his or her ideas cannot be separated. You have to love them both or reject them both. What a stealthy tactic of the enemy! If this were true, then God could not love any of us.

Lie #2: Differences Are More Important Than Similarities

In identity politics, people are taught to focus on their differences and their individual communities rather than their collective and shared experiences. Newsflash: *Everyone* has felt powerless. *Everyone* has felt invisible. *Everyone* has felt small or like they can't catch a break. Our shared experiences are manifest in different ways, but these are all universal human conditions. Which brings me to my next point.

Lie #3: People Can Be Generalized

When people are lumped together as "white people" or "black people" or "rich people" or "poor people," we have to ask: Which ones are you talking about? There are wealthy and poor people in every race and gender. Selfishness lurks in the heart of the investment banker, the housewife, and the gangbanger. No group has a monopoly on *any* vice or virtue.

Lie #4: A Person's Background Can Negate His or Her Opinion

Fill in the blanks: "You're only saying that because you are a [fill in religion], [fill in race] [fill in gender] who grew up [fill in background] with [fill in socioeconomic status]." Captain Obvious alert: Even people who are of the same gender, religion, race, and neighborhood differ widely in their perceptions.

Lie #5: Mankind Can Fix the Problems of Society

One of the greatest lies of Marxism is that man is both sinner and savior. When people focus on anything other than sin as the problem, they inevitably miss the solution. Sexism is not the problem. It is a *symptom* of the problem—the sin in our hearts. Racism is a symptom, but sin is the problem. Greed is a symptom, but sin is the problem. Any solution that proposes putting people into different circumstances to solve the symptoms of sin is doomed to fail. Sin is the problem, and the only solution is the One who deals with sin. Repentance, Christ's redemption, and the sanctifying work of the Holy Spirit are the only solutions for sin. Putting people in different circumstances might make it harder or easier for them to sin, but it won't remove their sin. Our human natures will emerge no matter what situation we are put into. (However, this is not to negate the legitimate role that environment plays in shaping us.)

Lie #6: Hierarchy Is Unjust

This is a big lie as well and affects many more areas than understood at first glance. While the SJWs will rage against the 1 percenters, they are taught to believe that all hierarchy necessarily leads to unfairness. Let us be clear: There is a hierarchy within the Godhead. God's first institution on earth was marriage, which consists of hierarchy within the family. God created hierarchy within the Judaic priesthood, as well as among the angels. The New Testament affirms a hierarchy within church government. There might even be hierarchy one day in heaven too (Matthew 19:28; Revelation 22:5). *So hierarchy and power are not the problem. Sinful people abusing their roles of power is the problem.*

When Marxists define hierarchy as the problem, economic hierarchy is the chief example. But Marxists don't just seek to do away with heirarchies. They are against anything that fosters an *instinct* for hierarchy. This is why Marxism is innately against any form of organized religions, strong nuclear families, or power structures within businesses, all three of which operate under a hierarchy with established authorities, whether that be God, parents, or bosses. In fact, Marxist literature faults the nuclear family and religion for "creating personalities habituated to authority," as if that were a bad thing.[17]

As Gottlieb explains, "The nuclear family tends to create people who think of themselves primarily as individuals rather than as members of communities or classes. This self-understanding makes political organizing and mass radical movements extremely difficult."[18]

Lie #7: Fostering Resentment Is a Great Foundation for Change

This seems to be the modus operandi of much of social justice ideology. Suffice it to say that resentment is *not* a biblical strategy for change.

According to Marxist theory, the only way to get the proletariat (the working class) to rise up and overthrow the "fat cats of oppression" is to make them angry enough to do so. Thus, much of undercover Marxism is aimed at creating divisions between the oppressed and the oppressor in hopes of unifying the oppressed under a single "class" who will revolt and demand to govern themselves. (This is what we saw played out in The Hunger Games franchise.) So far, all we have ever seen this do is make people susceptible to charismatic personalities who promise a world without injustice…who then go on to rule as totalitarian dictators.

There are more lies, and I can't go into all of them here. To see a list of communist goals as documented by an ex-FBI agent in the 1950s, go to the Mama Bear blog. You'll be surprised at how many have already been accomplished, and even more astonished to know that they are connected with communism!

> Our agenda is not to prove ourselves right. It is to love like Christ loved, and that includes knowing when to speak and when to be silent.

ARGUE for a Healthier Approach

There is a reason Colossians 2:8 warns us to not be taken "captive through hollow and deceptive philosophy, which depends on human tradition and the elemental spiritual forces of this world rather than on Christ." With most of the "isms" in this book, we are not dealing with willful rebels, but with *captives*—people held hostage to bad ideas. The first rule in hostage situations: If you don't have a clear shot at the captor, don't take the shot. Remember, we demolish ideas, not people. If a person is too close to their ideas, they will not be able to tell the difference between you attacking their ideas and you attacking their identity.

When addressing the lies inherent to Marxism and social justice, be prepared to be labeled as an oppressor. Do not play the game. Our agenda is not to prove ourselves right. It is to love like Christ loved, and that includes knowing when to speak and when to be silent.

Below are a few key ways to combat the lies.

1. *Recognize true injustice*—Where there is true injustice, speak up! However, don't let yourself be swayed by the word *injustice*. Not all claims of injustice are *actual* injustice. We here in America have it so good that so-called microaggressions are now used as examples of injustice. I'm sorry, but just *stop it*. We need to fight against true injustices in the world, like sex slavery, genocide, female genital mutilation, honor killings, dictatorships, kidnapping, true racism and sexism, and much more. If we make every tiny thing into an example of oppression, then the word loses its meaning and people become indifferent.

2. *Reject anything that ignores sin as the real problem or lumps people into a single group*—Often, people try to take symptoms of sin (sexism, racism, etc.) and make them the main problem. Or, they speak in generalities and pin certain sins onto an entire class of people (as if wealth and greed are a package deal). The efforts to pit one sin against another and assign it a demographic is just an endless cycle of "who is the bigger sinner." There are only two classes: non-sinner and sinner. God and humanity. Guess which class we all fall under?

3. *Unity over differences*—My mom once told me that God must love diversity because there are more than 200 species of roses. Let's appreciate our God-given differences, and remember that ultimately, our unity is to be found in Christ alone. The cross is the great equalizer. We all stand condemned as sinners, and we all (who have accepted the free gift of salvation) stand justified as children of God. At the foot of the cross, "there is no Gentile or Jew, circumcised or uncircumcised, barbarian, Scythian, slave or free, but Christ is all, and is in all" (Colossians 3:11). Will our ethnic backgrounds give us different experiences? Sure. Our gender? Absolutely. But when we are in Christ, we are no longer defined by our gender, race, education, or socioeconomic status. We are defined by Christ. Period.[19] Let's start acting like it.

REINFORCE Through Discussion, Discipleship, and Prayer

1. For young children: Play the "image of God" game. This game helps children understand that we are all made in the image of God and reminds them of our shared humanity as opposed to focusing on differences. Anytime you encounter someone different from you (skin color, hair color, age, body shape, disease, mental state), ask your kids, "Is that person made in the image of God?" Instill our collective identity as image-bearers of God no matter what our differences.[20]

2. Middle school and high school: Stay aware of buzzwords like *justice*, *injustice*, *equal*, and *unequal*. Ask your teens to define what is just, unjust, or unequal about a given situation. Read Matthew 25:14-30, the parable of the talents. What parts of this parable would our culture say are unjust? What point do you think Jesus was trying to make?

3. Identify who is using their power for good or evil. If you are watching a movie in which a husband mistreats a woman, ask your teens if the man is using his power for good or evil (duh—evil). When a leader makes a good decision, recognize how he or she has used power for good. Reinforce that power itself is neither good nor evil. Rather, it's how we use it that matters.

4. Ask your children if disagreeing with someone means that you hate them. Recall examples of times when you and your spouse or family have disagreed, but still loved each other. Reinforce that disagreement doesn't equal hate.

PAWS for Prayer

Praise

God Almighty, I praise You for ascribing worth to humans because we are created in Your image. You offer equal opportunity through the free gift of salvation to everyone who will call on Your name, confess their sins, and make You their Lord and Savior. You are a just God and the only arbiter of what is right. Your standard is objective and true and plays no favorites.

Admit

Lord, I am a sinner. We all sin and fall short of Your standard. Before Your cross, we all stand equally in need of a Savior. It is You—not the government—who is our Savior. Forgive us for trying to excuse the sin in our hearts by explaining it away.

Worship with Thanksgiving

Thank You, heavenly Father, that I am made in Your image, that I have a soul capable of accepting You as my redeemer. Thank You that I will be made perfect and complete when I am with You in heaven. Thank You for ordaining hierarchy as a means of order, responsibility, and accountability. When implemented properly and under Your control, hierarchy is a good thing.

Supplication

Help my children not to be influenced by the teachings of Marxism flooding our schools, especially our universities. Show me how to throw them the life preserver of Your Word. Help me proclaim with truth, clarity, and conviction that man cannot save himself. You are our only rescue. May I teach my kids to not equate power with privilege, but rather with responsibility. As an agent of peace, help me to model understanding instead of resentment, appreciate God-given differences, and commit to a work ethic that brings You glory. May those of us who have Christ share the good news of equality and unity in Him with others.

With praise to You, El Shaddai—almighty, all-sufficient God, Jehovah Shalom, our peace. Amen.

Discussion Questions

1. **Icebreaker:** Look in the footnotes for the links to the *Teen Vogue* articles. Read them aloud and discuss your thoughts.

2. **Main theme:** *When you ignore original sin as humankind's main problem, no solution you propose will work.* Imagine telling your kids to do their chores "for the good of all mankind." How effective do you think this would be? How do you think they would respond if you took away any rewards or allowance for performing their chores? What does this tell us about human motivation? Is this motive wrong? Why or why not? What do the following passages tell us about motives? See 1 Corinthians 9:24; 1 Corinthians 3:8; Matthew 5:10-12.

3. **Self-evaluation:** Most people long for a better life here on earth. Are there times when you are tempted to think that money or economic policies are more important than the Holy Spirit's influence on society? Why do you think we are inclined to pursue other solutions before going to Jesus?

4. **Brainstorm:** Read Acts 2:44-47 and 4:32-25. How might a Marxist interpret the Bible as advocating for communism?[21] Do you think it does? Read Matthew 25:14-30, the parable of the talents. How could this parable be seen as advocating for capitalism? Do you think it does? What can we learn by applying both principles advocated in Scripture? How does the Bible transcend politics?

5. **Release the bear:** Over dinner or during a long car trip, talk to your kids about what they think would happen if schools had no grades, or all the grades were averaged and distributed equally among students. Do they think students would work harder or less hard? Why? Read James 1:27 and discuss it. Orphans and widows were people who had no protection or power in Bible times. Ask your kids who God has put in their path to serve. What is the difference between asking individuals to serve versus asking the government to serve on a nation's behalf? Which one puts more responsibility on the individual? Is this a good or a bad thing?

Chapter 14

The Future Is Female

Feminism

REBEKAH VALERIUS, ALISA CHILDERS, AND
HILLARY MORGAN FERRER

"**I** am a nasty woman!" screamed actress Ashley Judd from the stage to a
sea of cheering women in pink hats meant to symbolize female geni-
talia.[1] They were part of a crowd of over 500,000 women who had gathered in Washington DC on January 21, 2017. "I am nasty like the blood
stains on my bedsheets," she continued, in a speech directed mostly at the
incoming US president.[2] Madonna added her voice, declaring (between
expletives), "I want to start a revolution of love," and "I've thought a lot
about blowing up the White House."

Marches occurred simultaneously in major cities all over the nation,
with organizers estimating that a wave of more than one million pink-
hatted women gathered across the country from sea to shining sea, hitting
the streets to march for women's rights...or was it equality? Or to protest
the patriarchy? Or to object to crass remarks from the newly elected president? The wide variety of responses given in media interviews seemed to
indicate no one was really sure.

According to the official website for the march, this "women-led
movement" brought "together people of all genders, ages, races, cultures,

political affiliations, disabilities and backgrounds in our nation's capital...to affirm [their] shared humanity and pronounce [their] bold message of resistance and self-determination."[3] Throughout the day, just about every news channel broadcasted continuous coverage of the event, hailing it as a historic moment for the cause of women's rights.

Did this represent a step forward or a giant leap backward for womankind? Might we suggest that millions of women wearing symbols of their privates on their head and gleefully screaming "I'm a nasty woman" was a massive failure for the cause of female empowerment and an especially devastating loss in the dignity department?

Don't get us wrong. Like all dutiful daughters of modernity, we're thankful for feminism. And as Christians, we are thankful for a God who gave woman-honoring mandates that broke with the traditions of culture.[4] Early feminists paved the way for the equality that women enjoy today. But we struggle to connect with many contemporary feminists, especially those who seem to be in a ceaseless state of agitation. Their talk of resisting the patriarchy seems strange to someone like me (Rebekah), who has brothers and who knows firsthand the struggles that men endure—often at the hands of women. And in my opinion, the latest version of the movement forfeited all moral high ground when it decided to die on the hill of abortion—a practice which, ironically, harms more baby girls than baby boys.

Still, protesting the president's crass comments by being equally crass in response is hardly productive. Historically, our feminist foremothers strove to *raise* the level of discourse. By contrast, today's feminists meet crudity on its own muddy turf.

Today, when a woman calls herself a feminist, it is not always clear what she means. The definition of feminism itself has changed a lot since its inception. Clearly, the pink-hatted protesters saw themselves as representing the cause of all women, but many women (like the three of us) felt left out and even repulsed. They wouldn't have welcomed us anyway.

Pro-life women were officially disinvited from their march (although some of them didn't get the memo).[5]

What does it mean to be a feminist today, and how has the meaning of the word changed over time? How do we prepare our little bears to think critically about a movement that would conduct such a march? To truly understand feminism, we need to look at its history and how its goals have changed over time. This is crucial for understanding how we arrived at the Women's March of 2017.

A Brief History of Feminism

The earliest roots of feminism date back a couple centuries. But the term *feminism*, in the sense that we know it, is largely a late-nineteenth century and twentieth-century phenomenon. As we examine modern-era feminism, we hope you will take note that feminism, even today, is not monolithic. Many of the critiques we present in this chapter have to do with the most vocal feminists of our day. Hopefully, as you come to understand feminism's history and the three waves of feminism, you will see not only the more redeeming aspects of ages past but learn how to advocate for a healthier feminism in times to come.

First-Wave Feminism

According to philosopher Christina Hoff Sommers (known as the Factual Feminist), first-wave feminism (early 1900s to late 1960s) could be divided into two groups she labeled as the *egalitarian* feminists and the *maternal* feminists.[6,7]

Egalitarian feminists argued for women's rights apart from their gender and fought for a woman's right to operate in the same roles as men. *Maternal feminists* argued for women's rights and equality *within* their unique roles as mothers and caregivers.

These two groups essentially fought for the same goals (voting rights, education, property rights, etc.). It was, however, the *way* they argued for these equalities that distinguished the two. The *egalitarian wing* was more like our current-day feminists. Equality for them meant women being able to act like men, do anything men could do, and go anywhere men could go. They downplayed the inherent differences between the sexes and promoted a woman's right to forge her own destiny to the extent that men could.

The early *maternal wing* is best represented by women like Hannah More and Frances Willard, who recognized that men and women are different. These feminists affirmed the unique role of women in society, especially as caregivers and nurturers. They argued for the same privileges as the egalitarians, but the maternal feminists were not vying for women to be *the same* as men. Rather, they fought for equal worth, dignity, and rights as fellow members of the human race without forfeiting their communal identity as women. The maternal feminists foresaw the implications of egalitarian feminism. They worried that if the egalitarians had their way, women might one day lose their current privileges, like chivalry, exemption from military drafts, and separate bathrooms.

Despite their differences, these two wings of feminism still managed to work together, and their efforts resulted in the 19th Amendment giving them the right to vote. They also opened doors for women to own property, attend universities, and run businesses. The first wave was, unfortunately, the last time these two groups worked together on a significant scale. The individualistic bent of the egalitarian feminists took a dangerous turn during the second and third waves, and the feminist movement as a whole left the maternal perspective behind, choosing instead to partner with Marxist thinking.

Second-Wave Feminism

The second wave, beginning in the early 1960s, and lasting about two decades, expanded the idea of women's rights by arguing for so-called "reproductive rights" and reducing workplace inequalities. It was here that fissures within the movement began to show. Second-wave feminists consistently downplayed the unique role of women in society and instead focused on the message of self-determination and autonomy. In other words, I am my own boss and I can do what I want...including with my own body (aka "My body, my choice"). The egalitarian feminists grew increasingly radical and forged new ties with those who advocated leftist policies. But why?

Women could now vote, run for office, attend the same colleges, and get the same jobs as men, but the numbers showed that many women still preferred domestic life. This left second-wave feminists scratching their heads. Why, after being given all these freedoms, were some women *still* choosing to (gasp!) stay home, keep a house, and raise families? And if they *did* choose the career path, why were they entering fields that paid less? Their only explanation was that there *must* be some kind of oppressive system in place that was invisibly holding women back—"the patriarchy" became public enemy #1, much like capitalism was to Marx.

Second-wave activists argued that equal pay was not enough to be considered equal to men. They also required full access to birth control and abortion, a key argument that demonstrated the cultural shift toward devaluing home life. In 1963, Betty Friedan wrote a bestselling book titled *The Feminine Mystique*. Granted, she made several legitimate critiques of the 1950s housewife stereotype. But, as in most corrective movements, she swung the pendulum too far in the opposite direction, comparing the life of the average American housewife to being in a "comfortable concentration camp."[8] (As if decorating a Pinterest board with fun meal ideas is at all comparable to the Holocaust?) Friedan chastised housewives for giving in to what she saw as an artificial and oppressive stereotype. She wrote,

> Have not women who live in the image of the feminine mystique trapped themselves within the narrow walls of their homes? They have learned to "adjust" to their biological role. They have become dependent, passive, childlike; they have given up their adult frame of reference to live at the lower human level of food and things. The work they do does not

require adult capabilities; it is endless, monotonous, unrewarding…they are suffering a slow death of mind and spirit.
Just as with the prisoners in the concentration camps, there
are American women who have resisted that death, who have
managed to retain a core of self, who have not lost touch with
the outside world, who use their abilities to some creative
purpose. They are women of spirit and intelligence who have
refused to "adjust" as housewives.[9]

That's not condescending at all, is it? (We hope you detect our sar-
casm here!) Apparently growing human beings in our bodies, birthing
them, feeding them (often with our bodies), creating a warm and loving
home, and basically teaching all new humans how to be, well, human, is
monotonous and unrewarding? We like how G.K. Chesterton put it: "Ten
thousand women marched through the streets shouting, 'We will not be
dictated to,' and went off and became stenographers."[10]
    Maternal feminists of the second wave recognized this attack on tradi-
tional femininity for what it was: radical activism that sought to eliminate
gender roles in its obsession with equality. The job of these new feminists
was to awaken women out of their allegedly complacent slumber and recognize their bondage to the insidious patriarchy.[11]

Third-Wave Feminism (This Means War!)

The third wave started around the 1980s and continues to this day.[12]
Even though the first two waves were wildly successful at achieving their
goals, third-wave feminists have declared all-out war on the supposed
patriarchy. They believe only a complete transformation of society from
the ground up will free women from their oven mitts—I mean chains.
(Again, note the Marxist emphasis on total transformation.) They believe
that men—whether they realize it or not—are still part of a system of
oppression that holds women down. Never mind that women have broken into practically every male-only field, and successfully. The oppression is real, and they won't be told otherwise.

Christina Hoff Sommers notes that today the war has reached a point that the most vocal feminists no longer discuss how women can join men on equal terms. Rather, they proclaim that society must be completely overhauled so that women can be protected from a "relentless and vicious male backlash" that continues to oppress them—more Marxist rhetoric.[13] More than ever, these feminist activists attempt to use modern scientific research to further their agenda. In their zeal, they often interpret statistical data in a way that reinforces their biases, a phenomenon that Sommers chronicles on her Factual Feminist vlog.[14]

Today's third-wave feminists truly believe that once you're taught to look for systemic misogyny, you'll find it everywhere. They interpret even the slightest interaction between men and women through the lens of power differentials. (Did that guy just open a door for me? He is exerting his perceived superiority and physical dominance over me. Misogynist!)

ROAR Like a Mother!

RECOGNIZE the Message

Many of the messages coming out of modern feminism are confusing and contradictory. "Don't objectify women's bodies (and if you do, we'll go shirtless to protest it)!"[15] "Stop exploiting women (but we are going to march for sex workers' rights, and completely ignore how women are being stoned for disobeying their husbands in other parts of the world)."[16]

If you recall from the chapter on Marxism, this lack of clarity might be strategic. For brevity's sake, I (Hillary) will focus on some of the more popular and fundamental messages you'll likely hear.

1. *Girl power!*—You'll see this message on little girls' backpacks, trapper keepers, T-shirts, and more. There's nothing wrong with being proud of how God made you. It's when we raise one gender *above* the other that we start treading dangerous ground. You'll never see the term *boy power* on anything. That's called toxic masculinity, and they make pills for that these days.[17]

2. ***Stop the war on women!***—Abortion and feminism are currently so intertwined that prolife advocates are characterized as literally "waging war on women." (Ahem…linguistic theft?) Search that phrase online, and you'll come across a tsunami of articles. The commitment to abortion rights is one of the main aspects of third-wave feminism that has sidelined conservatives from the cause and made countless others uncomfortable with the movement.

3. ***Men are superfluous***—This one started in 1970 as "A woman needs a man like a fish needs a bicycle."[18] Pay attention to movies and TV shows (even kids' programming), and you'll see a constant stream of dialogue and storylines that reinforce the message of female autonomy and male incompetence.[19] Women don't need men for anything, not even to have children. The future is female!

4. ***Anything men can do, women can do better***[20]—Women are no longer trying to prove that they are as good as men, but rather that they are *better*. For an interesting take on what this is doing to our little boys' psyches, read Christina Hoff Summers' book *The War Against Boys*.[21]

OFFER Discernment

We cannot exercise discernment on this issue without first acknowledging that women have been mistreated in the past, are mistreated today, and most likely will be mistreated in the future. Not only is history teeming with examples, but our world is filled with child brides, sex slavery, female genital mutilation, women being treated as property, and sex-selective abortion. Even in our modern and supposedly enlightened West, we still deal with rape, domestic abuse, and sexual harassment, which are significantly fortified by the mass objectification and exploitation of women through pornography and prostitution.

> A victim who is desperate to be heard will overlook the flaws of a movement that is willing to listen and be angry on her behalf.

Sadly, the church is by no means an innocent party to the problem. When you get a chance, read pages 10 and 22 of the grand jury report regarding child sexual abuse in the Pennsylvania Diocese.[22] As you do so, put yourself in the place of the victims, and picture all the people who participated in the mass coverup of the events that destroyed their lives. Keep that picture in your mind when I say this next statement:

A victim who is desperate to be heard will overlook the flaws of a movement that is willing to listen and be angry on her behalf. Read that again. And again. Keep reading it until it fully sinks in. Do you see what's happening here? There are some women who have been so abused that they will align with anyone who is willing to listen to them, believe them, and share their anger no matter what. The abuse was bad enough, but the willing ignorance and cover-up that follows only does further damage.

The church is seeing only the tip of the iceberg with the Me Too movement. (And by the way, #MeToo for one of us.) Why did it take a secular movement to push the church to the point it finally recognized the need to clean their own house? There is an almost unforgivable number of stories emerging in the media of both Catholic and Protestant clergy covering up abusive leaders and allowing them to maintain positions of authority. Before we criticize modern feminism (and there is plenty to criticize!), we must first remove the massive logs from our own eyes. Denying the truth of these atrocities within the church is not the way to fight the cultural lies embedded within modern feminism. We can stand strong for the rights of women without swallowing the lies mixed in.

Second, we can be thankful for feminism's advocacy and protection of women in terms of economic opportunity. In the past, single women had limited means of providing for themselves, with some reverting to prostitution to survive. Marriage was the main way of being taken care of. But if women were getting beat up at home, tough. Too bad. You just had to sit and take it, or leave and be homeless, or maybe land yourself in an even worse situation. Yes, many women take their hard-won freedom and abuse it. But on behalf of those who have been able to escape truly violent situations, thank you, feminism.

Finally, remember our linguistic theft chapter? The word *patriarchy* has been hijacked. Historically, *patriarchy* has meant "rule of fathers." It does *not* mean "rule of men." In the Christian worldview, fathers are biblically commanded to lead, serve, and protect their families—and they are expected to do this in a way that reflects God's love and care. They are to do this with gentleness and in full dependence upon God's guidance and strength. In Bible times, there was no welfare system, Department of Education, or Department of Finance. Everything happened within the context of a family. Given that environment, there needed to be a sense of order and authority. The patriarchal structure was intended to be protective, not oppressive.

Tragically, there are men who abuse their role and exploit and mistreat women. Thus we as Christians can wholeheartedly agree with modern feminists who say this is morally wrong. This is exactly what first-wave feminism was all about. (For the purposes of this chapter, we'll use the term *patriarchy* the way modern feminists use it, but we won't like it—#TakeBackPatriarchy!)

What are some of the most common lies of contemporary feminism?

Lie #1: Our Seemingly Democratic Society Is Really About Men Controlling Women

Women who resist this message are seen by third-wave feminists as proof that the patriarchy is alive and well and highly effective at blinding women to their oppression. Alisa had a *lovely* two-day Twitter battle with a bunch of dudes mansplaining feminism to her, insisting that she recognize how oppressed she was. We almost drowned in the irony.

Lie #2: Biology Is Unfair

Rather than seeing the differences between men and women as beautiful and complimentary, things like pregnancy are seen as a disadvantage—a disease, nay, a tumor that must be removed. The ability to terminate a pregnancy supposedly levels the playing field between men and women. To this we respond that if women need surgery to be made equal to men, then that's basically an admission that we weren't born equal to men. That presumed inequality is really offensive to us as women, and yet it is women peddling this nonsense. Abortion "on demand and without apology" has become a sacred right for the modern feminist. Forget the patriarchy, we now have to fight our own bodies in order to achieve equality. But once we start denying biology, the idea of gender becomes nothing more than an oppressive social construct. *Friend, if you have to deny reality to win the fight, you've lost the fight.*

Lie #3: The Traditionally Masculine Domain Is More Important

Work outside the home is viewed as the masculine domain, and the private realm of hearth and home is viewed as feminine. The subtle message pushed on women today is that if you are a stay-at-home mom or work in a traditionally feminine job (like nursing or teaching), then you are settling for a lesser realm. Sadly, modern feminists do not see how they are degrading femininity itself by devaluing the areas in which women are often quite gifted.

Lie #4: The Right to Complete Autonomy Trumps Even the Right to Life

Nowhere in society are we guaranteed the right to do whatever we want with our bodies. Just ask anyone who has ever gotten a traffic ticket for not wearing his or her seatbelt. You'll never see feminists protesting *that*, though. Feminists fight for supposed equality at any cost—even the cost of the unborn. Recall in the chapter on moral relativism how society often picks one virtue—in this case, free will—and elevates it above all others? That's what's happening here.

Lie #5: Feminism Freed Women

This is partially true. It is very true for first-wave feminism and partially true for second-wave, which fought harassment in the workplace. As for the third wave, we believe a much stronger argument could be made that feminism freed *men* more than it did women. Women moved into the workforce, but men did not move into the kitchen in equal numbers. As a result, many women have the equivalent of two full-time jobs—one in the home, and the other outside. Women didn't win in the bedroom either. As sexual promiscuity became the norm, many men stopped feeling pressure to commit and instead live lives of extended adolescence, playing video-games and getting all the guilt-free, consequence-free sex they could ever want. *How is this better for women?*[23,24]

Lie #6: Anger Is Power

This trend within feminism is something that all three of us have noticed—and I (Hillary) have a theory. When the fight-or-flight response is activated in us, we experience a biochemical rush that mimics energy and provides hyper focus. As we learned in chapter 3, when a person is in fight-or-flight mode, he or she is less able to think rationally. Our problem today is that people are purposely whipping themselves into this frenzied state, and I think it's because they are mistaking that biological "high" for a feeling of *empowerment*. To stay empowered, one has to stay angry. I could be wrong, but this description *might* explain the caricature of "the angry feminist."

ARGUE for a Healthier Approach

We hope you can see now that feminism is a lot more complex than most people might give it credit for. So how do we help our cubs navigate through the minefield of feminist thinking?

1. ***Recognize that there is no one-size-fits-all version of feminism—*** Some women identify as feminists because they are reacting against the actual abuse of women. Other women are just straight-up man haters. Unfortunately, since these factions and more all come under

the very broad umbrella of feminism, it can be hard to separate the legit from the crazy. That's why discernment is crucial. Chew and spit, and teach your kids to do the same.

2. *Have compassion on angry feminists,* but not their ideas. If a woman feels more comfortable being in a perpetual state of fight or flight, assume that what she is avoiding is probably terrifying. Usually these women are scared, hurt, and bear emotional wounds buried deep within. It might be easy for us to mock them, but that doesn't set a good example for our kids. Demolish the ideas while loving the person.

3. *Male and female He created them*—As we raise our children, we must instill in them a biblical understanding of gender.[25] The message of equal dignity and value with regard to every human being—regardless of gender, race, religion, culture, ability, income, or developmental status—is actually a *Christian* message. The apostle Paul, in Galatians 3:28, declared, "There is neither Jew nor Gentile, neither slave nor free, *nor is there male and female,* for you are *all one* in Christ Jesus." This may not seem shocking now, but this was a revolutionary concept in the first-century Roman world.

REINFORCE Through Discussion, Discipleship, and Prayer

1. *Discuss God-given gender differences*—In fact, celebrate them! Show how these differences are complementary and often necessary. If you have boys, talk to them about how one day they will be bigger and stronger than you. How will they use their strength to protect rather than control and exploit? Talk to little girls about how they might one day be surrounded by men who are bigger and stronger than they are. How might they stand up for themselves and be strong without emasculating the men around them?

2. *Properly define "weaker vessel"*—Read 1 Peter 3:7 together. Some versions say "weaker partner" and others say "weaker vessel." Many people hear "weaker" and think that means "less than," or "feebler."

Find an object in your house that is delicate—like a plate from your great-grandmother's wedding china. Talk about how you would treat that plate differently than you would plastic plates. Ask your kids, "Does the fact the plate must be handled more carefully make it less valuable?" Use this example to explain how the word "weaker" isn't being used in a negative sense.

3. *Teach healthy gender perspectives*—One of the triggers for unhealthy feminism is illegitimate stereotyping. Reinforcing gender does not mean that we tell little girls how pretty they are and little boys how strong they are, as if girls are only as valuable as their looks, and boys are no more than their abilities. You might have a daughter who loves sports, science, and rolling in the mud, or a son who loves to dance, cook, and paint. Show your children how their masculinity and femininity fit into their God-given interests and talents, not the other way around.

4. *Healthy gender relationships begin in the home*—It is not enough to merely criticize what our culture gets wrong. We must model and embody a better way. Let our kids see us treating their fathers and our husbands with respect. Let them see what it looks like to submit to leadership without being doormats or losing our unique voice. If you have boys, ask yourself, "Is the way I treat their father the way I would want my son's wife to treat him?" If you have girls, ask yourself if the way you are treated by your husband models healthy expectations for how she should be treated by her future husband. If you are a man reading this book, show your children what it looks like to live in an understanding way with their mother, loving her as Christ loved the church.

A Final Thought

The challenge we have as moms is to elevate femininity without denigrating masculinity. God made male and female *both* in His image. Just as men and women are equal in value, we are equally touched by the Fall and in need of redemption. The cross of Christ is the great equalizer of all humankind.

We shouldn't fight for women to be identical to men because we're not. Nor should we shame men for not being more like women. They never will be. Personally, we Mama Bears like the differences between us and our husbands. Vive la différence!

Enjoy the tension, yet at the same time, remember that we're on this crazy boat ride together, passing through stormier and stormier seas as our culture grows more confused. We men and women of God owe a profound loyalty to each other despite our differences. We must labor together to keep the boat from sinking so that we may rescue as many drowning souls as possible.

PAWS for Prayer

Praise

I praise You, the Triune God—Father, Son, and Holy Spirit—for having different roles yet being equal. You are purposeful in Your design, creating us male and female in Your image and You declared us "very good" (Genesis 1:31).

Admit

Forgive us for our dissatisfaction with our God-given roles, for distorting the goodness of complementary differences. We are sorry for reducing one another to stereotypes and not honoring the unique talents and skills you have given to both men and women. More personally, forgive me when my desire for autonomy and self-determination overrides submission to Your plan for me. Father, may I not be among those who denigrate men and their masculinity; I ask for Your forgiveness and correction. Save me from the denying of biology and the gender roles You endowed us with.

Worship with Thanksgiving

I praise You, Father, that You made women and men unique, with innate differences—that You designed us like puzzle pieces that complement one another. Thank You that *feminine* does not mean "weak," and that in Your eyes, both genders have equal dignity, worth, and value. Thank You for those who, in the past, fought for the rights I enjoy today.

Supplication

Lord, help me be content in my calling and not judge other women for theirs, especially other sisters in Christ who choose to pursue different home and work situations than I. May I protect the sacredness of my home, complement and not compete with my husband, and model healthy gender relationships to my children. Help me to see the unique ways You have gifted my children so that I can encourage them in their masculinity and femininity within those gifts, talents, and interests without imposing my own ideas. You created them, not I. Protect my children from the lies being taught about gender and equip them to be secure in who they are and Whose they are. In the name of the Father, Son, and Holy Spirit. Amen.

Discussion Questions

1. **Icebreaker:** What are some of the best things about being a woman, and some of the most frustrating things?

2. **Main theme:** *Feminists have gone from addressing legitimate grievances to being grievance collectors. Ultimately, men and women are created with equal worth and dignity in the image of God.* Do you think Christians should call themselves feminists? Why or why not?

3. **Self-evaluation:** Let's consider another spectrum. On a sheet of paper, draw a line. Label one end "Doormat Doris," and the other "Manhater Molly." Where do you think you fall on the spectrum, and why?

4. **Brainstorm:** Compile a list of as many positive effects of feminism that you can think of. Now do the same with negative effects. How can we stand up for a biblical femininity without affirming the lies in modern feminism?

5. **Release the bear:** Read Sue Bohlin's article *Raising Gender Healthy Kids* (see endnote 25 on page 287). Pick one way that you can encourage your child within his or her gender and within his or her talents and skill sets.

Chapter 15

Christianity Needs a Makeover
Progressive Christianity

ALISA CHILDERS

When I was a kid, our family had a tradition of going to a local pizzeria to binge on pizza, soda, and arcade-style video games. I loved the food and games, but what I looked forward to most was the self-serve soda dispenser. I would grab a cup and gleefully go down the line putting in a little bit of every soda option. A little bit of Coca-Cola. A little bit of Dr. Pepper. A little bit of Sunkist Orange soda. Fanta Grape. Sprite. By the end of the line, I had created an entirely new concoction that had an odd color and an even odder taste. And. I. Loved it.

It wasn't the taste that I loved so much, although it wasn't bad. It was the sense of *independence* I got from doing something different—something that deviated from the norm. I suppose at twelve or thirteen years old, that was about as rebellious as this well-behaved church girl was willing to get.

Now imagine that all the "isms" you've read about so far in this book are options in a soda dispenser. Grab a cup labeled "Christian," go down the line and put in a little bit of everything. A little bit of new spirituality, pluralism, self-helpism, feminism, Marxism, relativism, naturalism, skepticism, postmodernism, and emotionalism. What new libation will you have created? You will be quenching your spiritual thirst with an effervescent fusion of ideas called—progressive Christianity. But be warned: *This* mixture isn't harmless like the one I made at the pizza joint. These ideas have life-and-death consequences. This is a lesson I would eventually learn the hard way.

When progressive Christianity first came into full bloom in the late 2000s, I was married with a new baby in tow. The influx of all these new teachings flew past my radar because my days were spent nursing, changing diapers, and making baby food. Nights were spent sleeplessly attending to a sweet yet fussy little girl who never seemed to want to rest. Whatever intellectual energy I had left over was spent researching the latest nipple cream, cloth diapers, and organic mattress options. I was exhausted. Put simply, I wasn't contemplating the deep theological complexities of my Christianity—I was just trying to survive.

When our pastor invited me to be a part of a small and exclusive ministry training study class at the nondenominational church our family attended, it sounded like the perfect escape from my everyday routines— a chance to engage my intellectual side, which, let's be honest, was seriously starving. You can imagine my excitement when I left the baby with grandma and headed off to the first class.

I eagerly found my seat and waited for the meeting to start. The pastor opened by saying, "You are all here because in some way, you are peculiar." (Who me?) He explained to the dozen or so of us that we were all out-of-the-box thinkers, and that the class would be an opportunity for us to work through our questions and re-examine the theological paradigms that had defined what we believed about Christianity. Then, in an effort to squash any notion we might have that he had everything figured out, he announced, "I like to call myself a hopeful agnostic." A class that brought ancient Christian beliefs and doctrines into question led by an agnostic pastor—what could possibly go wrong?

Little did I know at the same time there were groups, classes, meetings, online forums, and conversations happening all over the country flooded with people questioning historic Christian beliefs such as the atonement, the exclusivity of Christianity, the authority of the Bible, the literal resurrection of Jesus, the nature of sin, the definition of heaven, and the reality of hell. With the explosion of social media and a few brave souls willing to take these new ideas public, these seekers found each other, "deconstructed" together (remember that from the chapter on postmodernism?) and united together. Thus a new movement was born: progressive Christianity.

The group I was a part of went on to question everything I had ever believed about God, Jesus, and the Bible. It rocked me to my core. It sent me into a time of doubt that felt like I had been thrown into a stormy ocean with no lifejacket or lifeboat in sight. I am so thankful that God walked me through it, His sovereign hand evident at every turn. As a result of this theological upheaval, I discovered apologetics and a deep, robust intellectual faith. As far as I know, I am the only soul in that class who came out with his or her faith intact. The rest went on to identify, along with the church itself, as a progressive Christian community.

A Brief History of Progressive Christianity

The participants in that class thought they had found something new, but in reality, all they had done was dust off old ideologies. Finding its roots in the "isms" we've looked at already, progressive Christianity echoes the unbiblical ways of thinking that began creeping into mainline Christian denominations in the early twentieth century. During that time, there was a growing tension between Christians committed to biblical thinking and the challenges brought about by Darwinian evolution and German higher criticism, both of which called traditional understandings of the Bible into question. Christians who held firmly to key Bible teachings began retreating from mainline denominations and forming their own churches and schools, leaving Christian ideas isolated from the rest of the world. Christianity was at a crossroads.

Once again we find ourselves at a crossroads. Will historic Christian doctrines survive the skepticism of naturalism and scientism? Will it out-live the subjective experiences of postmodernism, relativism, self-helpism, and emotionalism? Will it stand up against the ideologies of Marxism, feminism, and the new spirituality? I have some good news: The gospel has already survived all of these systems of thought, and it will survive pro-gressive Christianity.

ROAR Like a Mother!

RECOGNIZE the Message

What do progressive Christians believe? Unlike historic Christianity, there are no creeds or official belief statements that outline a common and unifying set of doctrines. In fact, nothing will send progressives running faster than the dreaded "sin of certainty" which creeds tend to encourage.[1]

Progressive Christians David Felten and Jeff Procter-Murphy candidly admit this in their comprehensive survey of progressive Christianity:

> Traditional understandings of Christology, Atonement, and the Incarnation are all in flux. In fact, many people find these concepts to be irrelevant to contemporary spirituality. Yet thinking theologically creates a disequilibrium that makes us continually rethink our beliefs in light of our changing understanding and ongoing experiences.[2]

But in abandoning the essential doctrines of the faith, this rethinking will inevitably result in a religion that has its own dogmas—only these dogmas will be fashioned according to the whims of culture and personal preference. The new sacred cow is...no sacred cows.

J. Gresham Machen, a Christian theologian writing against the lib-eralism of the early twentieth century, recognized this contradiction. He wrote, "There are doctrines of modern liberalism, just as tenaciously and intolerantly upheld as any doctrines that find a place in the historic creeds...in seeming to object to all theology, the liberal preacher is often merely objecting to one system of theology in the interests of another."[3]

So what are some of these tenaciously held doctrines of progressive Christianity? There are five key beliefs:

1. A rejection of the exclusivity of Christianity (that Jesus is the only way to God)

For example, in his 2016 "Everything Is Spiritual" tour, Rob Bell gave a lecture in which he described God in terms of an "energy" and "force" that connects all things.[4] When he got to the Jesus part of his story, he declared that when the apostles referred to "the Christ," they were referring to "a universal animating energy that holds the whole universe together." Here, Rob loosely referenced Colossians 1:17: "He existed before anything else, and he holds all creation together." Rob described this as "Christ consciousness" (remember that from the New Spirituality chapter?).

2. A rejection of the atoning blood sacrifice of Jesus on the cross

In the Rob Bell lecture cited above, the only reference to the blood atonement of Jesus was his explanation of the Eucharist (communion for Protestants). He explained that the defining characteristic of eating the bread and wine was to invite all people to "realize that there is this common humanity we share that trumps any of the ways we have cooked up to divide ourselves." So the Last Supper was really more of a small dinner party Jesus hosted in the hopes of motivating people to get along?

Bell even mockingly quipped that the 2,000-year-old Christian doctrine of atonement could be summed up in seven words: "God is less grumpy because of Jesus." Everyone in the audience had a good chuckle as Bell went on to explain *that* isn't what it's about. We pass the bread and wine specifically to "heighten our senses to our bonds with our brothers and sisters in our shared humanity." There was no mention of Jesus's blood, sin, sacrifice, or salvation.

In his final "benediction," Bell exhorted the crowd, "May you line yourself up with the fundamental energies of the universe which always move forward and beyond in love, complexity, depth, and unity."

In a blog post about how to talk to kids about Easter, a progressive Christian children's pastor wrote that telling kids Jesus died for their sins could be "psychologically damaging."[5] She went on to say that Jesus didn't specifically die for people. Rather, He died because He was a political and religious threat to those in power. Removing the notion of sin from the vocabulary sends the message that we are just fine all by ourselves—that we don't need to be saved from our sin.

3. A lowered view of Scripture

Historically, Christians have viewed the Bible as inspired by God and authoritative for their lives. However, many Christians are abandoning biblical authority and turning to their own thoughts, feelings, and instincts as the final sources of truth. But make no mistake: If we evict the one true God from our throne of worship, we will replace Him with ourselves. If we are the final source for "our truth," we can easily make God into our own image instead of the other way around.

Speaking of making God into our own image, progressive leader Brian McLaren suggests that Christians should change the way they read the Bible. Instead of reading it as an authoritative source for truth, he recommends it be read as an "inspired library" that preserves the best attempts of our (apparently less enlightened) spiritual ancestors to understand God in their own cultures and times. He compares Scripture with fossils to be dusted off and observed, rather than a revelation from God that we are to obey. In other words, as we grow and become more enlightened, we can look back on what the biblical writers communicated, and understand better what they believed about God, even if what they wrote about Him wasn't completely accurate.[6]

David Felton and Jeff Procter-Murphy put it like this: "The Bible is the witness of generations of faithful people recording their own understandings of the divine in their particular time, place, and culture. This theological pluralism reveals changing, developing, and sometimes conflicting ideas about God."[7] This is just a Christianized version of the "live your truth" message.

4. A redefining of words (linguistic theft)

Progressives often engage in linguistic theft when talking about historic Christian doctrines. For example, when I told my agnostic pastor that I was uncomfortable with where some of our class discussions were heading, he encouraged me to ask him any question I had. He promised to answer honestly and said that no inquiry was off limits. I asked, "Do you believe in hell?" and "Do you believe the Bible is divinely inspired?" He answered unequivocally yes to both. That put me at ease enough to continue in the class, although I was very confused as to how he could believe the Bible was divinely inspired yet question its truthfulness.

A few months later, I came to discover what he meant by "divinely inspired." He believed the Bible was inspired much like the writings of C.S. Lewis or A.W. Tozer, but not in any special kind of way. And hell? He meant it in a figurative sense—as in living out the negative consequences of bad choices we make here on earth.

5. A focus on social justice

As we've learned earlier in the book, doing true biblical justice is good. Jesus came to save the outcasts. In Mark 2:17, He said, "Those who are healthy don't need a physician, but those who are sick do. I have not come to call the righteous, but sinners."

All Christians recognize the need to reach the outcasts—to bring love and justice to the oppressed and to accept people just as they are. Progressive Christians, however, have elevated social justice, confusing it for the gospel. Popular progressive blogger, author, and pastor John Pavlovitz plainly admits this. In his blog post defining progressive Christianity, he wrote, "We believe that social justice is the heart of the Gospel."[8]

Love and justice are biblical concepts and attributes of God—as long as we defer to the biblical definitions of those words. But *social justice* is a cultural term that carries a lot of baggage. Aristotle defined justice as giving each person what was due to him or her. Today, however, this term tends to be applied to whatever is the liberal cause du jour. Progressive Christians have adopted the cultural definition of social justice and retrofitted it to reinterpret Jesus's teachings. But in reality, Jesus never affirmed sinful *behaviors*. He affirmed *people*, who were invited to repent, take up their cross, and follow Him.

Without a biblical definition of justice, social justice becomes an entirely subjective and culturally adapted term. This is why so many progressive Christians are fighting for the acceptance of LGBTQ behavior, modern feminism, and abortion—all in the name of Christ.

OFFER Discernment

When progressive Christians first came on the scene, they offered some critiques of evangelical Christian culture that were valid and sorely needed. They recognized the hypocrisy of condemning homosexuality while winking at the sin of gluttony. They acknowledged spiritual abuses and the damaging effects of legalism. They rightly pointed out that we shouldn't be afraid to ask questions and think hard about what we believe and why. This is what makes progressive Christianity so attractive to so many people—it appears to provide a safe place to process these concerns.

However, instead of staying within the bounds of orthodox Christianity and bringing reform from within, progressives set their aim on the actual doctrines of Christianity rather than the abuses committed by Christians. Doctrine doesn't abuse people; people abuse people. Instead of identifying how people have taken the truths of Christ and used them to beat others over the head, progressives have called the essential doctrines of the faith into question. To them, everything is fair game. Nothing is off the table.

I once met a woman who had been horribly abused by her father. As a child, he demeaned her constantly and was quick to fly into a rage at even the smallest misstep she committed. She told me that thinking about God's acceptance of Jesus's sacrifice on the cross made her feel confused and uncomfortable. How could a loving Father require that His own Son shed His blood? She related her own father's sinful anger and abuse with the perfect love and justice of God, and I certainly understood where she was coming from. Thankfully, she chose to struggle through that tension and not abandon a belief in the atoning work of Jesus on the cross. But for many progressive Christians, this isn't the case.

Many have left historic Christianity due to abusive experiences in hyperfundamentalist churches. Others have left due to hypocrisy and lack of character in their church leaders. Others have found biblical morality to be too demanding or difficult. These reasons for departing the faith are understandable, but it's important to recognize that we can't judge a belief system based on the abuses of some, and we can't abandon objective truth because it appears too difficult to follow or seems to ask too much of us.

ARGUE for a Healthier Approach

As Christians, how can we avoid extremes and develop a biblical and healthy faith? First, we need to be aware of the swinging pendulum.

At some point, we have all walked into an office and seen what's called a Newton's cradle. At the top are two thin metal rods parallel to each other. From them are suspended five steel balls. When you pull of one of the outside balls outward then let it go, it collides into the next ball, which creates momentum that sends the outside ball on the *opposite* end swinging outward, while the three balls in the middle stay relatively still. Then the outside ball swings down again and collides into the three middle balls, sending the outside ball on the opposite end outward. The outside balls continue to swing back and forth for quite a while, leaving the middle three balls fairly motionless.

If we imagine progressive Christianity as being one outside ball and hyperfundamentalism as being the opposite outside ball, we have a perfect picture of what can happen when people react to extreme ideas with opposite extreme ideas. Those two extremes will go on colliding and swinging endlessly as the three balls in the middle continue to stay still, absorbing the impact.

The lesson we can learn from this is that we have all kinds of information crashing into us, but it doesn't have to send us swinging. This is why we have the Word of God. It is vital that we adhere to the doctrine of biblical authority (that the Bible has final say when it comes to the issues relating to our faith) if we want to have a healthy Christian life. Believing in Scripture's authority is the only way to assure that your worldview is in line with reality. In his book *Unbreakable*, Andrew Wilson put it this way: "Many of us, when faced with a biblical difficulty—and there are plenty of those!—conclude that the Scriptures are broken…But if the Scriptures are the unbreakable word of God, as Jesus seems to have thought they were, then a different approach is needed…Maybe I'm the one who is broken, rather than the Bible."[9]

This is the key difference between progressive Christianity and historic Christianity. Through the ages, Christians have sought to submit their lives to the teachings of the Bible. Progressive Christians, however, see the Bible as a helpful resource but subject it to their own opinions and preferences.

Holding firmly to the doctrine of biblical authority will ensure that we are the *middle* ball in Newton's cradle. In the storm between progressive Christianity and hyperfundamentalism, we can remain steadfast in the truth—crashed, bashed, and bumped, but ultimately undisturbed.

REINFORCE by Discussion, Discipleship, and Prayer

At the beginning of my talk titled "Almost the Real Thing: How Progressive Christianity Is Hijacking the Gospel," I show the audience a picture of my daughter on the big screen. At the end of the talk, I try to help the audience learn how to spot progressive Christian ideas in books, blog posts, and social media content. I explain that the best way we can equip ourselves to recognize these wrong ideas is to know the real thing. To drive this point home, I show another picture of my daughter. Only this time, unbeknownst to the audience, it's *not* a picture of my daughter. Rather, it's a picture of a little girl who looks like my daughter. She is the same age, she has the same wavy brown hair, brown eyes, creamy skin, and perky smile. The audience usually oohs and ahhs about how cute she is until I drop the bomb: "This is not my daughter. But you didn't realize that because you don't know my daughter. But I know her, and no one would ever fool me into thinking this is her." I go on to explain that the best way to spot counterfeit Christianity in any form is to know the real thing.

We can *teach* our kids about doctrine, church history, apologetics, and warn them about all the "isms" in this book until we're blue in the face (and we should!). But they will actually *learn* what we ourselves *embody*. Are we, as moms, loving the people around us as we engage them in conversations about faith? Are we modeling an authentic faith outside of church on Sunday mornings? Are we taking care of the poor and standing up for the abused? Are we living out the teachings of the Bible with love and grace?

When I was in the class that challenged my beliefs, one of the main reasons I was able to endure was because of the genuine faith my parents had modeled for me and my three sisters. They were not perfect, but they prayed with us, read the Bible with us, repented in front of us, and put their faith in action in many ways, including caring for the homeless and less fortunate. Loving Jesus was what their whole life was about. They didn't give me a tepid, shallow, fake Christianity to rebel against. It was the real thing.

This stood in stark contrast to almost everyone else in the class. Some had been raised in loveless, legalistic churches. Others grew up in the midst of spiritual abuse. Still others had only known Christians to be artificial and hypocritical. They didn't know the real thing, which made them vulnerable to *almost* the real thing.

Progressive Christianity is just that—almost the real thing. The best and most convincing lies are packaged in truth, and there is enough truth in progressive Christianity to make it attractive and persuasive to the undiscerning believer. But the path it can lead to is another "ism" we talked about in the skepticism chapter: atheism.

How do we get from progressive Christianity to atheism? Isn't that a bit of a leap? Former progressive Christian and now secular humanist Bart Campolo doesn't think so. Son of the famous Christian (now progressive) teacher and author Tony Campolo, Bart began abandoning historic

Christian doctrines when he couldn't reconcile them with the poverty and suffering he encountered in urban ministry. After his faith began unraveling, he said that his belief in God "died the death of a thousand unanswered prayers."[10]

Campolo believes that the transition from historic Christian to progressive Christian naturally leads to full-blown atheism. This makes perfect sense considering the fact that most progressive objections to Christian doctrines mirror the objections voiced by atheists and agnostics. Campolo notes that letting go of historic teachings on hell, God's sovereignty, biblical authority and inspiration, and sexuality is addictive—and once you start, you can't stop.

This is a sober reminder to us as moms that we need to teach our kids to not let their hardships, sufferings, or perceived unanswered prayers dictate their theology. What we believe about God should be informed by the Bible, not our feelings, perceptions, and experiences. In fact, in our times of trial and tears, it is comforting to know that historic Christianity is true—whether or not we feel like it's "working."

As individuals, we might progress in our understanding of God's truth and His ways, but God Himself and His truth never change. God has revealed Himself in Scripture as He was, is, and forever will be. Christianity is not progressive; it's eternal.

PAWS for Prayer

Praise

God of history and time, You alone are the one true God—the real thing. You are the author of history as well as its creator and sustainer. You have given us sound doctrine. Your ways, Word, statutes, and laws are perfect. They do not change, nor do they need changing. There is no shadow of turning with Thee. You do not change on my whim. Great is Your faithfulness, Lord, unto me.

Admit

Forgive me, my family, and others for any spirit of rebellion that prefers Your Word done our way. Help us to be diligent about discerning heresy. Forgive those who "will not tolerate sound doctrine and accurate instruction that challenges them with God's truth," but who want "to have their ears tickled with something pleasing," who "accumulate for themselves many teachers…chosen to satisfy their own desires and to support the errors they hold" (2 Timothy 4:3 AMP). Forgive us for looking to self as a source of truth and trying to improve on Your ways.

Worship with Thanksgiving

Father God, I thank You that we have an intellectual faith with historical veracity and proven principles. I am in awe of the way that Christian values have been a force for good in the world. Thank You for the atonement, the authority of the Bible, the gift and promise of heaven. Thank You for the creeds and doctrines that have encapsulated and preserved through the centuries the orthodox tenets of the faith. Because of Your unchanging nature and perfect work, nothing new is needed with regard to Your precepts, promises, and principles.

Supplication

Lord, instill in me and Your church a high view of Scripture. Help me teach my children to examine ideas and teachings and understand terms correctly and not be deceived by slick-sounding lies. Help me teach my children to hold to biblical rather than cultural definitions. May my children never align their Bible to their thinking, but rather, align their thinking to Your Word. Give us insight to recognize the convincing lies and near-truths that are touted as Christian. Protect my children from starting on a path that would take them on the slow descent to atheism. And in the unchanging name of Jesus, don't let our feelings or experiences dictate our theology.

In the name of the eternal God, amen.

Discussion Questions

1. **Icebreaker:** When you were a kid, did you ever create a soda concoction like the one Alisa described? Why did you like it? Was it the taste or the freedom?

2. **Main theme:** *People are changing historic Christian doctrines to accommodate the times.* Do you think the Bible is out of step with society? Do you think adherence to societal norms is the test of truth? Why or why not?

3. **Self-evaluation:** Do you find yourself drawn to progressive Christianity or repulsed by it? How strong is your reaction? Why do you think you react the way you do? In what ways can you be discerning about what you read and listen to?

4. **Brainstorm:** Where have you seen these ideas in books, conferences, or devotionals? Why do you think the message of progressive Christianity is so attractive? Can you think of specific examples of progressive Christian thinking that you've read or heard?

5. **Release the bear:** If you find yourself conversing with a person (or your kids) who have been influenced by progressive Christian thinking, ask him or her, "How did you come to your conclusions?" Keep in mind all the "isms" you've learned. Do they believe truth is relative (postmodernism)? Is he or she skeptical of miracles (naturalism)? Does he or she say that the truths in the Bible are too harsh (emotionalism)?

Chapter 16

How to Take All This Information and #RoarLikeAMother

You did it—you made it to the end! By now you may be scratching your head and saying, "Okay, that was a lot for me to learn. Where do I go from here?" Here are some tips from each of our Mama Bears regarding how you can take the information you just read and #RoarLikeAMother!

Hillary Morgan Ferrer

Many apologetics books deal with specific questions and answers, or provide historical evidence for what we believe. This book is more foundational. My main advice for you is to gain a clear understanding of each "ism" so that you can start recognizing which ones are at play when they surface around you. How is naturalism affecting your children's questions about science? Is postmodernism affecting their ability to believe that truth exists or is knowable? Is a hyperskepticism preventing them from accepting answers because they expect absolute certainty?

For Mama Bears with older kids, I hope this book helps you understand *where* your kids' questions are coming from—that is, where is their foundation cracking? For those with younger kids, I hope this book helps you build your children's foundations strong, so that when they encounter the tough questions, they will recognize a faulty premise from the start. Christianity, though it prompts tough questions, has even tougher answers, and the foundation on which we build our answers is firm.

Julie Loos

Mama Bears, you have taken your first step toward teaching yourself and training your children to love God with their minds. Bravo! No matter what age your kids (or grandkids) are, it is never too late to start. Neither is it ever too early. And do not underestimate the value of prayer in this endeavor; our battle is spiritual. We can labor in the natural realm through apologetics, and in the spiritual realm through prayer. As Francis Schaeffer said in his book *The God Who Is There*, "It is important to remember, first of all, that we cannot separate true apologetics from the work of the Holy Spirit, nor from a living relationship in prayer to the Lord on the part of the Christian. We must understand that eventually the battle is not just against flesh and blood."[1] Finally, we Mama Bears must remember that when it comes to our cubs, our best apologetic is our life. (Nod to William Lane Craig on that thought.)

Hillary Short

If this is your first taste of Christian apologetics, you may find yourself feeling overwhelmed. Don't let unfamiliar terms and ideas intimidate you—with a willingness to learn, you are on the path to becoming equipped to help your kids (and yourself) recognize error and respond to it. Too many people shut the door to growing in biblical knowledge and wisdom because they think that knowing it *all* is a requirement for being effective. That's not true. I shudder to think where my view of and relationship with Christ and life's biggest questions would be had I never been introduced to apologetics and taken the time to learn about the robust academic and historic fortitude of the Christian faith (thank you, Howard!). Push forward. Become comfortable with looking things up and asking questions (because it never ends). And don't look back.

Teasi Cannon

My biggest encouragement is that you be kind and gracious to yourself as you digest all the information you've just read. This may have been the first time you've heard some of the terms in this book or to think more deeply about the issues we've addressed, and that's totally okay! Instead of beating yourself up over what you don't know (something I'm prone to do if I'm not on guard), be encouraged that you are *learning*. You are choosing to love God with your mind, which isn't always easy. Not everyone is willing to do the hard mental work that you've just done. (Kudos!) Every single one of us starts by learning one new concept that leads to another, and so on. Some learn faster than others, some retain more than others, and some are just plain brainiacs (definitely *not* me). But remember, this isn't a competition. It's a journey, and we're all in this together.

Rebekah Valerius

Remember that all the "isms" you have learned in this book—though seemingly powerful—are ultimately powerless against Him who has been raised from the grave. Our Lord has already overcome the world, and that includes naturalism, skepticism, feminism, postmodernism, etc. Take heart, Mama Bear, and be encouraged. I'll leave you with some wise words from one of my favorite books: "Some believe it is only great power that can hold evil in check, but that is not what I have found. It is the small everyday deeds of ordinary folk that keep the darkness at bay. Small acts of kindness and love" (from *The Lord of the Rings* by J.R.R. Tolkien).

Cathryn Buse

Thank you, Mama Bears, for taking the time to read this book. It means that you want to prepare your children for engaging in the overwhelming world of ideas. I applaud you for wanting to show your kids that the Christian faith described in Hebrews 11:1 is not blind faith. It is a faith that is unafraid of questions because it stands on a solid foundation of truth.

Don't worry if you don't have all the answers—just welcome the inquiries! Allow your children to ask questions, and then dig in with them to find the answers. Doing this will show them we are never too old to learn, and that we are to continue to grow in our faith and knowledge of God. Remember, God made biology, chemistry, physics, geology, time, space, matter, and everything else. We don't need to be afraid to look for Him in any of those disciplines. We don't have to be afraid of trying to answer those tough questions that the world throws at us—and at our children. "Be strong and courageous. Do not be afraid; do not be discouraged, for the LORD your God will be with you wherever you go" (Joshua 1:9).

Alisa Childers

I'll never forget that class in which my Christian faith was challenged by an agnostic pastor. I sat there wondering, *Why didn't anyone prepare me for this?* I want to congratulate you for taking the time and intellectual energy to read this book. You have just done your kids a huge favor and taken necessary steps toward preparing them to handle everything from a college evolutionary biology class to an atheist philosophy professor to an agnostic pastor. Remember the story from chapter 2 about the mama bear hoisting her grown adult daughter back into the raft? If you've read this book, that's you! High five. I want to encourage you to keep learning. Even though the amount of information to learn can seem overwhelming at times, I'm always amazed at how God takes the one thing I studied last week to help answer a question from a friend or loved one this week. Take advantage of the incredible resources we've listed in the recommended reading list on page 271 so you can continue this journey. As Hillary F. always says, "We're all in this together."

Reading Resources
for Each Chapter

Chapter 1: Calling All Mama Bears

Cultural Captives: The Beliefs and Behavior of American Young Adults—Stephen Cable

The Jesus Survey: What Christian Teens Really Believe and Why—Mike Nappa

Meet Generation Z: Understanding and Reaching the New Post-Christian World—James Emery White

Chapter 2: How to be a Mama Bear

Tactics: A Game Plan for Discussing Your Christian Convictions—Greg Koukl

Talking with Your Kids About God: 30 Conversations Every Christian Parent Must Have—Natasha Crain

Chapter 3: The Discerning Mama Bear

The Discipline of Spiritual Discernment—Tim Challies

Chapter 4: Linguistic Theft

The Fallacy Detective: Thirty-Eight Lessons on How to Recognize Bad Reasoning—Nathaniel Bluedorn and Hans Bluedorn

Chapter 5: Self-Helpism

The Grand Weaver: How God Shapes Us Through the Events of Our Lives—Ravi Zacharias

Chapter 6: Naturalism

Darwin's House of Cards: A Journalist's Odyssey Through the Darwin Debates—Tom Bethell

Science and the Mind of the Maker: What the Conversation Between Faith and Science Reveals About God—Melissa Cain Travis

Chapter 7: Skepticism

Atheism's New Clothes: Exploring and Exposing the Claims of the New Atheists—David Glass

True Reason: Confronting the Irrationality of the New Atheism—Tom Gilson and Carson Weitnauer

Chapters 8, 9 and 10: Postmodernism, Moral Relativism, and Emotionalism

Not a Day Care: The Devastating Consequences of Abandoning Truth— Dr. Everett Piper

How Now Shall We Live?—Charles Colson with Nancy Pearcey

Relativism: Feet Firmly Planted in Mid-Air—Francis Beckwith and Gregory Koukl

True for You, But Not for Me: Overcoming Objections to Christian Faith—Paul Copan

Saving Truth: Finding Meaning and Clarity in a Post-Truth World— Abdu Murray

Chapter 11: Pluralism

God Among Sages: Why Jesus Is Not Just Another Religious Leader— Kenneth Richard Samples

Understanding the Times: A Survey of Competing Worldviews—Jeff Myers and David Noebel (includes sections on Marxism)

Teaching Others to Defend Christianity: What Every Christian Should Know—Cathryn Buse

Chapter 12: New Spirituality

Why Jesus? Rediscovering His Truth in an Age of Mass Marketed Spirituality—Ravi Zacharias

Spellbound: The Paranormal Seduction of Today's Kids—Marcia Montenegro

"O" God: A Dialogue on Truth and Oprah's Spirituality—Josh McDowell and Dave Sterrett

Chapter 13: Marxism

Rules for Radicals: A Practical Primer for Realistic Radicals—Saul D. Alinsky (basically a Marxist how-to manual)

Marxism 1844–1990: Origins, Betrayal, Rebirth—Roger S. Gottlieb (great explanation of Marxism, but from a pro-Marxist, non-Christian perspective)

"Understanding Critical Theory and Christian Apologetics"—Neil Shenvi and Patrick Sawyer, *Ratio Christi: Campus Apologetics Alliance*, https://ratiochristi.org/blog/post/understanding-critical-theory -and-christian-apologetics/6371?fbclid=IwAR3CqEnl8IKsFx7AxrKL GISNbNd10CR_F8Npb161hV4aUli8QbWyTEP0zGU#

"Christianity and Social Justice"—Neil Shenvi, *Neil Shenvi— Apologetics*, https://shenviapologetics.wordpress.com/ christianity-and-social-justice/

Chapter 14: Feminism

The War Against Boys: How Misguided Policies Are Harming Our Young Men—Christina Hoff Sommers

Who Stole Feminism? How Women Have Betrayed Women—Christina Hoff Sommers

Chapter 15: Progressive Christianity

Distortion: How the New Christian Left Is Twisting the Gospel and Damaging the Faith—Chelsen Vicari

Prayer:

Moms in Prayer: Standing in the Gap for Your Children—Fern Nichols

Notes

Chapter 1—Rise Up, Mama Bears

1. Ronald Tiersky, "Whose God Is the One True God?" *Huffington Post* (July 24, 2014; updated September 23, 2014), https://www.huffingtonpost.com/ronald-tiersky/whose-god-is-the-one-true_b_5618066.

2. A Lifeway study reported that while 60% leave, around two-thirds of those finally return. That sounds encouraging until you do the math and realize that still means we are losing 45% of our youth *for good* every generation. When you get to numbers that high, you start seeing exponential loss because those 45% are now raising their own kids, and those kids are interacting with *your* kids. See Lifeway Research, "Reasons 18-22 Year Olds Drop Out of Church," *Lifeway Research* (August 7, 2007), https://lifewayresearch.com/2007/08/07/reasons-18-to-22-year-olds-drop-out-of-church/.

3. David Kinnaman, *You Lost Me: Why Young Christians Are Leaving Church…and Rethinking Faith* (Grand Rapids, MI: Baker, 2011), 23.

4. Alexander W. Astin, Helen S. Astin, and Jennifer A. Lindholm, *Cultivating the Spirit: How College Can Enhance Students' Inner Lives* (San Francisco, CA: Jossey-Bass, 2011), 89.

5. Barna study, "Most Twentysomethings Put Christianity on the Shelf Following Spiritually Active Teen Years," *Barna* (September 11, 2006), https://www.barna.com/research/most-twentysomethings-put-christianity-on-the-shelf-following-spiritually-active-teen-years/.

6. T.C. Pinckney, "We Are Losing Our Children: Remarks to the Southern Baptist Convention Executive Committee," *Alliance for the Separation of School and State* (September 18, 2001), http://www.schoolandstate.org/SBC/Pinckney-WeAreLosingOurChildren.htm.

7. Pew Research Center, "Choosing a New Church or House of Worship," *Pew Research Center* (August 23, 2016), http://www.pewforum.org/2016/08/23/choosing-a-new-church-or-house-of-worship/.

8. Christian Smith and Melinda Lundquist Denton, *Soul Searching: The Religious and Spiritual Lives of American Teenagers* (New York: Oxford, 2005), 133, 162-163.

9. Lifeway Research, *2016 State of American Theology Study: Research Report*, commissioned by Ligonier Ministries, *The State of Theology*, https://thestateoftheology.com/assets/downloads/2016-state-of-america-white-paper.pdf.

10. Mike Nappa, *The Jesus Survey* (Grand Rapids, MI: Baker, 2012), 60.

11. Josh McDowell and David H. Bellis, *The Last Christian Generation* (Holiday, FL: Green Key, 2006), 15.

12. Nappa, *The Jesus Survey*, 15.

13. Nappa, *The Jesus Survey*, 81.

14. Nappa, *The Jesus Survey*, 117.

15. Barna Group, "Six Megathemes Emerge from Barna Group Research in 2010, " *Barna*, (December 13, 2010), https://www.barna.com/research/six-mega themes-emerge-from-barna-group-research-in-2010.

16. Nappa, *The Jesus Survey*, 10.

17. Nappa, *The Jesus Survey*, 11.

18. Barry A. Kosmin and Juhem Navarro-Rivera, *The Transformation of Generation X: Shifts in Religious and Political Self-Identification, 1990–2008* (Hartford, CT: Trinity College, May 22, 2012), 17, http://commons.trincoll.edu/aris/files/2012/09/GENX report2012_05_22.pdf.

19. Lifeway, "Reasons 18-22 Year Olds Drop Out of Church," 2007.

20. Stephen Cable, *Cultural Captives—the Beliefs and Behavior of American Young Adults* (Plano, TX: Probe Ministries, 2012), 7.

21. Pew Research, "US Public Becoming Less Religious," *Pew Research Center* (November 3, 2015), https://www.pewforum.org/2015//11/03/u-s-public-becoming-less-religious/.

22. James Emery White, *Meet Generation Z—Understanding and Reaching the New Post-Christian World* (Grand Rapids, MI: Baker, 2017), 49.

23. Ken Ham, Britt Beemer, and Todd Hillard, *Already Gone—Why Your Kids Will Quit Church and What You Can Do to Stop It* (Green Forest, AR: Master Books, 2009), 38, 41.

24. Frank Turek, "The Seeker Church: Is Anyone Making Disciples?" *CrossExamined.org*, https://crossexamined.org/church-beliefs/#toggle-id-1. Emphasis added.

25. Ed Stetzer, "Why Many Young Adults Quit," *CT Pastors*, Fall 2007, https://www.christi anitytoday.com/pastors/2007/fall/10.15.html.

26. Cable, *Cultural Captives*, 78.

27. Cable, *Cultural Captives*, 78.

28. Ham, Beemer, and Hillard, *Already Gone*, 31,32.

29. National Association of Evangelicals, "When Americans Become Christians," *National Association of Evangelicals* (Spring 2015), https://www.nae.net/when-americans-become-christians.

30. Jen Oshman, "Worldview Is Formed by Age 13: Who's Shaping Your Kids?," *The Oshman Odyssey* (July 25, 2017), https://www.oshmanodyssey.com/jensblog/n6pb5opplj5kaql2ihl4gahklx7ocl.

Chapter 2—How to Be a Mama Bear

1. Melanie Shankle, *Sparkly Green Earrings: Catching the Light at Every Turn* (Carol Stream, IL: Tyndale, 2013), 175-176.

2. Michael Shermer, "The Number of Americans with No Religious Affiliation Is Rising: The Rise of the Atheists," *Scientific American* (April 1, 2018), www.scientificamerican .com/article/the-number-of-americans-with-no-religious-affiliation-is-rising/.

3. Natasha Crain, *Talking With Your Kids About God: 30 Conversations Every Christian Parent Must Have* (Grand Rapids, MI: Baker, 2017), 87-88.

4. Martin D. Tullai, "Theodore Roosevelt: A Man for All Ages," *World and I* (April 1998), 327.

5. Thomas S. Mayhinney and Laura L. Sagan, "The Power of Personal Relationships," *Kaleidoscope: Contemporary and Classic Readings in Education,* eds. Kevin Ryan and James M. Cooper (Belmont, CA: Wadsworth, 2009), 16.

Chapter 3—The Discerning Mama Bear

1. 2 Samuel 12.

2. James 1:27.

3. To be fair, I must qualify my statement about there being few things that can be labeled "all dangerous." Much like the fatty parts that I cut off my steak, there are certain elements of pop culture that can be tossed outright, like pornography. We can safely discard pornography without any fear that we are missing out on a nugget of truth. Most of our culture, however, is a mixture or truth and error.

4. Yes, I have chosen poorly before and as a result have images burned into my mind that I'll never be able to unsee. Thank God for websites like www.kidsinmind.com. There are some things you can't spit out, even if you try.

Chapter 4—Linguistic Theft

1. Holly Ordway, *Apologetics and the Imagination* (Steubenville, OH: Emmaus Road, 2017), 68.

2. Amy F.T. Arnsten, "Stress Signaling Pathways That Impair Prefrontal Cortex Structure and Function," *Neuroscience* 10, no. 6 (June 2009): 410-422, https://doi.org/10.1038/ nrn2648.

3. Jonathan Turley, "The Hypocrisy of Antifa," *The Hill* (August 29, 2017), http://the hill.com/blogs/pundits-blog/civil-rights/348389-opinion-antifa-threatens-to-turn -america-into-an.

4. Family Policy Institute of Washington, "Gender Identity: Can a 5'9, White Guy Be a 6'5, Chinese Woman?" (April 13, 2016), www.youtube.com/watch?v=xfO1veFs6Ho.

5. Psalm 133:1; John 17:23; 1 Corinthians 1:10; Ephesians 4:3; Colossians 3:13-14; 1 Peter 3:8.

6. Go to biblehub.net and search the words *justice* and *injustice*, and you will see how these concepts are peppered throughout Scripture.

7. Anemona Hartocollis and Stephanie Saul, "Affirmative Action Battle Has a New Focus: Asian-Americans," *The New York Times* (August 3, 2017), https://www.nytimes.com/2017/08/02/us/affirmative-action-battle-has-a-new-focus-asian-americans.html.

8. Erik Ortiz, "The Dept. of Justice Could Review Asian-Americans' Complaint against Harvard Admissions," *NBC News* (August 3, 2017), https://www.nbcnews.com/news/asian-america/asian-americans-complaint-against-harvard-could-get-dept-justice-review-n789266.

Chapter 5—God Helps Those Who Help Themselves

1. John LaRosa, "What's Next for the $9.9 Billion Personal Development Industry," *Mar ketResearch.com* (January 17, 2018), https://blog.marketresearch.com/whats-next-for-the-9-9-billion-personal-development-industry.

2. A Hellenistic philosophy of the third century BC that promoted the power of the human mind and logic as the ultimate source of human happiness.

3. Samuel Smiles, *Self Help* (Boston: Ticknor and Fields, 1863), https://www.econlib.org/library/YPDBooks/Smiles/smlSH.html?chapter_num=3#book-reader.

4. James Allen, *As a Man Thinketh* (N.P.: CreateSpace, 2006), https://www.amazon.com/As-Man-Thinketh-Complete-Original/dp/1523643536.

5. 2 Corinthians 10:5.

6. Christian Science teaches the idea that illnesses are either an illusion or controllable by a person's mind. If people could change their thought life or say the right prayers, then they would be healed.

7. Norman Vincent Peale, *The Power of Positive Thinking: A Practical Guide to Mastering the Problems of Everyday Living* (London: The Quality Book Club, 1956; reprint Self-Improvement eBooks, 2006), 6, http://www.makemoneywithpyxism.info/join stevehawk.com/PowerOfPositiveThinking.pdf.

8. *Humanism* is the belief system that man can essentially be his or her own god. It encourages people to look to themselves and not to a divine or supernatural being. Humanists believe that people are born good and that, given the right circumstances and skill sets, they can be good again.

9. If you want to read someone who truly understands the fullness of sin, look up Jonathan Edwards's sermon "Sinners in the Hands of an Angry God." I wouldn't read it as gospel, and it robs the gospel of love, but the man understood sin very well.

10. Jonathan Edwards, *Sinners in the Hands of an Angry God: a sermon, preached at Enfield, July 8, 1741, at a time of great awakenings; and attended with remarkable Impressions on Many of the Hearers* (Boston: S. Kneeland and T. Green, 1741), reprinted by ed. Reiner Smolinski (Lincoln, NE: University of Nebraska, Lincoln—Digital Commons, n.d.), https://digitalcommons.unl.edu/cgi/viewcontent.cgi?article=1053&context=etas.

11. Matthew 10:39.

12. Psalm 121:2; Zechariah 4:6; John 15:5.

Chapter 6—My Brain Is Trustworthy…According to My Brain

1. Technically, material things can also be things that are too small for any of these senses to detect but can still be used to create repeatable reactions in the lab—reactions that can be detected by the senses.

2. There are people who have experiences where they have interacted with angels or demons, but these experiences are not the norm, nor can they be reliably or repeatedly reproduced.

3. There's also an immaterial form of naturalism, where a person believes that all things are nature, but that nature includes both material and immaterial things. This distinction is not as common, so we aren't addressing it here.

4. Richard Dawkins, speech at the Edinburgh International Science Festival (April 15, 1992), quoted in "A scientist's case against God," *The Independent* (April 20, 1992), 17.

5. Scientists would refer to this kind of thinking as an "open system" rather than a "closed system." A closed system cannot have interference from outside of the system, which means that God could not interact with creation. An open system allows that things outside our system (like God) can interact. There is more than just natural laws, though natural laws are sufficient causes for most things we study.

6. AD 1543 was the year that Copernicus published *On the Revolutions of the Heavenly Spheres,* the first scientific treatise asserting a heliocentric (sun-centered) rather than geocentric (earth-centered) model.

7. A great reference is Ken Sample, *A World of Difference* (Grand Rapids, MI: Baker, 2007).

8. Malachi 3:6 (KJV).

9. Charles Darwin, *The Origin of Species* (originally published 1859; reprinted New York: Barnes & Noble Classics, 2008), 77 (emphasis added).

10. This expectation is an important theme and will come into play as we discuss skepticism and postmodernism in the next few chapters. Absolute certainty is attained when something is proven beyond even a possible doubt.

11. We in the modern West have realized that there are only two areas in which absolute certainty can be achieved: logic and mathematics. Even our personal experiences can be philosophized away as just elaborate dreams of a brain in a vat.

12. The word *eugenics* means "good" (*eu*) "genes" (*genics*). It was basically taking Darwin's natural selection and using it on humans in the same way that dog breeders selectively breed dogs: sterilize the people who have less desirable genes. About 60,000 people were sterilized (many against their will) in the early part of the twentieth century. Many of them were mentally handicapped or had birth defects. It was the United States' applications of Darwinism to "purify the genepool" that was responsible for not only Planned Parenthood, but also for the atrocities perpetrated by Hitler. The word *eugenics* became much less popular after WWII when we saw how far Hitler took it, but the ideas behind it live on in Planned Parenthood, and with the growing movement to legalize physician-assisted suicide.

13. "Jesus Christ is the same yesterday, today, and forever" (Hebrews 13:8; HCSB).

14. I should mention that the eternal universe hypothesis (also called *steady-state theory*) was smashed to bits when Hubble discovered that the universe was expanding. Something expanding *must* eventually be traced back to a starting point.

15. For a complete list, see Hugh Ross, "Part 1: Fine Tuning for Life in the Universe," *Reasons to Believe* (Covina, CA: Reasons to Believe, 2008), http://d4bge0zxg5qba.cloudfront .net/files/compendium/compendium_part1.pdf.

16. There are many places where you can see Lennox describe this exchange, like here: https://www.youtube.com/watch?v=CwwUnsqA5gI.

17. We cannot dismiss the fact that science progresses slowly. I am not saying that because we have just scratched the surface that we will never get to the bottom of this. I am saying that we know pretty well what natural processes can and can't do, and the leap between these too isn't based on ignorance; it's based on knowledge. This is not an argument from ignorance. It is an inductive argument based on the best explanation of what we currently know, which is ideally what science should limit itself to.

18. If you would like a terrifying picture of what this looks like when you infuse this belief into the justice system, check out John West, *Darwin Day in America* (Wilmington, DE: Intercollegiate Studies Institute, 2007).

19. Not His plan for salvation though—that is found only in Scripture.

20. Ben Stein, in the documentary *Expelled*, got Richard Dawkins to admit that aliens were his best guess. See Ben Stein, *Expelled* (Premise Media and Rampant Films, 2008), 1:27:25-1:33:08, https://www.youtube.com/watch?v=V5EPymcWp-g.

21. Baruch A. Shalev, *100 Years of Nobel Prizes* (Los Angeles, CA: The Americas Group, 2002), 46, 57.

22. Robert Jastrow, *God and the Astronomers* (New York: W.W. Norton, 1992), 116.

Chapter 7—I'd Believe in God If There Were Any Shred of Evidence

1. Dan Wallace, "Has the New Testament Text Been Hopelessly Corrupted?," *A Defense of the Bible: A Comprehensive Apologetic for the Authority of Scripture*, eds. Stephen B. Cowan and Terry L. Wilder (Nashville, TN: Broadman & Holman, 2013), 156-57.

2. We *do* have original documents like shipping logs and receipts, but no original documents of *literature* that would have been copied and circulated.

3. Josh McDowell and Sean McDowell, *The New Evidence that Demands a Verdict* (Nashville, TN: Thomas Nelson, 2017), 52-56.

4. David Hume, *On Human Nature and the Understanding*, Antony Flew, ed. (New York: Collier Books, 1962), 163.

5. Hillary Short, "Playground Apologetics: Apologetics Tactics for Busy Moms," *Mama Bear Apologetics* (February 14, 2018), http://mamabearapologetics.com/ playground-apologetics-intro/.

6. Bertrand Russell, "The Free Man's Worship," *The Independent Review*, vol. 1 (December 1903), 415-24.

7. Richard Dawkins, "Thought for the Day," *BBC Radio* (January 2003), quoted in Alister McGrath, *The Dawkins Delusion?* (Downers Grove, IL: InterVarsity, 2007), 19.

8. If you have never seen the Bob Newhart skit "Just Stop It," search for it online. Trust me, it's worth your time.

9. Christopher Hitchens, interview, *ABC Lateline* (November 18, 2010), 11:10, https://www.youtube.com/watch?v=6ulJhUhPTFs.

10. Anna Skates, "The Trouble with Easter: How To (and Not To) Talk to Kids About Easter—Unfundamentalist Parenting," *Patheos* (April 12, 2017), http://www.patheos.com/blogs/unfundamentalistparenting/2017/04/trouble-easter-not-talk-kids-easter/.

11. Richard Dawkins, "Physical Versus Mental Child Abuse," *Richard Dawkins Foundation* (January 1, 2013), https://www.richarddawkins.net/2013/01/physical-versus-mental-child-abuse/.

12. Rebekah Valerius, "Is It Abusive to Teach Children About Hell?," *Christian Research Journal* 40, no. 3 (2018): 34-39.

13. Richard Dawkins, *The God Delusion* (New York: Houghton Mifflin, 2006), 135.

14. Richard Dawkins, "Richard Dawkins: The Rational Revolutionary," video hosted by *Intelligence*[2] (July 14, 2016), 1:09:07-1:11:02, https://www.youtube.com/watch?v=aWIQ5nWKyNc.

15. Dr. John D. Ferrer, "Rejecting a Rembrandt?," *Intelligent Christian Faith* (April 29, 2016), https://intelligentchristianfaith.com/2015/11/19/rejecting-a-rembrandt/.

16. Richard Dawkins, "God Under the Microscope," video "Heart of the Matter," *BBC One* (September 29, 1996), https://www.youtube.com/watch?v=2gTYFolrpNU.

17. Christopher Hitchens, "The Fanatic, Fraudulent Mother Teresa," *Slate* (October 20, 2003), http://www.slate.com/articles/news_and_politics/fighting_words/2003/10/mommie_dearest.html.

Chapter 8—The Truth Is, There Is No Truth

1. Gilbert K. Chesterton, "The Revival of Philosophy—Why?," *Common Man* (New York: Sheed & Ward), para. 1.

2. Nancy R. Pearcey, *Total Truth* (Wheaton, IL: Crossway, 2004), 103.

3. Stephen Hicks, *Explaining Postmodernism: Skepticism and Socialism from Rousseau to Foucault* (Loves Park, IL: Ockham's Razor, 2014), 2.

4. Yes, my mind *does* interpret the wavelength of light to tell me that it's purple, but my perception can't change the objective wavelengths of light being emitted.

5. Hicks, *Explaining Postmodernism*, 3.

6. As my friend Beth was reading through a draft of this chapter, she commented on how her friend's child came home from college claiming that his *religion* professor at his *Christian* college told him that Jesus was a homosexual and he could prove it from the Bible. I'd like to say that reports like this are uncommon, but they're not.

Chapter 9—You're Wrong to Tell Me that I'm Wrong!
1. C.S. Lewis, *Mere Christianity* (New York: Touchstone, 1996), 45.

2. Timothy Keller, *The Reason for God: Belief in an Age of Skepticism* (New York: Riverhead, 2008), 73.

3. Richard C. Lewontin, "Billions and Billions of Demons," *New York Review of Books* (January 9, 1997), https://www.nybooks.com/articles/1997/01/09/billions-and-billions-of -demons/ (emphasis added).

4. Jonathan Merritt, "The Death of Moral Relativism," *The Atlantic* (March 24, 2016), https://www.theatlantic.com/politics/archive/2016/03/the-death-of-moral-relativism /475221/.

Chapter 10—Follow Your Heart—It Never Lies!
1. Fredric Heidemann, "I Was an Atheist Until I Read 'The Lord of the Rings,'" *Strange Notions* (December 19, 2016), https://strangenotions.com/i-was-an-atheist-until-i -read-the-lord-of-the-rings/.

Chapter 11—Just Worship Something
1. Brandon Showalter, "Only 1 in 10 Americans Have Biblical Worldview, Just 4 Percent of Millennials: Barna," *The Christian Post* (February 28, 2017), https://www.christianpost .com/news/1-in-10-americans-have-biblical-worldview-just-4-percent-of-millennials- barna-176184/.

2. For more information about what St. Francis of Assisi may have said or not said, see Jamie Arpin-Ricci, "Preach the Gospel at All Times?," *Huffington Post* (August 31, 2012), https://www.huffingtonpost.com/jamie-arpinricci/preach-the-gospel-at-all-times-st- francis_b_1627781.html.

3. 2 Corinthians 10:5.

4. Cathryn Buse, *Teaching Others to Defend Christianity* (Denver, CO: CrossLink, 2016), 73-98.

5. John 14:6.

6. Buse, *Teaching Others*, 93-96.

7. Luke 12:51-53.

8. Acts 4:20.

9. Nabeel Qureshi, *Seeking Allah, Finding Jesus* (Grand Rapids, MI: Zondervan, 2016), 90.

Chapter 12—I'm Not Religious; I'm Spiritual!
1. Otto Friedrich, "New Age Harmonies," *Time* (December 7, 1987), 62-72.

2. Joseph Liu, "'Nones' on the Rise," *Pew Research Center* (October 9, 2012), http://www
    .pewforum.org/2012/10/09/nones-on-the-rise/.

3. Marianne Williamson, "How to Apply a Course in Miracles in your Daily Life,"
    posted by Hay House on YouTube (March 14, 2016), https://www.youtube.com/
    watch?v=bgWBmiqR4pI.

4. Helen Schucman, *Manual for Teachers* in *A Course in Miracles* (Mill Valley, CA: Founda-
    tion for Inner Peace, 1975; reprint 2007), 91, http://stobblehouse.com/text/ACIM.pdf.

5. Helen Shuchman, *A Course in Miracles* [primary text] in *A Course in Miracles, Combined
    Volume*, 3d ed. (Mill Valley, CA: Foundation for Inner Peace, 1975; reprint 2007), ch. 4,
    intro., para. 3.

6. Shuchman, *Manual for Teachers*, 2007, sect. 23, para. 4.

7. Shuchman, *Course in Miracles, 1975*, ch. 3, intro., para. 4.

8. Shuchman, *Workbook for Students* in *A Course in Miracles, Combined Volume*, 3d ed.
    (Mill Valley, CA: Foundation for Inner Peace, 1975; reprint 2007), lesson 61, para. 1.

9. Shuchman, *Workbook*, lesson 259, para. 1.

10. Shuchman, *Workbook*, lesson 70, para. 1.

11. Todd Gilchrist, "Star Wars Speeches: Yoda," *IGN.US* (August 29, 2006), https://www
    .ign.com/articles/2006/08/29/star-wars-speeches-yoda.

12. Bill Moyers and George Lucas. "Of Myth and Men," *Time* (April 18, 1999), http://con
    tent.time.com/time/magazine/article/0,9171,23298,00.html.

13. Rob Bell, *What We Talk About When We Talk About God* (New York: HarperCollins,
    2014), 106.

14. Bell, *What We Talk About*, 118.

15. Ekhart Tolle, *The Power of Now: A Guide to Spiritual Enlightenment* (Vancouver, BC,
    Canada: Namaste, 2004), 104.

16. Deepak Chopra, *The Third Jesus: The Christ We Cannot Ignore* (New York: Random
    House, 2008), 9.

17. Marcia Montenegro, "Mindfulness: Taming the Monkey, Part 1," *Midwest Christian Out-
    reach Journal*, vol. 20, no. 1 (Fall 2014), para. 12, http://www.christiananswersforthenew
    age.org/Articles_MindfulnessMonkey.html.

18. For more on this, see chapter 3 of Clay Jones's book *Why Does God Allow Evil?* (Eugene,
    OR: Harvest House, 2017).

19. Mary Poplin, "As a New Age Enthusiast, I Fancied Myself a Free Spirit and a Good Per-
    son," *Christianitytoday.com* (December 21, 2017), http://www.christianitytoday.com/
    ct/2018/january-february/as-new-age-enthusiast-i-fancied-myself-free-spirit-and-good
    .html.

Chapter 13—Communism Failed Because Nobody Did It Right

1. Danielle Corcione, "Everything You Should Know About Karl Marx," *Teen Vogue* (May 10, 2018), https://www.teenvogue.com/story/who-is-karl-marx.

2. Kim Kelly, "Everything You Need to Know About Capitalism," *Teen Vogue* (April 11, 2018), https://www.teenvogue.com/story/what-capitalism-is.

3. Karl Marx and Frederick Engels, *Manifesto of the Communist Party* (1848), translated by Samuel Moore and Frederick Engels, in *Marx/Engels Selected Works, vol. 1* (Moscow: Progress Publishers, 1969), 98-137, revised English translation edited by Andy Blunden (Online: Marxists Internet Archive, 2004), 40.

4. *Marx/Engels Selected Works*, 26.

5. *Marx/Engels Selected Works*, 24.

6. Bruce Mazlish, *The Meaning of Karl Marx* (New York: Oxford University Press, 1987), 8.

7. William Z. Foster, *Towards Soviet America* (London: Forgotten Books & Ltd., 2015), 326.

8. W.A. Suchting, *Marx: An Introduction* (New York: New York University Press, 1983), xviii.

9. Roger S. Gottlieb, *Marxism: 1844-1990* (New York: Routledge, Chaplain & Hall, 1992), 34.

10. Bertell Ollman, "Marx's Vision of Communism: The First Stage," *Dialectical Marxism: The Writings of Bertell Ollman,* https://www.nyu.edu/projects/ollman/docs/marxs_vision.php.

11. Robert Harvey, *A Short History of Communism* (New York: Thomas Dunne Books, 2004), 25.

12. Karl Marx and Frederick Engels, *Manifesto of the Communist Party* (1848), translated by Samuel Moore and Frederick Engels, in *Marx/Engels Selected Works, vol. 1*, pgs. 98-137, (Moscow: Progress Publishers, 1969), revised English translation edited by Andy Blunden (Online: Marxists Internet Archive, 2004), 18.

13. *Marx/Engels Selected Works*, 25.

14. *Marx/Engels Selected Works*, 14.

15. Robert Harvey, *A Short History of Communism* (New York: Thomas Dunne Books, 2004), 25.

16. Saul Alinsky, *Rules for Radicals* (New York: Vintage Books, 1971), 66.

17. Roger S. Gottlieb, *Marxism: 1844–1990* (New York: Routledge, Chaplain & Hall, 1992), 124.

18. Gottlieb, *Marxism*, 137.

19. John MacArthur has a good series on this. Here's the first message in the series: John MacArthur, "Social Injustice and the Gospel," Grace to You Ministries (August 13, 2018), https://www.gty.org/library/blog/B180813.

20. I got this idea through Kim Van Vlear's *DeepRoots Bible Curriculum*, which can be found at https://deeprootsbible.com/.

21. I have to point out that these passages do not support communism because communism is enforced by the government. Notice the people were not giving their proceeds to the government to distribute. They were giving it to the apostles—the religious leaders. Thus, if this passage advocates for anything, it is a self-imposed theocracy (meaning a government in which priests rule according to divine guidance). Ancient Israel was a theocracy. Any government that operates with freedom of religion cannot be a theocracy. However, we *can* operate within the church governance in the manner that the early church did.

Chapter 14—The Future Is Female

1. Diana Bruk, "Ashley Judd Gave an Incredibly Fiery Speech at the Women's March. Here's the Full Transcript," *Cosmopolitan* (October 8, 2017), www.cosmopolitan.com/entertainment/a8625295/ashley-judd-womens-march-speech/.

2. Bruk, "Ashley Judd."

3. The Organizers, "Our Mission," *Women's March* (2017), www.womensmarch.com/mission/.

4. In Genesis 1:27, God declares both men and women as made in His image. In Genesis 16:10, God uses the same covenant language with Hagar, an Egyptian slave, as He does with Abraham. In the ancient Near East, women were little more than property, yet God commanded children to honor their mothers (listed first) as well as their fathers (Leviticus 19:3). In the New Testament, only students were allowed to sit at the feet of a rabbi, and yet that's where we see Mary, the sister of Martha, in Luke 10:38. Jesus broke cultural taboos when He spoke to the woman at the well (John 4), and He chose women to be the first witnesses to the resurrection (Matthew 28) during a time when the testimony of a woman was said to be worthless, according to Josephus and the Talmud (Josephus, *Antiquities of the Jews,* 4.8.15; Talmud, Rose Hashannah 1:8).

5. Kelly Riddell, "Pro-life Women Banned from Anti-Trump Women's March on Washington," *The Washington Times* (January 17, 2017), https://www.washingtontimes.com/news/2017/jan/17/pro-life-women-banned-anti-trump-womens-march-wash/.

6. Christian Hoff Sommers, *Freedom Feminism* (Lanham, MD: Rowan & Littlefield, 2013), 10-12.

7. The beliefs of egalitarian and maternal first-wave feminism are similar, but not identical, to the church's current debate between egalitarian and complementarian models of marriage.

8. Betty Friedan, *The Feminine Mystique,* 50th anniversary ed. (New York: W.W. Norton, 2013), 337.

9. Friedan, *The Feminine Mystique*, 368.

10. Attributed to G.K. Chesterton.

11. By the way, has anyone ever *seen* the patriarchy? Where does this infamous boys' club meet? Who are they? When asked at the women's march to identify this nefarious group,

feminists responded with their best deer-in-the-headlights impressions. See Summer White, "Feminism Implodes at Women's March," Video *Apologia Studios*, YouTube (January 23, 2017), https://www.youtube.com/watch?v=B5yI42X9-Yw.

12. Some people claim we are in the fourth or fifth wave, but time has yet to confirm if they are separate waves, or just ripples from the third.

13. Christian Hoff Sommers, *Who Stole Feminism? How Women Have Betrayed Women* (New York: Touchstone, 1995), 25.

14. Christina Hoff Sommers, *Factual Feminist*, YouTube, https://www.youtube.com/playlist?list=PLytTJqkSQqtr7BqC1Jf4nv3g2yDfu7Xmd.

15. Caroline Mortimer, "Women's Rights Group Strips Naked in Protest Against Objectification," *The Independent* (September 22, 2016), https://www.independent.co.uk/news/world/americas/women-naked-nude-female-body-protest-objectification-urbanudismo-argentina-feminism-sexuality-a7323376.html.

16. Hillary Morgan Ferrer, "So You 'Marched for Women' This Weekend? 8 Things You Probably Didn't Know You Were Marching For…," *Mama Bear Apologetics* (February 14, 2018), https://mamabearapologetics.com/marched-women-weekend-8-things-probably-didnt-know-marching/.

17. By "pills," I am referring to the overabundance of boys on ADD pills. See Peg Tyre's *The Trouble with Boys* (New York: Harmony, 2009) and Christina Hoff Sommers, *The War Against Boys,* rev. and upd. (New York: Simon & Schuster, 2015).

18. According to one source, this feminist proverb was first coined by Irina Dunn, which she wrote on a bathroom wall in 1970. Jennifer Baumgardner, and Amy Richards, *Manifesta: Young Women, Feminists, and the Future*, 10th anniversary ed. (New York: Farrar, Straus, Giroux, 2010), 41.

19. Even though I liked *The Simpsons*, I believe it helped paved the way to spread this model with all of Homer's buffoonery.

20. For the record, I'll agree with this when it comes to certain types of dance. Whatever the guy does, the woman has to do backward…and in heels.

21. Christina Hoff Sommers, *War Against Boys: How Misguided Policies Are Harming Our Young Men* (New York: Simon & Schuster, 2013).

22. To download the victim's report, go to "Report I of the 40th Statewide Investigating Grand Jury," *Pennsylvania Diocese Victim's Report* (August 27, 2018), https://www.attorneygeneral.gov/wp-content/uploads/2018/08/A-Report-of-the-Fortieth-Statewide-Investigating-Grand-Jury_Cleland-Redactions-8-12-08_Redacted.pdf.

23. Emily Badger, "The Unbelievable Rise of Single Motherhood in America over the Last 50 Years," *The Washington Post* (December 18, 2014), https://www.washingtonpost.com/news/wonk/wp/2014/12/18/the-unbelievable-rise-of-single-motherhood-in-america-over-the-last-50-years/?utm_term=.16c1ec4ce1ae.

24. John Ferrer, "Unwaging the War on Women," *Intelligent Christian Faith* (August 6,

2016), www.intelligentchristianfaith.com/2016/08/06/unwaging-the-war-on-women-2/amp/.

25. I recommend Sue Bohlin's article "Raising Gender Healthy Kids" at https://probe.org/raising-gender-healthy-kids/.

Chapter 15—Christianity Needs a Makeover

1. An influential scholar in the Progressive movement, Pete Enns, developed this idea in his book *The Sin of Certainty: Why God Desires Our Trust More Than Our "Correct" Beliefs* (New York: HarperOne, 2016).

2. David M. Felten and Jeff Procter-Murphy, *Living the Questions: The Wisdom of Progressive Christianity* (Toronto, Canada: HarperCollins, 2012), 23-24.

3. J. Gresham Machen, *Christianity and Liberalism* (Grand Rapids, MI: Eerdmans, 2009), 16.

4. Rob Bell, "Everything Is Spiritual," *RobBell.com*, YouTube (May 1, 2016), https://www.youtube.com/watch?v=JT09JbaEh_I.

5. Anna Skates, "The Trouble with Easter: How To (and Not To) Talk to Kids About Easter—Unfundamentalist Parenting," *Patheos* (April 12, 2017), http://www.patheos.com/blogs/unfundamentalistparenting/2017/04/trouble-easter-not-talk-kids-easter/.

6. Brian D. McLaren, *A New Kind of Christianity: Ten Questions That Are Transforming the Faith* (New York: HarperCollins, 2010), 103.

7. Felten and Procter-Murphy, *Living the Questions*, 24.

8. John Pavlovitz, "Explaining Progressive Christianity (Otherwise Known as Christianity)," *John Pavlovitz* (October 5, 2016), https://johnpavlovitz.com/2016/10/05/explaining-progressive-christianity-otherwise-known-as-christianity/.

9. Andrew Wilson, *Unbreakable: What the Son of God Said About the Word of God* (Leyland, UK: 10 Publishing, 2014) 9-10.

10. Sam Hailes, "Bart Campolo Says Progressive Christians Turn into Atheists. Maybe He's Right," *Premiere Christianity* (September 25, 2017), https://www.premierchristianity.com/Blog/Bart-Campolo-says-progressive-Christians-turn-into-atheists.-Maybe-he-s-right.

Chapter 16—How to Take All This Information and #RoarLikeAMother

1. Francis Schaeffer, *The God Who Is There* (Downers Grove, IL: InterVarsity Press, 1998), 153.

To learn more about Harvest House books and
to read sample chapters, visit our website:

www.harvesthousepublishers.com

HARVEST HOUSE PUBLISHERS
EUGENE, OREGON